THE GROWTH OF AFRICAN CIVILISATION

A History of West Africa 1000-1800

OTHER BOOKS BY BASIL DAVIDSON:

Old Africa Rediscovered
Black Mother: *Africa, the Years of the Slave Trade*
The African Past: *Chronicles from Antiquity to Modern Times*
Africa in History: *Themes and Outlines*
A History of East and Central Africa to the Late Nineteenth Century
The Africans: *an Entry to Social and Cultural History*
The African Awakening
The Liberation of Guiné: *Aspects of an African Revolution*
In the Eye of the Storm: *Angola's People*

OTHER BOOKS BY PROFESSOR AJAYI:

Christian Missions in Nigeria 1841-91
Milestones in Nigerian History
Yoruba Warfare in the Nineteenth Century (with R. S. Smith)

OTHER BOOKS BY F. K. BUAH:

Modern World History since 1750
History Notes: West Africa since A.D. 1000 (2 vols)
An Elementary History for Schools (5 vols)
A New History for Schools and Colleges (2 vols)

OTHER BOOKS IN THE GROWTH OF AFRICAN CIVILISATION SERIES

The Revolutionary Years: West Africa Since 1800 by Professor J. B. Webster and Professor A. A. Boahen with a contribution by H. O. Idowu

The Making of Modern Africa 1800-1960 (2 vols) by Professor J. D. Omer-Cooper, Dr A. E. Afigbo, Dr E. A. Ayandele and Professor R. J. Gavin

East Africa to the Late Nineteenth Century by Basil Davidson with J. E. F. Mhina and the advice of Professor B. A. Ogot

BASIL DAVIDSON Hon DLitt Ibadan
in collaboration with
F. K. BUAH MA
Headmaster Tema Secondary School, Ghana
and with the advice of
J. F. ADE AJAYI BA PhD
Vice Chancellor,
University of Lagos, Nigeria

THE GROWTH OF AFRICAN CIVILISATION

A History of West Africa 1000-1800

LONGMAN

Longman Group Limited
Longman House
Burnt Mill
Harlow Essex U.K.

First published 1965
Revised edition 1967
New revised edition 1977
Fifth impression 1981

ISBN 0 582 60340 4

Printed in Singapore by
Kyodo Shing Loong Printing Industries Pte Ltd

089376

Acknowledgements

I should like to express my warm thanks to Professor Ajayi for his guidance and advice on many points. To my colleague in the writing of this book, Mr Buah, go my thanks for his work in grading the text for secondary school students and for providing the questions and relevant historical advice. Among other historians for whose instruction and correction we are especially grateful are Mr Christopher Fyfe of the University of Edinburgh and Professor Ivor Wilks, now at North-Western University, while many more, whom I may perhaps be allowed to thank anonymously, will recognise the influence of their pioneering work in a book whose design excludes a full list of references.

For this entirely new and revised edition, we also gratefully acknowledge the work of Mr Paul Thatcher (Government College, Keffi, Nigeria) for revising the questions in line with the latest syllabi and for preparing a new note on sources and appropriate lists of reading materials. We should also like to thank, for guidance and advice: Dr G. O. Ogunremi, Professor E. J. Alagoa and Dr E. A. Oroge.

For some of the maps Mr Buah and I found sturdy guidance in Professor Fage's invaluable *Atlas of African History* (Edward Arnold Ltd., 1958); while for other maps we have followed those in Professor K. O. Dike's *Trade and Politics in the Niger Delta, 1930-85* (Oxford 1956); Dr Colin Newbury's *The Western Slave Coast and Its Rulers* (Oxford 1961); Professor Raymond Mauny's *Tableau Géographique de l'Ouest Africain au Moyen Age* (IFAN 1961); M. Jean Rouch's *Contribution à l'Histoire des Songhay* (IFAN 1953); Professor Jean Suret-Canale's *Afrique Noire* (Editions Sociales, 1958) and *Zur Geschichte und sozialen Bedeutung der Fulbe-Hegemonie* (Akademie Verlag, 1960); the late Louis Tauxier's *Histoire des Bambara* (Paul Geuthner 1942); the late Yves Urvoy's *Histoire de l'Empire du Bornou* (IFAN 1949); and Professor Ivor Wilks's 'Rise of the Akwamu Empire' in the *Transactions* of the Historical Society of Ghana, 1957, while Professor Wilks has also kindly provided our map of Asante expansion. To all these and their publishers we tender our thanks. At the same time we should like to explain that our maps are not intended as more than broad guides to comparative positions, frontiers and lines of movement.

BASIL DAVIDSON

The publishers are indebted to the following for their help and permission to reproduce photographs:

J. Allan Cash for pages 148 and 150; Courtesy of the American Numismatic Society for pages 152 and 283; Bibliotheque Nationale for page 197; British Museum for pages 88, 91, 114, 134, 149 (right), 149 (left), 153, 170, 202; Camera Press for page 263 (Michele Da Silva); Crown Copyright/Wallace Collection for page 175; Basil Davidson for pages 15, 16, 17 (top), 17 (bottom), 21, 231, 279; Mary Evans for pages 79, 155, 158; Werner Forman Archive for pages 10, 19, 51, 75, 76, 82, 110, 122, 125, 128, 129, 130, 133, 156 (top), 156 (bottom), 165, 167 (British Museum), 176, 219 (John Friede Collection, New York), 242, 243 (British Museum), 249 (Private Collection, New York), 269; Fotomas Index for page 200; Ghana Film Industry Corporation for page 22; Ghana Information Services for page 241; Hoa-Qui for pages 168 and 169; IFAN for page 11; A. H. M. Kirk-Greene for page 101; The Mansell Collection for page 85; Musee De L'Homme, Paris for page 104; Popperfoto for page 32; R. A. Reuter for page 161; Royal Commonwealth Society for page 211; West African Newspapers for page 234; Ivor Wilkes for page 80.

The Cover Photograph was kindly supplied by Werner Forman.

The publishers are also grateful to the West African Examinations Council for permission to reproduce 12 questions from past History 'O' level papers and to Professor R. Mauny for permission to reproduce the diagram on page 37 which first appeared in *Afrique au Moyen Age*.

Contents

List of Maps

Preface

This book is for students of history in West Africa preparing for the West African School Certificate and similar public examinations. We hope that it will also prove of use to many other persons who are interested in the historical growth and value of the civilisation of West Africa.

In this new edition, revised to meet the growing demands of history courses, we have made many changes. We have added new sections so as to make the book still more directly useful to present examination papers. We have brought the information into line with the latest trends of research.

J. F. A. AJAYI
F. K. BUAH
BASIL DAVIDSON

June 1977

Mefrɛ Sika,   *I call Gold,*
Sika ngye so.   *Gold is mute.*
Mefrɛ Ntama,   *I call Cloth,*
Ntama Gye so.   *Cloth is mute.*
Onipa ne asɛm.   *It is Mankind that matters.*

INTRODUCTION
Early Times

CHAPTER ONE

The background of History

Africa through the ages

History is about people, the people of the past: about how they lived and worked, about what they did in their lives. So history is about our ancestors: about our parents' parents for many generations before us.

Why do we have to know about history? It is because the history of our ancestors is also the history of ourselves, of all of us today. In order to understand the world of today, we need to understand the world of yesterday as well. For the world of yesterday helped to make the world of today.

Many different peoples live in West Africa. Each has a very long history of its own. Why is that? Why is the history of one people different from the history of other peoples: the history of the Yoruba different

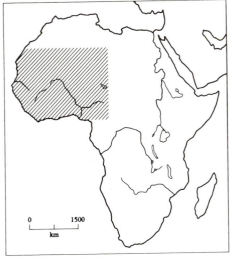

1 West Africa: the area considered in this book.

from the history of the Fulani, the history of the Akan different from the history of the Ga, the history of the Mende different from the history of their neighbours of Sierra Leone, and so on?

But all these peoples and their neighbours are West Africans. They all share the same West African history. Their histories are different from each other, but they are also like each other. In what ways are they like each other?

All our peoples are West Africans. But they have become united into different nations. Why is that? How did it happen?

Why does one people live and work in one way, and another people in different ways? Why are some people strong, and others weak? Why are some people rich, and others poor? And why, in spite of many differences, do all West Africans belong to one great civilisation, the civilisation of West Africa, itself a part of the still bigger civilisation of the Africans everywhere?

All such questions are the business of the study of history.

Here we study the history of all the West Africans. But we do this within limits marked by three points.

1 We study the main lines of our history, the big events, the leading developments. That is the way to begin.
2 We study what is now known about our history. Many facts are known. But more facts will become known. The work of discovering history is never ended.
3 We study one great period of our history, the centuries between AD 1000 and 1800.[1] These are the centuries when our ancestors built up our civilisation of the past, the civilisation that we inherit today.

We begin by looking briefly at a still earlier history: at the ways in which West Africans lived and worked in times even long before AD 1000.

Geographical divisions of West Africa

The ways in which people have developed in the past have always depended, to quite a large extent, on the kind of countryside and climate they have lived in. So the history of West Africa, as of any other part of the world, is closely connected with its geography. We must therefore begin by looking at the geographical background of West Africa.

[1] Christian dates are used in this book. Muslims count their years by a different calendar, beginning with the foundation of Islam in the year 622 of the Christian calendar.

West Africa is divided by nature into a number of belts of varying land and climate. These belts run across the map of Africa between west and east, with the Atlantic Ocean at one end and the valley of the River Nile and then the Red Sea at the other end. In other words, looking at them from north to south, these belts form a number of zones. How many zones? A *soil map* of West Africa shows five main zones of different soils. These range from the desert of the Sahara to the red-brown tropical soil and the laterite soil that form, between them, much of the region's surface.

A *rainfall map* shows even more belts or zones, reckoning these by the average amount of rain that falls every year in each of them. In the southern Sahara this average is less than 25 centimetres a year. In western Guinea and the Niger Delta, at the other extreme, the average rainfall is more than ten times as much.

These wide differences in natural conditions — in *environment* — can be seen by all of us. Anyone who makes a journey from the Sahara down to the coast will pass through belt after belt of differing vegetation, ranging from open plains to dense forest. There are very many such variations. For our purposes, however, we can group them together into *two big zones*: the land and climate of the open plains of the north, and the land and climate of the forest and coastal areas of the south. The first of these we call the *Central and Western Sudan*; the second we call *Guinea.*

Of course, each of these big zones of different land and climate

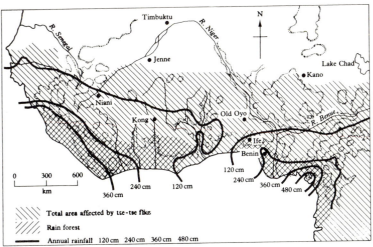

2 Rainfall in West Africa, vegetation, and total areas affected by the tse-tse fly.

contains many lesser zones: the waterways of the great Niger River-system, the Niger Delta itself, the mountain ranges of eastern Nigeria and western Guinea, the islands that lie along the coast of Sierra Leone, the course and estuary of the Gambia River, and many others.

Besides these two main zones we should also note another zone of historical importance. This is formed by the open country between the Pra River in modern Ghana and the Yewa River in modern Nigeria. Here it is that the grasslands of the north push down almost to the coast, thus splitting the great forest belt of West Africa into two parts.

Different zones have different advantages and handicaps. The West African forest belt is often good for growing valuable crops, yet bad for cattle. The plains of the north are good for cattle, but no good for certain valuable crops like cocoa. Soil and rainfall both play their part. So, for example, do pests like the tse-tse fly. This pest is also part of West African history. Tse-tse flies have been common in many parts of West Africa from very early times. They have strictly limited the areas in which people could keep cattle and horses, or develop the use of ploughs.

These *natural* variations have led to many contrasting ways of life. They help to explain why northern farmers and their neighbours have been so successful with raising cattle; or, to take another example, why Ịjọ fishermen of the Niger Delta have proved so skilful in catching fish; or why Akan farmers have done so well with the growing of forest crops. And all these variations in ways of living and of working have gone hand-in-hand with different ways of community life, different methods of government, different ideas about how to keep law and order, and much else besides. *Natural* variations, in short, have helped to lead to *social* variations.

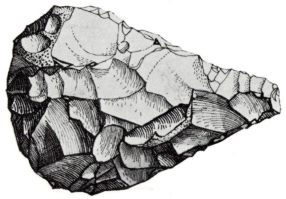

Early man used this like an axe but he held it in his hand, 15 cm long.

Way of life of early man

The origins of African history are extremely old. Recent discoveries suggest that Africa may have been the birthplace of mankind. These discoveries indicate that it was in Africa that early types of men, very different from ourselves, first developed the use of tools, and that this occurred several million years ago. The tools they made were lumps of chipped stone, and so the times in which these early peoples lived are called the Stone Age.

Equipped with these primitive tools, early man made progress. Slowly but surely, they grew stronger in their efforts to live and prosper. Their numbers became larger. They wandered across Africa. But they were still very rare. Life for them and their families remained dangerous and difficult.

About eight thousand years ago, some of these early folk made another big discovery. They had already learned how to make and use fire, stone tools, and stone weapons, as well as how to hunt for food and gather food from wild plants. Now they learned how to *grow* food by planting seeds and by raising cattle.

This growing of food was one of humanity's most revolutionary discoveries. It introduced what is called the Neolithic or *New Stone Age*. It enabled people to live in different ways from before. They could now settle in one place for quite long periods, make permanent villages, and give up a good deal of their wandering in search of game and wild plants. This great discovery occurred only after many centuries of trial and error. And it occurred at different times in different places.

Harpoon-head made of bone by early man, 30 cm long.

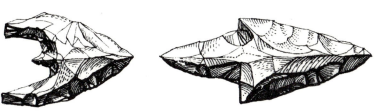

Arrowheads made of flint by early man, 8 and 12 cm long.

7

The habit of living by agriculture, by growing food instead of hunting game and gathering wild plants, occurred first in the Middle East and was adopted by northern Africans some 6,000 years ago. Africans of other regions started agriculture in somewhat later times. Knowledge of how to farm and raise cattle spread gradually across the open plains. This knowledge came to the southern lands of West and Central Africa about 3,000 years ago.

At this point we should notice an important natural difference between the Africa of New Stone Age times and the Africa of today. West Africa today is divided from North Africa and the Nile by the Sahara Desert. But this was not always the case. In New Stone Age times, parts of this vast desert were rich and fertile land. The Sahara then had areas of tall trees and green pastures. Broad rivers flowed through them. Game and cattle were plentiful there. So were fish.

From one end of the Sahara to the other, from Mauretania to Egypt, scientists have found stone tools and bone harpoons and fishing hooks, as well as pictures and drawings on rock of animals and men and gods. All these were made and left behind by many settlements and groups of vanished people. The Old Sahara was in fact a cradle of early African

A rock painting of a chariot and horses. The man holding the spear is hunting animals. The other two are driving the chariot. This scene may have have been painted more than 1,000 years before Christ.

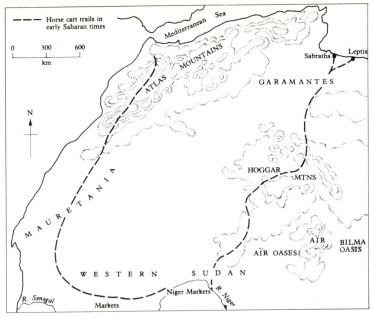

3 Horse-cart (chariot) trails across the ancient Sahara.

civilisation. Far from being a natural barrier between the peoples of
West and North Africa, the Old Sahara joined these peoples together.
All could share in the same ideas and discoveries.

Many travellers journeyed through the green Sahara in New Stone
Age times. They used horses and carts. Ancient rock pictures of these
horses and carts have been found along two main trails between North
and West Africa. One of these trails passed through Mauretania in the
western Sahara, while another went through the central Sahara between
the middle section of the Niger River and modern Tunisia. We can be
sure that new ideas and discoveries were taken back and forth by these
old travellers.

Around 2000 BC there began a great natural change. The climate
gradually became much drier. The Sahara received less and less rain. Its
rivers began to fail. Little by little, its farming peoples had to move away
and find new homes. Some went northwards, and helped to form the
Berber peoples of North Africa. Others pushed eastwards to the margins
of the fertile valley of the Nile. Others again came southwards into West
Africa. By about 500 BC this complicated movement of peoples was
already in the past, and the Sahara had become the dry and stony
wasteland that we know today. The horse made way for the camel,

widely used from about two thousand years ago, because the camel, with its broad feet, could move better over sand and could walk further without water than the horse.

The southward movement of peoples may have helped to bring the discoveries of the New Stone Age into West Africa. But there was certainly a great deal of West African invention. There is evidence, even though it does not yet add up to proof, that the peoples of West Africa made their own discovery of agriculture several thousand years ago. Scientists believe that African types of rice, as distinct from Asian types brought in much later, were first cultivated by early farmers in the region of the Middle Niger lakes, perhaps as long ago as 1500 BC. From there these rice crops are thought to have spread to farmers in other regions, notably in Senegambia.

Food growing in the forest country became important only after 500 BC, and remained for a long time on a small scale, partly because the forest peoples had good supplies of wild fruit and wild vegetables. Yet here, too, farming gradually went through a technological revolution which adapted its methods to African tropical conditions.

A rock engraving from Tassili Mountains in the Central Sahara.

This is a well known French archaeologist, Professor Raymond Mauny, pointing at ancient drawings of chariots at Es-Souk in the Sahara.

The spread and expansion of farming steadily enlarged the supplies of food. This in turn helped to increase the size of the populations, and to enable these populations to support persons who neither grew nor gathered food, but who worked at specialised jobs such as the making of tools. Settlements grew bigger. All this was part of the growth of early forms of civilisation.

11

Early peoples of West Africa

Who were the peoples of West Africa who adapted and invented new methods of farming and metal-working two thousand years ago and more? The answer is that they were the descendants of Stone Age peoples who had already been living in West Africa for thousands of years. They were the ancestors of the peoples of West Africa today.

Many West African peoples have legends and traditions which say that their ancestors came from another homeland in the distant east or north, or from some part of West Africa other than where they live today. In central Guinea, for example, the Akan and the Nzima say that their ancestors came from far in the north. The Ga and Ewe hold that theirs came from the east. The Yoruba likewise have a tradition which explains that their ancestors originated far in the east. Why is this?

Nearly always, these legends and traditions must be taken as referring only to very small groups of incoming ancestors. When they really occurred, such movements were made only by a small minority of people, by a few clans or families, or by a few warriors under strong leaders who, leaving their homeland, entered new territory, merged there with the more numerous peoples whom they found, and began a new tradition about where all these people had come from.

We shall find plenty of examples of the way in which history combines what is new with what is old. We shall see how new ideas, combined with old ideas, start new ways of government. We shall see how new skills, combined with old skills, start new methods of earning a livelihood. And it may be useful for us, at this stage, to think of this constant combining of what is new with what is old, this interplay of history, as being like a man who weaves. He stretches first of all his long threads, tying them to a stake in the ground or perhaps a tree trunk. He pulls them taut and sits at his loom. Then he threads his shuttle and begins weaving it back and forth between the stretched threads. Out of this interplay there comes a cloth. The finished cloth is composed of the two sets of threads, and yet it is an entirely new thing. It is different from any of the threads, and it is more than any of them.

If we use this illustration to explain the history of West Africa, as we could use it to explain the history of any other region of the world, then the long threads represent the inhabitants of West Africa, together with the beliefs, ideas, skills and customs they have worked out for themselves. The shuttle threads are all the new beliefs, ideas, skills and customs that have come into West Africa from time to time, or have been invented or created in West Africa. Woven together, all these threads make what we can call the cloth of history.

Through the course of time the cloth of history in West Africa, as elsewhere, has been constantly rewoven in a rich process of change and development. New designs and patterns have constantly appeared in it. It has been during this never-ceasing process of change that many traditions about the distant origins of various peoples have come into being. But nearly all the inhabitants of West Africa today are in fact the descendants of peoples who have lived in this region for countless centuries.

The importance of iron

The discovery of agriculture was a big advance in the early history of men. It wove many new patterns and designs into the cloth of history. Another big advance was the discovery of how to use metals.

The ancient Egyptians, like some of their Asian neighbours, were using copper and gold more than five thousand years ago. This was long before other Africans knew anything about the use of metals. But copper and gold, though excellent for making jewels and pots, were not much use for hunting, warfare, or tilling the soil. They were too soft. Egyptian and Asian metalworkers then learned how they could get a harder metal if they mixed copper with tin. The result was bronze, which is tougher than copper. The disadvantage still remained that copper and tin, like gold, were rare metals. Kings and famous warriors could afford bronze weapons and tools. Ordinary folk could not.

Some time around 1500 BC an Asian people called the Hittites, who lived in the country that is Turkey today, found out how to use iron. This was a discovery of enormous value for two reasons. First of all, iron was a metal out of which hard tools and weapons could be forged. Secondly, iron was a plentiful metal. Once men had understood how to use iron, good tools and weapons could be made in large quantities by many different peoples.

One people after another of the ancient world adopted the use of iron. These peoples are said by historians to have entered their *Iron Age.* So far as Africa is concerned, iron began to be commonly used in the countries of the Nile Valley, along the coast of North Africa, and in Ethiopia, soon after about 600 BC. West African peoples began entering their Iron Age a little later, soon after 300 BC.

The main evidence for West Africa's early use of iron comes from Nigeria. Scientists have shown how people who lived in the region of the Niger and Benue Rivers, began using iron more than two thousand years ago. They have been able to demonstrate this from the evidence of iron-working left behind by these people, who also modelled skilfully in baked clay. The name given to this early Iron Age way of life in central

13

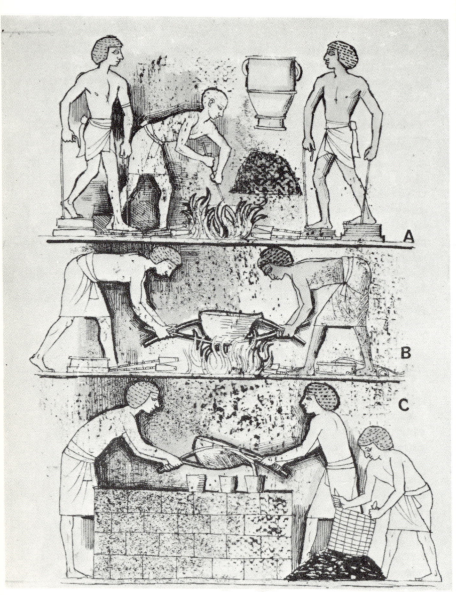

In picture A two Egyptians are using foot-bellows to heat the metal. The third man stirs the melting metal. Picture B shows the molten metal being lifted from the fire. Picture C shows the metal being poured into moulds. These scenes are taken from an Egyptian tomb that is more than 3,000 years old.

14

Above and on page 16: the Kushites of Meroe built handsome temples to their gods at their capital near the Nile, and 100 kms north of modern Khartoum. Some of these buildings were begun as early as 500 BC; others at a somewhat later date. Their ruins are still there.

Nigeria is the Nok Culture, after the village of Nok where some of the evidence was first discovered fifty years ago.

The importance of iron was so great in those distant times that the reasons for this must be examined in more detail. *The first reason* was that it gave West Africans better weapons and tools. Iron-pointed spears were more useful than sharp sticks or stones. Iron-headed hoes, probably invented some time after iron-pointed spears, were better than stone or wooden ones. Iron-headed axes could fell trees and shape wood much better than stone axes.

These improvements in equipment made it possible to produce more food. Having more food, people lived better than before. They became more numerous. But more people needed more land. Here lay *a second reason* why iron was important, and why its use marked the opening of a new stage of development. With iron spears and iron tools, Africans could attack some of the great natural barriers of their continent. They could penetrate the deep forests, open new trails, defend themselves against wild animals, and generally move about with more safety. There are grounds for thinking that the early Iron Age peoples of West Africa sent out many groups of wanderers, of migrants who moved from one homeland to a new homeland, through the forests of the Congo Basin and neighbouring lands.

Iron also brought *a new source of military power.* Those who first learnt to use it were able to rule their neighbours, especially if they also succeeded in keeping the secrets of its making to themselves. Stronger peoples began to rule weaker peoples.

And at the same time as people grew more numerous, there came a need to find new ways of keeping law and order. Little by little, many peoples in West Africa began forming themselves into *states.* Men began to feel the need for organised *government.*

There were various reasons for this. With iron tools there could be

Farmers of Ancient Egypt shown transplanting an incense tree.

Head of Prince Arka, the son of a Kushite king who ruled in about 250 BC.

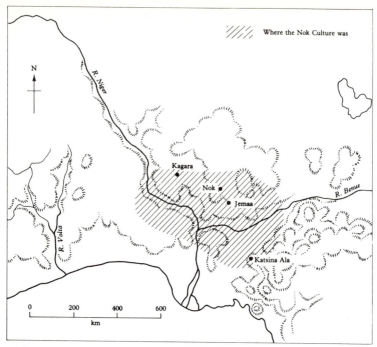

4 The Nok people lived in the areas shown and fragments of their work, in the shape of clay figures and other objects, have been found at the places marked.

more and better farming. With more farming there began to be enough food to maintain specialists who worked at making tools, weapons and other hand-made things. This *division of labour* encouraged trade, at first local and then long-distance, by producing a wide range of goods. All this, together with the growing size of populations, called for more complex forms of political organisation.

These early states were of many kinds. They were very simple in their government compared with those we know today. Some were ruled by a single chief or king and his counsellors. Others were governed by a council of chiefs or elders. Others again were formed by several neighbouring peoples whose chiefs were bound in loyalty to one another. Elsewhere, at the same time, there were peoples who found it better to get along without any chiefs. Traditional groups such as clans, families descended from common ancestors, or age-sets of people born at about the same time, had influence in these early states, as in later times, because they could help to maintain law and order. Of course it is important to remember that no one kind of state or community is more to be admired than another. A people with a strong central government

A baked clay (terra cotta) head from Nok.

was not necessarily more intelligent than another people who had no such government. The reason why there were different kinds of states, some with kings and some without, was that people lived under different conditions, and faced different problems. So they had to solve these problems in different ways.

The possibilities of *trade* were also important in deciding what kind of states were formed. Most peoples who lived on the main routes of developing trade tended to form themselves into states with a central king or government. One important reason for this was that taking part in long-distance trade called for the kind of united decisions, especially on conditions of purchase and sale of goods, which a king or central government could best take. But other peoples who lived far off these routes, and so had little interest in trade, tended to accept much looser forms of rule. They carried on living by the old family and clan customs of earlier times.

Early states

The earliest of West Africa's big states was named Wagadu, although the Berber traders of the Saharan trading towns called it Aoukar. We know it as Ancient Ghana, for Ghana was the title of its king. North African and other Arabic writers began mentioning Ghana in their books during the eighth century AD. Soon after AD 770, Al-Fazari named it as 'the land of gold'. In about AD 830 Al-Kwarizmi marked it on a map. We shall come back to Ancient Ghana in the next chapter. Meanwhile there are a few things to say about it here which illustrate the importance of iron and trade.

The origins of Ancient Ghana go back much further than AD 800. This state grew out of its peoples' need to protect their trade. If you consider the geographical position of Ancient Ghana, you will see why.

The heart of Ancient Ghana lay in its market-centres. These were placed in the grasslands to the north of the upper waters of the Niger and Senegal Rivers. Their commercial position was a strong one. They stood at the *southern end* of the trading-caravan routes which crossed the Sahara from North Africa. But they also stood at the *northern end* of the trading routes which came northward from the gold-producing country of West Africa. The traders of these market-centres bought gold and ivory from the traders of West Africa, and sold these goods to the traders of North Africa in exchange for Saharan salt and North African goods. Being powerful in trade, they needed to be powerful in government. They certainly succeeded in this.

The ruins of Kumbi Saleh, the capital of Ancient Ghana.

What took place in the lands of Ancient Ghana, in the north-western region of West Africa, also took place elsewhere. Trading states were formed along the course of the Niger River. Others emerged in neighbouring regions. Among these were the small trading states of Takrur and Sila in the Futa Toro region along the Senegal River, and Gao along the Niger River. By the time our main period begins in about AD 1000, the peoples of West Africa had already passed through many stages of civilised development.

This civilisation did not live entirely by itself, cut off from contact

Kumbi Saleh.

with other civilisations. It was part of a wider African civilisation. Although the Sahara was now a dried-up wilderness, West Africa remained in touch with North Africa and with the lands of the Nile Valley. Those ancient contacts were never broken. They ensured that these three great regions — West Africa, the Nile Valley, and North Africa — should develop together even though, because of the Sahara lying between them, they also developed separately. So the wider picture is one of three great African regions learning from each other, teaching each other, trading with each other through the centuries.

If we were to try to compare West Africa then with West Africa today, we should notice many contrasts. There were far fewer people. Most of them lived by growing food, but their crops were much less varied. They had no maize in those times, no pineapples, no sweet-potatoes: all these crops arrived in European ships from the Americas after AD 1500. They had few towns as yet, and no great cities. But even then, a thousand years ago, many important features of West African civilisation were already in existence. Many religious beliefs, social manners and ways of behaviour, and other aspects of our daily life, had already come to birth.

PART ONE
Six dynamic centuries
AD 1000-1600

CHAPTER TWO
West Africa in about AD *1000*

Some general notes

Between about AD 1000 and 1600 the peoples of West Africa passed through a great and memorable period of their history.

Many West African communities developed more useful methods of government during this period. They worked out new ways of organising their community life, and of enforcing law and order. Some of them went ahead without chiefs and kings and central governments, while others founded large states and empires. Cities grew in number, size and wealth, and became the home of new kinds of craftsmen and traders, politicians, priests, soldiers, writers and men of learning. With their export of gold and ivory, these trading cities and states became a valuable part of the whole wide network of international trade that was composed of West and North Africa, southern Europe and western Asia.

There was plenty of war and ruin in this period, as well as peace and prosperity. Yet we can often think of this period as one in which splendid things were done. Travelling through the empire of Mali in the fourteenth century, a famous Moroccan traveller, Ibn Batuta, praised its good government. There was, he found, 'complete and general safety in the land. The traveller has no more reason than the man who stays at home to fear brigands, thieves, or violent gangs'. Such security showed great political and social achievement, and it was by no means the only one of its kind.

What is really meant by a 'period of history'? This long and sometimes brilliant period of West African history did not, of course, begin in AD 1000 or end in 1600. History has no such neat beginnings and endings. It is the writers of history who divide the past into periods. They do this because there is no other clear and sensible way of writing about the past, especially the distant past. The people who lived in those days certainly had no idea that they might be beginning one period or ending another. We make these divisions in time only for our own convenience. In truth, the growth of West African civilisation after the tenth century AD was the fruit of all that had happened in earlier times. And in many important ways this 'period of greatness' lasted for a long time after the year 1600.

If these centuries were a 'period of greatness', does this mean that they were followed by a 'period of smallness', of decay and decline and disaster? History is more complicated than that. There were great disasters after the end of this period. There were big changes and upheavals. But there were continued growth and development as well, though in new ways. The period after the sixteenth century was a time of *transition*, of changes toward new forms of social life. This time of transition will be considered in Part Three.

Three main regions

To avoid getting confused by a mass of names and dates, we shall make another division. We have already divided the past into periods. Now we shall divide West Africa into regions and sub-regions. Needless to say, this division on the map is as artificial as the division of past years into periods. Nobody in the past recognised any such regions. But they are useful for the purpose of study.

West Africa, as noted on page 5 above, has two principal zones of climate and vegetation: the grasslands of the Central and Western

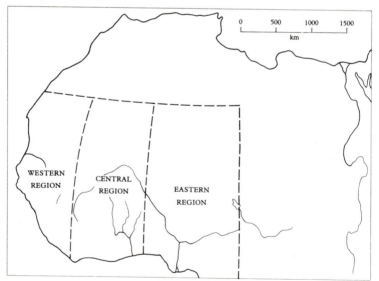

5 *The three regions of West Africa adopted for convenience of study in this book.*

Sudan, and the forest country of Guinea. European historians have usually divided West Africa 'horizontally' in this way. But this can be a confusing way of studying West African history, for it can suggest the false conclusion that grassland peoples and forest peoples were without influence on each other. It is therefore better to divide West Africa, for purposes of studying history, into 'vertical' sections or regions, each of which has grassland *and* forest peoples. The map shows the 'vertical' divisions adopted in this book.

The 'western region', lying mainly between the Senegal and Gambia Rivers, may also be called *Senegambia.*

The 'central region' consists of the Middle Niger country of the *Western Sudan,* together with the forest lands of Ivory Coast and Ghana.

The 'eastern region' includes the *Central Sudan,* together with southern Nigeria, the Niger Delta, and neighbouring countries.

These divisions are only for the convenience of study. The history of the western region was connected with that of the central region, and that of the central region with the eastern region.

The great trading empires of the Sudan

Geographers have usually divided the wide belt of grasslands known as the Sudan into two big 'halves': the Eastern Sudan from east of Lake Chad to the Red Sea, and the Western Sudan from west of Lake Chad to the Atlantic Ocean. It is with the history of the second 'half' that these chapters are concerned: that is with the regions which we can also call the Western and the Central Sudan. But we should remember that the peoples of both 'halves' of the Sudan have always been in contact with each other, often very fruitfully, just as they have always been in contact with their northern neighbours of the Saharan oases and the peoples of North Africa, as well as with their southern neighbours of Guinea: that is, of the West African coastal regions.

Introduction

Many different populations have inhabited the grasslands of the Sudan. Yet they have all shared the same kind of history because they have also shared the same kind of country: rolling plains dotted sparsely with baobab trees or bushes, and watered by a few large rivers of which the greatest is the Niger.

The most important peoples of the Western Sudan in this period were, from west to east, the Wolof; the Mande-language peoples (including the Soninke of Ancient Ghana and the Mandinka of Mali); the Songhay of Gao; the Fulani; the Hausa of northern Nigeria; and the Kanuri of Bornu and the country east of Lake Chad.

These peoples had their own names for the countries where they dwelt. The word Sudan is from Arabic: it came into use when the Berbers of North Africa began changing to the Arabic language after the Muslim conquests of the eighth century AD. They began to call the southern grasslands the Bilad as-Sudan, the Country of the Blacks. They were intensely interested in this distant country beyond the Sahara Desert, mainly for reasons of trade. They sent down trading expeditions and went into partnership with Sudanese peoples. Exploit-

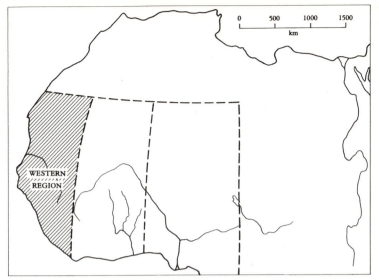

6 *The western region (Senegambia).*

ing this partnership in trade, leading Sudanese peoples formed large states and empires. Three preliminary points about these states should be noted.

Firstly, Western Sudanese peoples and their Guinea neighbours had many forms of wealth which were valuable in long-distance trade.

Secondly, communications across the Sahara improved when Asian camels began to be widely used. Camels are better for use in sandy desert than horses, mainly because they have broader feet, and sink in less. Camels were increasingly used after about AD 100.

Thirdly, technical progress in West Africa led to an expansion in production, and therefore in trade, after about the beginning of the Christian Era. This was especially true of mining.

Early trade

Gold and ivory were the products of old West Africa that were desired above all else by the traders of the north. Trans-Saharan commerce in these items helped to build the comfort and splendour of large North African cities such as Carthage, Leptis, and Sabratha, back in the times of Phoenician and Roman rule before about AD 400. But the main expansion of the trans-Saharan long distance trade came after the

29

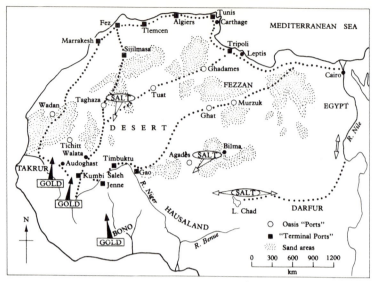

7 *Trade and trading-routes across the Sahara in the times of the great trading empires and terminal and oasis 'ports'.*

Muslim conquests of North Africa in the eighth century AD. It was from this time onwards that the trade began to have important results for the Western and Central Sudan.

This trade was to everyone's advantage. The peoples of West Africa, for example, had one great need which the peoples of the Sahara, or those beyond the Sahara, could help to supply. This was salt. It is probably true that salt was no less valued by the peoples of West Africa than gold by the peoples who lived to the north of the desert.

So the basis of trade between the Sudan and the Berbers of the Sahara oases lay in the exchange of salt for gold. But this was only the basis of trade. The whole system was much wider. For the Saharan Berbers sold the goods they bought from the Sudan to the Arab traders of North Africa, and the traders of North Africa sold them again to Europeans and Asians. European and Asian goods came down into West Africa by the same methods.

There were many other items of trade besides gold and salt. West Africa, for example, also needed copper, silks, and more metalware (such as pots and pans and swords) than West Africans could make themselves. West Africa also supplied ivory and kola nuts. Both sides bought a few slaves.

All this trade led to the founding of cities. Most of these cities were especially concerned with the trade across the Sahara. They began as small trading settlements, but grew bigger as more traders came and went. They became centres for craftsmen who worked in leather, wood, ivory and metals.

Then city governments were needed, as well as men trained to be put in charge of keeping accounts, of maintaining law and order, of looking after the safety of citizens.

Then the rulers of these cities began to extend their power to ever wider regions of neighbouring countryside. Gradually the cities grew into states, and the states grew into empires.

This long historical process, from trading settlements to trading empires, also occurred to the north and east of the Sahara. Trading settlements and cities also appeared in the stony lands of the Sahara itself. These were Berber cities. Some of them are alive to this day: Agadès, Ghat and Murzuk, for example. Others, like Walata and Tichitt, still exist but have lost their wealth and importance. Others again, such as Audoghast and Sijilmasa, have entirely disappeared.

The same process of city-founding and empire-building went on in the grasslands to the south of the Sahara. Here, too, some of the old cities of the Western and Central Sudan have disappeared, while others, like Timbuktu, Gao and Jenne, are still there. And the main business of these old cities of the Sudan was also to conduct the trade that came and went across the Sahara, and was fed by the wealth of West Africa.

Crossing the Sahara

It was always hard and dangerous to conduct this trade. Ibn Batuta has left a vivid description of how he crossed the desert in 1352. He tells how he travelled down from Fez to Sijilmasa, then one of the greatest of the market-centres on the northern side of the Sahara. There in Sijilmasa he purchased four months' supply of food for his camels. Together with a company of Moroccan merchants who were also travelling to the Western Sudan, Ibn Batuta journeyed on to Taghaza, a principal salt-producing centre of the great desert. At Taghaza, he tells us, 'We passed ten days of discomfort, because the water there is bitter and the place is plagued with flies. And there, at Taghaza, water supplies are laid on (by the caravan captains) for the crossing of the desert that lies beyond it, which is a ten nights' journey with no water on the way except on rare occasions.'

'We indeed had the good fortune to find water in plenty, in pools left by the rain,' Ibn Batuta continues. 'One day we found a pool of fresh

Part of a camel caravan crossing the Sahara desert.

water between two rocky hills. We quenched our thirst at it, and washed our clothes.

'At that time we used to go ahead of the caravan, and when we found a place suitable for pasturage we would graze our beasts. We went on doing this until one of our party was lost in the desert; after that I neither went ahead nor lagged behind. We passed a caravan on the way, and they told us that some of their party had become separated from them. We found one of them dead under a shrub, of the sort that grows on the sand, with his clothes on and a whip in his hand. . . .' Many brave men died on those harsh trading journeys.

The trade continued in spite of all the dangers and difficulties. It brought many changes to all the peoples who had a part in it. This was the trade that shaped the growth of states and empires in the Western Sudan.

Foremost among these early states was Ancient Ghana.

SUMMARY

Facts about the trans-Saharan trade

1 It began a very long time ago. The earliest 'markers' on trans-desert ('cross'-desert) caravan trails were put there by Berbers who lived more than 2,500 years before now. But this long-distance trade became much bigger and more important for many peoples after the rise of powerful Muslim states in North Africa: after, that is, about AD 650. The trade reached its height around AD 1500. It lost much of its importance after the rise of a big coastal trade with Europeans round the shores of West Africa: after, that is, about AD 1650.

2 For the Western and Central Sudan, there were three impoitant groups of trails across the desert between West and North Africa. One group was in the far west, linking Morocco with West African markets along the Senegal River and the upper reaches of the Niger River. A second group was in the centre, linking Algeria with West African markets on the middle reaches of the Niger: markets such as Jenne and Timbuktu. A third group of trails was further east, linking Tunisia and the Fezzan with the markets of Kanem-Bornu.

   Further east again there were other trails linking Libya and Egypt with the states of the Eastern Sudan, including Darfur. Another important route, running west-east, linked the markets of Kanem-Bornu with Darfur, and onward to the Nile.

3 West African exports along these routes were gold, ivory, and other products, as well as domestic servants who were treated as slaves. The most important West African imports were salt and copper, but these imports also included many luxury goods for privileged and wealthy people: horses, fine cloths, silk garments, steel weapons, as well as books for Muslim scholars.

CHAPTER FOUR
The empire of Ghana

Soninke and Berber traders

Our three main sources of knowledge about the ancient Sudan —
archaeology, oral history, and the books written by Africans or Arabs —
tell us a good deal about the famous empire of Ghana.

We can be sure of some of the things they tell us; other things must be
left in doubt. What we can be sure of is that early West Africans who
lived to the north of the upper waters of the Niger River formed
themselves into a strong trading state. This state spread its power over
many neighbouring peoples: in other words, the state became an
empire. It commanded a large region of trade, security and strong
government. It lasted for several hundred years. It was deeply respected
by travellers who came within its borders, and by others, living far
beyond Ghana's borders, who heard of it or read about it.

We can be fairly sure, too, that the peoples who formed this state and
empire were Soninke who spoke one of the languages of the Mande
group; languages that are spoken today by many of the peoples of the
westerly regions of the Western Sudan. These founders of Ghana had
good trading relations with the Berber chiefs and traders who lived to
the north of them, in oasis towns in the Sahara; and it was through them
that they conducted their trade across the desert.

Growth of Ghana

The Soninke certainly built their state before AD 773, the date of the
first North African reference to it. But exactly how long before we do not
know. It is possible that they were traders in this region in very distant
times. A tradition recorded in the *Tarikh as-Sudan,* an important history

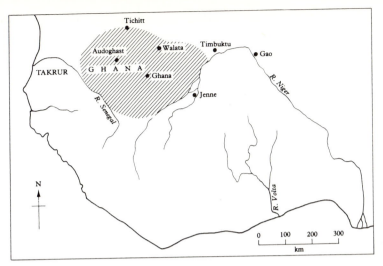

8 Ancient Ghana (very approximate frontiers).

book that was written in Timbuktu about AD 1650, says that there were twenty-two kings of Ghana before the beginning of the Muslim Era (AD 622) and twenty-two kings after that. If this were true, it could place the origins of the Ghana kingdom in about AD 300.

By 800, in any case, Ghana had become a powerful trading state. Called Wagadu by its rulers, the name of Ghana came into general use because of one of the king's titles, *ghana* or war chief.[1] Each succeeding king was known by his own name, and also by the title of *ghana*. Another of his titles was *kaya maghan*. This means 'lord of the gold', because the king controlled the export of that precious metal.

Nothing is known about the political methods or history of Ghana under its early kings. What probably happened was that heads of large families or descent-lines[2] among the Soninke, encouraged by the needs and opportunities of the trade in gold and other goods with Berber

---

[1] There are two reasons why the modern state of Ghana, though situated far away from Ancient Ghana, has the same name. One reason is that the old traditions speak of a movement of some of the people of Ancient Ghana southward into the region of Asante. Another reason is that the modern leaders of Ghana wished to celebrate the independence of their country — formerly called the Gold Coast — by linking their new freedom to the glorious traditions of the past.

[2] This term will be used often in these pages. A descent-line or lineage means just what it says: a line of family descent, through fathers or through mothers, which links one generation to another, and goes on for several or for many generations. This means that all the successive members of a descent-line look back to the same 'founding ancestors'. Nearly always, they revered these ancestors as persons of great authority and power in the world of the spirits.

35

merchants of the Sahara, saw an advantage in having a single ruler. So they elected a king from among themselves. This king's duty was to organise the trade and keep good relations with the Saharan traders, as well as acting as senior religious leader and as representative on earth of the 'founding ancestors' of the Soninke people.

In this way the king gathered power. He controlled the trade within Soninke territory. He made gifts and gave rewards to all who served him.

Next came an expansion of Soninke power over neighbouring peoples who were also busy with trade: the wider the territory the Soninke could control, the more prosperous they would be. By 800, the king of Ghana was able to make lesser kings or chiefs obey his laws and pay him taxes. And so the king's wealth increased. With more wealth, he also had more power. He could command the services of many descent-lines. He could raise big armies. He could employ large numbers of messengers and other servants. He could pay for the needs of a growing empire.

Some account of how this was done for the later kings of Ghana is given in books written by North African and Spanish Arab authors during the eleventh and twelfth centuries AD.

One of these books offers a brilliantly clear picture of the court of the emperor of Ghana in about AD 1065, and of the way in which that emperor, whose name was Tunka Manin, organised his power and wealth. This book was the work of a Spanish Arab called Al-Bakri.[1] He finished it in 1067.

The achievement of Ghana

From this account of Al-Bakri's we can know a little more about what had happened during earlier times. It appears that many of the North African and Berber traders of the Sahara accepted Islam after the Arab conquest of the eighth century. They abandoned their old religions and became Muslims. They were made welcome at the capital of the emperor of Ghana. He was not a Muslim; he believed in Ghana's own religion, but he allowed the Muslims to build a town of their own.

The 'town of the Muslim traders' was ten kilometres away from the emperor's own town with its surrounding settlements. While the latter were built in the traditional materials of West Africa — hardened clay, thatch, and wooden beams — the most successful Muslim traders

---

[1] Al-Bakri did not visit Ghana himself, but collected information from North African travellers who did.

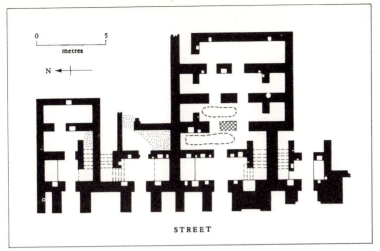

Group of houses excavated at Kumbi Saleh. Note the narrow rooms, staircases and thick walls giving on to streets.

preferred to build their houses in stone, according to their own customs in North Africa. It is not known exactly where the capital was when Al-Bakri wrote his book. In the course of Ghana's long history, the king's capital was undoubtedly moved from one place to another. But we can add a good deal to Al-Bakri's picture by studying the remains of Ghana's last capital, which lay at Kumbi Saleh about 320 kilometres north of modern Bamako. Here too there was a town where the king of Ghana lived, and another nearby town where the Muslim traders had their houses and stables. At the height of its prosperity, before AD 1240, this city of Kumbi was evidently the biggest West African city of its day, and had as many as 15,000 inhabitants or even more.

So long as they obeyed the laws of Ghana and paid their taxes, the traders from the north were sure of safety and hospitality. This was a partnership in long-distance trade that went on for a very long time. Its safety depended on the strength of the emperor and his government. Al-Bakri has left us a description of all that. King Tunka Manin, he wrote, 'is the master of a large empire and of a formidable power'. So powerful was this king, that he could put out '200,000 warriors in the field, more than 40,000 of them being armed with bow and arrow'. But the real strength of the Ghana armies, as we know from other North African sources, came from their power in iron-pointed spears. Their weapons, like their government, were stronger than those of their neighbouring peoples; and it was this strength which helped to build their empire.

37

Working from eyewitness accounts which he had received from Muslim travellers, Al-Bakri described the pomp and majesty of King Tunka Manin:

> When the king gives audience to his people, to listen to their complaints and to set them to rights, he sits in a pavilion around which stand ten pages holding shields and gold-mounted swords. On his right hand are the sons of the princes of his empire, splendidly clad and with gold plaited in their hair.
>
> The governor of the city is seated on the ground in front of the king, and all around him are his counsellors in the same position. The gate of the chamber is guarded by dogs of an excellent breed. These dogs never leave their place of duty. They wear collars of gold and silver, ornamented with metals.
>
> The beginning of a royal meeting is announced by the beating of a kind of drum they call *deba*. This drum is made of a long piece of hollowed wood. The people gather when they hear its sound...

The memory of these old glories were long remembered among the peoples of the Western Sudan. Five hundred years later, for example, a writer of Timbuktu called Mahmud Kati entertained his readers with the stories of those ancient days. In his valuable history book, the *Tarikh al-Fattash*, he tells how a certain king of Ghana of the seventh century, called Kanissa'ai, possessed one thousand horses, and how each of these horses 'slept only on a carpet, with a silken rope for halter', and had three personal attendants, and was looked after as though it were itself a king.

These old stories, magnified and embroidered with the passing of the years, also tell how the kings of Ghana used to give great banquets to their subjects, feeding ten thousand people at a time, and dispensing gifts and justice to all who came. Such stories give an idea of the greatness of Ghana's reputation in the years of its power.

Government of the empire

If we look carefully behind the travellers' information collected and written down by Al-Bakri and other Arab writers, and behind the stories that were afterwards told in countless homes for many years, we can trace several developments in ways of life. These were of great importance to West Africa. They must be clearly understood.

With the growth of Ghana, and of other states like Ghana, the peoples of West Africa were inventing new methods of living together, of governing themselves, of raising money to pay for government, and of producing wealth. These ways needed a single strong authority or government which could rule over many lesser authorities or governments. This central authority or government could only, in the thought and customs of the times, be a king.[1]

In states like Ancient Ghana, the power of government increased still further. Important kings became kings over lesser kings. They became what are called emperors. At the heart of the explanation of why this happened there was the growth, as we have seen, of international trade. Occupying the lands to the north of the upper waters of the Niger, the old Ghana rulers and their people enjoyed a position of great power and value. Their towns and trading settlements became the go-betweens or middlemen between the Berber and Arab traders of the north and the gold and ivory producers of the south.

It was this *middleman position* which made Ghana strong and prosperous. It was this that gave its rulers gold and glory. It was this that paid for its armies, and made its civilisation shine with a light whose dazzling brilliance we can still glimpse in the writings of Al-Bakri. Little by little, the people of Ghana and their rulers felt the need for a strong government not only over themselves, but also over their neighbours, so that they could ensure peace and order throughout a wide region of the Western Sudan. For only in this way could they make the best use of their middleman position. And at the same time as they felt this need, they also had the chance of realising it. They were skilled workers in iron. They were able to use iron weapons against neighbours who generally did not have any.

As time passed, the ruling men of Ghana, the Soninke people of the Mande group, further extended their political power. They strengthened their middleman position by bringing lesser states like Takrur (in modern Senegal) under their control. They pushed their borders southeastward in the direction of the land of the gold producers, and they also pushed their influence northward into the Sahara. They took control of south-Saharan cities like Audoghast, a famous market which, as we noted before, has long since disappeared. In this way the emperors of Ghana wielded power and commanded wealth. They were among the greatest men of their time.

Their system of government expanded with their success in trade. As it expanded, it became more complicated. A king and his counsellors

[1] Today, of course, a central government can be many things besides a king. In fact, kings have almost disappeared from the modern world. They have disappeared because the *stage of social organisation,* which required kings in the old days, requires them no longer. People have invented more modern ways of government.

could rule over a small country. They could not rule over a large one unless they could also rule through lesser kings and counsellors. Even with the swift horses of the Western Sudan, a king's orders would have gone too slowly through the land, and would not have been obeyed. So the king of Ghana needed governors whom he could place in charge of distant provinces.

In this way there grew up a number of lesser governments, under lesser kings or governors. These gave loyalty and paid taxes to a single central government. Compared with what we have today, all this was a simple and crude sort of government. Ordinary folk ran many dangers. They were often bullied or plundered. But the growth and conduct of trade over a wide region meant peace and security over this region; and many people of Ghana benefited from this. The formation of Ghana and its growth into a large empire therefore marked an important stage in social development. It was a big political and economic achievement.

Revenue and wealth of Ghana

Before leaving this subject we must look a little more closely at how the emperors ruled, maintained their public services, and met the expenses of keeping law and order. For they established ways of government which appeared again and again, afterwards, in the Sudan.

Where did King Tunka Manin and the emperors who ruled before him find the wealth to pay many soldiers, and to feed and arm them? Where did they get the means to make rich gifts to strangers from other lands? Questions like these take us back to the economic system of the Ghana empire. And it is Al-Bakri, once again, who gives the answers. He explains how the rulers of Ghana used their control of the long-distance trade.

The ruler of Ghana, Al-Bakri tells us, had two main sources of revenue,[1] of wealth with which to pay for government. These were taxes of two kinds. The first of these was what we should today call an *import and export tax*. This tax consisted of sums of money (or more probably their equal in goods) which traders had to pay for the right to bring goods into Ghana, or to take other goods out of the empire. 'The king of Ghana', wrote Al-Bakri, 'places a tax of one dinar of gold on each donkey-load of salt that comes into his country'. But he also 'places a tax of two dinars of gold on each load of salt that goes out'. Similar taxes,

---

[1] 'Revenue' means the money or other kinds of wealth that governments get from taxes.

higher or lower in value as the case might be, were applied to loads of copper and other goods.[1]

The second kind of tax was what we should call a *production tax*. It was applied to gold, the most valuable of all the products of the country. 'All pieces of gold that are found in the empire,' says Al-Bakri on this point, 'belong to the emperor'. But this regulation was more than a means of collecting royal wealth. It was also a way of keeping up the price of gold. For if the emperor had not insisted on taking possession of all pieces of gold, Al-Bakri explains, then 'gold would become so abundant as practically to lose its value'.

Ancient Ghana, in short, adopted the monopoly system that is employed to this day for another precious commodity, diamonds. Most of the diamonds of the world are mined by a handful of big companies. These companies work hand-in-hand with each other. They have agreed among themselves not to put all the diamonds they mine on the market. If they did, they would drive down the price, for diamonds would then cease to be scarce; and what is not scarce is not expensive. Instead, the diamond companies sell their diamonds in small quantities, according to the demand for them, so their price stays high. The old emperors of Ghana did much the same with their pieces or nuggets of gold.

They were able to do this because of Ghana's strong trading position. West African gold was important to Europe as well as to North Africa and the Near East. In earlier times the Europeans had obtained the gold they needed, whether for money, ornaments, or the display of personal wealth, from mines in Europe or in western Asia. These mines were becoming worked out at about the time of the rise of Ghana. Where else could Europeans and North Africans obtain gold? Only, as history shows, from West Africa.

And so it came about that the gold used in North Africa and Europe was largely supplied, century after century, by the producers of West Africa. Even kings in distant England had to buy West African gold before they could order their craftsmen to make coins in this precious metal. It was on this steady demand for gold that the states and empires of the Western Sudan founded their prosperity.

Ghana began the trade in gold. As time went by, other peoples began to copy Ghana's success. When Ghana disappeared in the thirteenth century AD, its place was eventually taken by another great empire built on the same foundations and by much the same methods. This new

---

[1] The dinar was a gold coin of North Africa.

empire was called Mali. It carried the progress made under Ghana to a new level of development.

The fall of Ghana: the Almoravids

But a long period of confusion came between the fall of Ghana and the triumph of Mali.

After about 1050, Ghana began to be invaded by Berber warriors from the north-west, from the Mauretanian Sahara. These Berbers were driven by troubles of their own, mainly poverty, into striving for a share in the wealth of more prosperous neighbours. Soon after AD 1000 they began to look for a new means of livelihood.

The solution they found, as so often in history, took a religious form. There arose among them a devout and very strict Muslim leader called Abdullah ibn Yasin. He established a centre of religious teaching, called a hermitage. He and those who followed him became known as the people of the hermitage, Al-Murabethin, or the Almoravids. Gradually, ibn Yasin brought the Berber communities of the far western lands under his influence. At the same time his missionaries set about the task of converting the rulers of those states in far western Africa whom they could reach, especially in Takrur (or Futa Toro), and in this they had

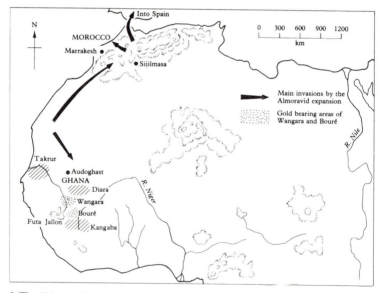

9 The Almoravid invasions.

some success. In 1056, moving northwards into Morocco, the Almoravids captured the great city of Sijilmasa, the main northern trading centre for West African gold. From there they went further to the north, conquering the rest of Morocco. Then they crossed the Straits of Gibraltar, and took over Al-Andalus, or Muslim Spain.

A southern section of the Almoravid movement meanwhile moved against Ghana. Its leader, Abu Bakr, put himself at the head of a Berber confederation, made an alliance with the people of Takrur, whom we shall discuss in a moment, and waged a long war against Ghana. In 1054 he took the city of Audoghast. In 1076, after many battles, the Almoravids seized the capital of the empire.

But these invaders, like others after them, could not hold the West African lands they had taken. There was much resistance. There were many revolts. Abu Bakr was killed while attempting to suppress one of these in 1087. By this time, however, the Ghana empire had fallen apart. Its last kings had authority over only a few of its former provinces, and we know almost nothing about them. Great changes were on the way.

The successor states of Ghana

In this time of confusion, set in motion by the Almoravid Berbers but soon bringing other peoples into action, the Ghana empire broke up, and some smaller states tried to build small empires of their own. One was the state of Takrur. Another was Diara. A third was Kaniaga. In some of these, a new name now enters on the scene, that of the Peul (or Pullo in the singular) whom in English we call Fulani (or Fulah in the singular).

These Fulani were to make several big contributions to West African history. The biggest of these will be described later on. Meanwhile we should note that the Fulani were and are a West African people of a somewhat different physical stock from most of their neighbours, but who spoke (and speak) a language related to the languages of Senegal.

They seem to have originated in the lands that lie near the upper waters of the Niger and Senegal Rivers, and to have shared these lands with peoples like the Soninke who played a leading part in the formation of Ghana. They appear to have begun as cattle-keeping farmers, which is what many of them remain to this day.

When Ghana suffered the blows of Abu Bakr and his armies, the Fulani of Takrur (in the northern part of modern Senegal) became independent. They in turn set out upon the road of conquest. After about AD 1200 they took control of the kingdom of Diara, once a

The door to a chief's house in Walata. This kind of decoration has not changed for hundreds of years.

province of Ghana. Their most successful leader, whose name was Sumanguru, seized Kumbi Saleh, then the capital of Ghana, in about 1203. Meanwhile other Fulani and allied peoples became powerful in another old Ghana province, the kingdom of Kaniaga.

But this new attempt at building an empire out of the ruins of Ghana met with no better fortune than the Berber efforts led by Abu Bakr. Two developments brought Sumanguru's enterprise to defeat. The first was that the Muslim traders of Kumbi Saleh, Ghana's last capital, rejected Sumanguru's overlordship. For reasons that were no doubt partly religious and partly commercial, they left Kumbi Saleh and travelled northward, to form a new trading centre at Walata,[1] far beyond the reach of Sumanguru's soldiers. Secondly, in about 1240 or maybe a few years earlier, Sumanguru was challenged by the Mandinka people of the little state of Kangaba, near the headwaters of the River Niger. The two armies fought each other at a famous battle. Sumanguru was defeated and killed. His chiefs and generals retreated to Takrur, where they and their successors continued to rule for many years.

Sumanguru's defeat opened a new chapter in history. For the little state of Kangaba was the heart and core of the future empire of Mali. It was to be the Mandinka people who would now bring peace and order to wide regions of the Western Sudan.

[1] See map on page 35.

Summary of Ghana dates

Some time after AD 300	Origins of Ghana.
Soon after 700	New trade begins with Muslims of North Africa and Sahara.
About 1050	Ghana at height of its power. Al-Bakri describes King Tunka Manin (in 1067).
1054	Beginning of Almoravid invasion. Almoravids capture Audaghost, one of Ghana's important trading towns.
1076	Almoravids capture Ghana capital (probably Kumbi Saleh).
About 1203	Sumanguru takes Kumbi Saleh.
About 1240	End of Ghana empire.

WESTERN REGION II

CHAPTER FIVE

The empire of Mali

Kangaba

The old traditions of the Western Sudan suggest that Kangaba, the little state that was to grow into the mighty empire of Mali, was founded some time before AD 1000. What is certain is that the Mandinka people of Kangaba were also middlemen in the gold trade during the later period of Ancient Ghana. They were important among those who carried to the north the gold of Wangara, the gold-bearing country that is now the northern part of the Republic of Guinea, to the market centres of Ghana. Probably it was through these gold-traders of Kangaba that the rulers of Ghana and their agents were able to secure their main supplies of gold.

In later times the traders of Mali, the Dyula or Wangara as they are still called, were to become famous for their skill and enterprise. There is reason to think that they were similarly active in the days of Ancient Ghana as well. It is likely that while Kangaba was a subject country of the Ghana empire, perhaps sending yearly gifts to its ruler in exchange for friendly protection against enemies and rivals, the traders of Kangaba enjoyed positions of privilege within the empire.

There was a two-sided interest here. The government of Ghana needed gold, and it was largely from Wangara that Ghana's gold must come. But the traders who dealt in the gold of Wangara also needed a market, and it was only in Ghana that they could find this market.[1]

When the empire of Ghana was split into pieces by attacks from without and revolts from within, this peaceful system of two-way interest was destroyed. All was then in the melting-pot for new rivalries for power. Eventually, as we have seen, Sumanguru prevailed. Once

[1] See map on page 42.

Sumanguru had mastered Kumbi and the main caravan routes, it was with him and his agents that the Mandinka of Kangaba had to conduct their business.

Yet Sumanguru, as we have also noted, was never able to set up a firm and lasting system of law and order over the lands he had conquered. Others challenged his power. The caravan routes ceased to be safe and peaceful. And no doubt the people of Kangaba, whose livelihood was thus threatened and who were increasingly oppressed by Sumanguru, were troubled by all this. In about 1240, at any rate, they decided to enter the struggle themselves. They made a bid for their own independence, and they won.

Growth of Mali

The legends tell the story in more colourful and personal terms. They speak of Sumanguru's harsh taxation, of his bad government, of his seizure of Mandinka women. These abuses caused the Mandinka to revolt. Fearing reprisals by Sumanguru, who had a frightening reputation for dangerous witchcraft, the ruler of Kangaba fled. But the situation was saved for him by a brother whom he had exiled. This

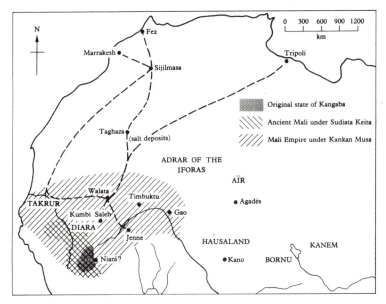

10 *The expansion of the empire of Mali (very approximate frontiers).*

brother was Sundiata Keita. Returning from exile with an army, Sundiata gathered friends and allies, increased his forces, gave them fresh heart and courage, and marched boldly against the dreaded Sumanguru.

'As Sundiata advanced with his army to meet Sumanguru', say the old legends,

> he learned that Sumanguru was also coming against him with an army prepared for battle. They met in a place called Kirina [not far from the modern Kulikoro]. When Sundiata turned his eyes on the army of Sumanguru, he believed they were a cloud and he said: 'What is this cloud on the eastern side?' They told him it was the army of Sumanguru. As for Sumanguru, when he saw the army of Sundiata, he exclaimed: 'What is that mountain of stone?' For he thought it was a mountain. And they told him: 'It is the army of Sundiata, which lies to the west of us.'
>
> Then the two columns came together and fought a terrible battle. In the thick of the fight, Sundiata uttered a great shout in the face of the warriors of Sumanguru, and at once these ran to get behind Sumanguru. The latter, in his turn, uttered a great shout in the face of the warriors of Sundiata, all of whom fled to get behind Sundiata. Usually, when Sumanguru shouted, eight heads would rise above his own head.

But Sumanguru's witchcraft, the legends say, proved less powerful than the witchcraft of Sundiata. Sumanguru was struck with an arrow bearing the spur of a white cock, fatal to his power, and 'Sumanguru vanished and was seen no more. . .' After this victory, Sundiata became the master of a new empire, governing through powerful and able men who were the heads of leading Mandinka descent-lines, each with a province under his control.

The capital of Kangaba at this time was at a place called Niani, a city that has long since disappeared but was located near the River Niger, not far from the frontier of Modern Guinea and modern Mali. And from about this time the name 'Mali', which meant 'where the king resides', absorbed the name Kangaba, and the empire of Mali was born.

The rulers of Mali

Sundiata was the founder of the empire of Mali, but not the first of Mali's kings. This was Barmandana, who is said to have ruled in about

1050. He became a Muslim, and made the pilgrimage to Mecca that all Muslims are supposed to make at least once in their lives. He was followed by other kings of whom we know nothing but their names.

Sundiata, sometimes called Mari-Diata, came to the throne in about 1245. He ruled for about 25 years, doing great deeds.

Next came his son Uli, who also took the royal title of *mansa* (lord in the Mandinka language), and followed in the conquering path of his more famous father. He ruled from about 1260 to about 1277. Like other Mali kings, he made the pilgrimage.

Then came two of Uli's brothers, Wati and Khalifa, but we do not know the dates of their reigns. They were said to be weak kings who ruled badly. Khalifa's subjects revolted against him, and killed him. Power then passed to Abu Bakr who ruled until 1298.

In 1298 the throne was seized by a freed 'slave of the court'. This was Sakuru who proved one of Mali's strongest rulers. He held power till 1308. After him came *Mansa* Qu and *Mansa* Muhammad.

In 1312 another great ruler came to power, *Mansa* Kankan Musa. He ruled till 1337[1], and was followed by *Mansa* Magha, who ruled for about four years, and then by *Mansa* Suleyman, who ruled with much success till about 1360. Then came another Mari-Diata who ruled for about thirteen years, and was followed by other kings of less importance. By about 1400 the great period of the Mali empire was drawing to a close.

The achievement of Mali

Mali repeated the achievement of Ancient Ghana on a still greater scale. Its rulers secured or regained control of the gold-producing lands of Wangara and Bambuk. They invaded most of Diara to the north-west. They pushed their power down the Niger River to the shores of Lake Deba. They formed one of the largest of the world's empires of those times.

Three periods of success occurred:
1 Under Sundiata (about 1235-60). He founded the empire.
2 Under *Mansa* Sakuru (about 1298-1308). He extended the empire. 'Under his powerful government,' wrote the great North African historian, ibn Khaldun, in about 1400, 'the power of Mali became mighty. All the nations of the Sudan stood in awe of Mali, and the merchants of North Africa travelled to his country.'

[1] The year of Musa's death is often given as 1332. But Ibn Khaldun (born Tunis 1332; died Cairo 1406) whose writings are our best source of information on the dates of the rulers of Mali, has recorded that Musa was still alive in 1337.

3 Under *Mansa* Kankan Musa (about 1312-37). He again extended the empire. His success was maintained by *Mansa* Suleyman (about 1340-60).

Mansa Kankan Musa

When *Mansa* Musa came to power, Mali already had firm control of the trade routes to the southern lands of gold and the northern lands of salt. Now Musa brought the lands of the Middle Niger under Mali's rule. He enclosed the cities of Timbuktu and Gao within his empire. He imposed his rule on southern trading towns such as Walata. He pushed his armies northward as far as the important salt-producing place called Taghaza, on the northern side of the great desert. He sent them eastward beyond Gao to the borders of Hausaland. He sent them westward into Takrur.

So it came about that Musa enclosed a large part of the Western Sudan within a single system of law and order. He did this so successfully that Ibn Batuta, travelling through Mali about twelve years after Musa's death, found 'complete and general safety in the land'. This was a big political success, and made *Mansa* Musa into one of the greatest statesmen in the history of Africa.

The Dyula (Wangara) traders were greatly helped by all this. Their trading companies began to travel in many parts of West Africa.

These Dyula traders were men of skill and energy. But they also drew strength from being Muslims. Belonging to Islam gave them unity. They stuck together even when members of their trading companies came from different clans or territories.

Islam was now important in the western Sudan (see page 136: *Islam and West Africa*).

Like the Mali kings before him, Musa was a Muslim. But most of his people were not Muslims. So he supported the religion of the Mandinka people as well as Islam. Different religious customs and ceremonies were allowed at his court.

Musa's pilgrimage to Mecca became famous. He began it in 1324. His magnificent journey through the Egyptian capital of Cairo was long remembered with admiration and surprise throughout Egypt and Arabia, for Musa took with him so much gold, and gave away so many golden gifts, that 'the people of Cairo earned very big sums' thanks to his visit. So generous was Musa with his gifts, indeed, that he upset the value of goods on the Cairo market. Gold became more plentiful and therefore worth less, and so prices rose.

The North African Scholar, Al-Omari, who lived in Cairo a few years after *Mansa* Musa's visit and wrote the words we have just quoted, declared that of all the Muslim rulers of West Africa Musa was 'the most powerful, the richest, the most fortunate, the most feared by his enemies and the most able to do good to those around him'. Behind these words of praise we can glimpse the power and reputation that Mali drew from its control of a very wide region of trade in precious goods such as gold, salt, ivory and kola nuts.

Mali was now a world power, and recognised as such. Under *Mansa* Musa, Mali ambassadors were established in Morocco, Egypt, and elsewhere. Mali's capital was visited by North African and Egyptian scholars. On returning from pilgrimage, Musa brought back with him a

The old Sankore Mosque at Timbuktu.

number of learned men from Egypt. These settled in Mali and Timbuktu. One of them, called As-Saheli, designed new mosques at Gao and Timbuktu, and built a palace for the emperor. The fashion of building houses in brick now began to be popular among wealthy people in the cities of the Western Sudan.

Niani, the capital of all this empire, has long since disappeared. Yet as late as the sixteenth century, the Moroccan traveller Leo Africanus (Hassan ibn Muhammad al-Wazzan az-Zayyati) could still describe it as a place of 'six thousand hearths', and its inhabitants as 'the most civilised, intelligent and respected' of all the peoples of the Western Sudan.

The spread of Islam also called for new methods of rule. *Mansa* Musa opened courts of law for Muslims, alongside the old courts of law for those who were not Muslims.

The government of Mali

Like Ghana before it, Mali was ruled by kings who were the heads of important descent-lines or leading families. (See note on page 35). The kings ruled the different parts of the empire, called provinces, through governors; these governors were also the heads of local descent-lines. As well as these persons of important families, who were persons of privilege because of their birth, the king had some officials who did not come from important families. Some of these came from families who 'belonged' to the king because they had lost their civic rights, usually through being captured in wars. Later on, as we shall see, such 'slave officials', or 'king's men', were to get more power.

In the capital, at Niani, there were various top officials. Most of these were noblemen: that is, they came from important families. One was the *hari-farma*, in charge of the fishing on the Niger. Another was the *sao-farma*, responsible for looking after the forests of the empire. A third was the *babili-farma*, the king's 'minister of agriculture', just as the *khalissi-farma* was the 'minister of finance'.

This was a more complicated kind of government than Ancient Ghana's. That was because populations had grown in size; trade was bigger than before; society had become more complicated.

Rivals and successors

But the very success of this far-reaching empire was also a reason for its decline. The spread of metal-working and of trade, the growth of the ideas of kingship and of strong central government, the pressures of wealth and trading rivalry — all these and similar influences stirred many peoples in West Africa. Some of these peoples saw that there were new advantages in being free to run their own affairs. The ruler and people of the city of Gao, for example, had to pay taxes to the emperor of Mali. Now they became determined to be rid of these taxes. They believed they could do better on their own. Others thought as they did.

The truth was that Mali had outgrown its political and military strength. Only supremely skilful leadership at the centre could hold this wide empire together. *Mansa* Musa commanded that skill. His successors, generally, did not. For a while, all remained well with the empire, especially under the rule of *Mansa* Suleyman (about 1340-60). Then the good days were over. *Mansa* Mari Diata II, who followed Suleyman, was described by Ibn Khaldun as 'a bad ruler who oppressed the people, depleted the treasury, and nearly pulled down the structure of the government'. He was followed by several other rulers who did little better than he had done.

Mali remained a powerful empire until about 1400. Then it ran into a host of troubles. Gao rebelled. The Tuareg nomads of the southern Sahara, always hoping to win control of the market cities of the Western Sudan, seized Walata and even Timbuktu. The peoples of Takrur and its neighbouring lands, notably the Wolof, threw off their subjection to Mali. Others in the south-western region of the empire, especially the Mossi in what is now the modern Republic of Upper Volta, began to harass the emperor's governors and garrisons.

Yet the grand old system, now more than two hundred years old if we reckon its life from the time of Sundiata Keita, still enjoyed widespread respect. Many peoples had grown accustomed to thinking of the Mali *mansa*, the Mali *koy*, as their rightful overlord. The habit of thinking this was slow to die. And so it came about that the fame and reputation of this once wide system of imperial rule lived on for a long while after it had become weak and defenceless.

Even in the time of the powerful Songhay emperor, *Askia* Muhammad (1493-1528), the traditional frontier of Songhay and Mali was still recognised as running through the region of Sibiridugu — astride of the upper Niger, that is, in the neighbourhood of the river-city of Segu. And Niani, the capital of the old empire, was still a large and prosperous city. Commercially, too, the traders of Mali, the famous Dyula companies, were the most enterprising and successful merchants of all the western and central regions of West Africa. They travelled far and wide, across the plains and through the forests, trading even on the distant coast of central Guinea.

But the political power was mostly gone. As early as 1400 the Songhay ruler of Gao is said to have pillaged Niani itself. In 1431 the Tuareg rushed into Timbuktu. By the end of the century Mali had no power to the east of Segu. Even within his homeland, the Mali emperor could seldom do more than stand aside and let things happen. Yet he certainly tried. In 1534 he sent an ambassador to the coast for help from the Portuguese, with whom he and his predecessors had enjoyed good diplomatic and trading relations. But the king of Portugal was unable to help, and did nothing except send messengers and gifts to his ally *Mansa* Muhammad II. The time was still far ahead when Europeans would be strong enough to have any direct influence on the affairs of West Africa.

WESTERN REGION III

CHAPTER SIX
Early Senegambia before 1600

Senegambia

The name Senegambia is used for the coastland between the Senegal and Gambia Rivers, and for some of the inland country as well.

Takrur (Futa Toro)

Long before 1000, the region of the River Senegal was the scene of political advances connected with the long-distance trade northward through Mauretania to the cities of what afterwards became Morocco. This encouraged the growth of market cities such as Takrur, Sila and Berissa. These have long since vanished from the map, for reasons to be discussed later in this book. But nine centuries ago they formed the state of Takrur along the south bank of the river.

When the Ghana empire reached its height towards AD 1050, Takrur was part of its dominions. Afterwards it fell to the overlordship of the emperor of Mali, and then emerged as an independent state under a new line of rulers of Fulani origin.[1] Throughout these centuries, Takrur was a small but important state of market towns along the Senegal River, and as such forming a valuable link in the chain of long-distance commerce between the Western Sudan and North Africa.

The Wolof empire

Soon after AD 1300 the Wolof people come into history as the makers of

[1] See below, *Futa Toro and the Fulani*, page 59.

11 The Wolof empire and some neighbouring states.

a small state, called Jolof, in the central part of inland Senegal. Though little is known about their relations with Ghana or other states of the Western Sudan, it seems that their political methods were influenced by their neighbours. Jolof was ruled by a king, whose title was *burba*, through ruling families in much the same way that had been adopted by the Soninke of Ghana and the Mandinka of Mali. Here again was a case where an important descent-line chief who had religious duties, as the leader of ceremonies by which one people linked themselves with their 'founding ancestors' in the world of the spirits, was given political duties as well. Exercising these political and religious duties, the king became powerful.

Like early Ghana long before, Jolof began to form a number of little 'daughter states' during the fourteenth century. This was a type of political development which happened in many lands. It occurred at much the same time, for example, among the Yoruba of Western Nigeria: the Yoruba 'mother state' of Ife set the pattern for the formation of other Yoruba states which were governed in the same way.[1] So the *Burba* Jolof, like the *Oni* of Ife, came to have religious and political power over lesser Wolof states of which the principal ones were Cayor, Walo, and Baol. These the *burba* and his government of Jolof joined into a powerful Wolof empire during the fifteenth century. At the same time a related people, the Serer, formed a state called Sine-Salum; this became an outlying part of the Wolof empire.

Wolof government and trade

Up to the middle of the sixteenth century the empire was held firmly together by the government of the *burbas*. This government may be described, again like that of the Yoruba, as an aristocratic one. It was ruled by privileged men or nobles who drew their power from being born into ruling families. Their political strength came from their leadership in warfare, their control of trade, and their close alliance with one another under the rule of the *burba*. They also had religious power that came from Wolof beliefs about the spiritual character of their rulers.

This aristocratic system was well described by the earliest European, a Venetian called Cadamosto, who wrote about the Wolof after a visit in 1455. He explained that the *Burba* Jolof was not chosen simply by birth. Usually, he said, 'three or four lords (of whom there are many in this country) choose a king whom they like. . .and who reigns as long as he pleases them. [But] they often dethrone their kings by force, and [on their side] the kings often try to make themselves so powerful that they cannot be dethroned. . .' Like other kings in other kingdoms that we shall examine in this book, the Wolof kings did this by appointing their own officials and servants to positions of power. These could serve the king by opposing the power of the nobles.

Most people had no political rights of much value. They were obliged to serve the nobles, pay tribute in cattle and other goods, and work for the nobles when required. Within these limits, however, the Wolof empire was prosperous and stable. It endured for many years. How strong it was is shown by a Portuguese report of 1506.[2] This says that the *Burba* Jolof had an army of 10,000 horsemen and 100,000 foot soldiers, no doubt an exaggeration but obviously pointing to the existence of a big military power.

With the development of European sea-trade along the coast of

---

[1] See Chapter 10, *Yoruba methods of government*, page 120.

[2] That of Duarte Pacheco Pereira, *Esmeraldo de Situ Orbis*.

Senegal, there came a gradual dissolution of Wolof power. European contacts had begun in the 1440s, at first as little more than piracy. Portuguese sailors and soldiers fortified the little island of Arguin, on the northerly coast of Mauretania, and raided the mainland for captives whom they took back to Portugal and sold into slavery. By the 1450s, however, this piracy had begun to give way to a regular partnership in trade between the Portuguese captains and the agents of the *Burba* Jolof and his subject-kings. Like other rulers, they proved willing to sell captives to the Europeans in exchange for the advantage of being able to buy European goods such as metalware, cotton cloth, and weapons.

Partnership in trade led to a political alliance with the Portuguese. One interesting example of how this worked occurred when Biram became *Burba* Jolof in 1481. Biram favoured as his heir a man who was his own mother's brother. This was resented by Biram's brothers who were the sons of other wives of his father. After Biram's death they revolted and deposed the prince whom Biram had chosen. This prince is known in the European records as Bemoy, from the Wolof word *bumi*, 'the chosen one'. Bemoy fled for help to Portugal. There in Lisbon he was splendidly welcomed and promised aid if he would become a Christian. The Portuguese records describe Bemoy as 'forty years old, a man of great stature, very dark, with a long beard, finely built and of a very noble appearance'.

Intending to make Bemoy their puppet ruler, and so gain indirect power in the Wolof empire, the Portuguese sent him back to Wolof with a fleet of 20 ships and many soldiers. But this attempt at warlike infiltration, a method which the Portuguese were afterwards to try in other African lands and sometimes with success, failed disastrously in Wolof. Bemoy was killed, and the expedition went home defeated.

Rivals to Jolof: the rise of Cayor

Although the Wolof proved strong enough to keep the Portuguese out of their country, they were unable to hold their empire together. The main reason for this lay in the advantages which the leading men of Cayor, the biggest of the 'daughter states' of Jolof, could now win from coastal trade with Europeans. As this trade expanded, the nobles of Cayor grew more powerful; and, growing more powerful, they became more independent. Finally, in about 1556, they rebelled against the *Burba* Jolof of that time and set up an independent kingdom under one of their number, whom they chose to be king, and whose royal title was *damel*. Encouraged by this success, Cayor then invaded Baol, and the *Damel* of

Cayor then became ruler of Baol as well. Their success in this was crowned a little later when Cayor defeated a Jolof army and killed the *burba* who was leading it.

From this time onwards the prosperity and therefore the power of Jolof declined because it was cut off by Cayor from contact with European trade.[1] Yet the *Damels* of Cayor proved incapable of building a strong empire. This was partly because Walo and Baol also shared in the advantages of European trade, and partly because they failed to form a firm alliance against Mauretanian Berbers, who repeatedly attacked these trading states from across the Senegal River.

In 1686, Baol threw off its subjection to Cayor. Not long afterwards Jolof again invaded Cayor, seeking to re-establish its former power, and this time with partial success because they were able to kill the *damel*. Many Cayor Wolof then fled to Baol. In subsequent fighting the *Burba* Jolof was himself killed in battle and his army thrown back. After this the king or *Teny* of Baol took control of Cayor and became its *damel*. This ruler, Latir Fal Sukabe, continued to rule over Baol and Cayor until 1702 when he was succeeded by two sons, the older of whom became *Damel* of Cayor while the younger became *Teny* of Baol.

Though with many wars such as these, and therefore with a great deal of misery for the mass of ordinary people, all these states maintained their independence of the Europeans until the late nineteenth century, when they were invaded and subjected by the French. They had formed a notable part of West African civilisation. But they had failed to overcome the quarrels between their aristocratic rulers, or to resolve the great conflict between the interests of the nobles and the interests of the majority of ordinary folk within their kingdoms.

Futa Toro and the Fulani

One other development in Senegal must be noticed. This was the rise of a new state in old Takrur, north-east of the Wolof states. With this the Fulani and their near-relations, the Tucolor,[2] now made a decisive entry on the scene of history.

We have come across the Fulani in earlier times. They were con-

---

[1] Here again, as explained in Chapter 10, there is an interesting parallel with Yoruba history. There, too, during the sixteenth century the Yoruba of Oyo, thanks to their command of long-distance trade with the Western Sudan, were able to outshine the power of Ife and its traditional ruler, the *oni*.

[2] Tucolor means 'people from Takrur'.

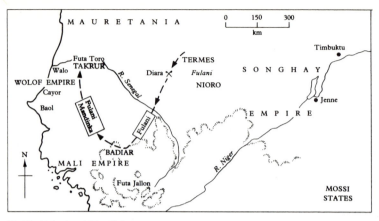

12 *The Fulani and Mandinka movements in the sixteenth century.*

cerned in the fall of Ancient Ghana and the rise of its successor states. But by this time they had spread far across the grasslands of West Africa from their original home near the upper Senegal River and the upper Niger.

They had sent out nomad groups of cattle-breeders both eastward and westward. These groups were certainly small in the beginning. But they built up their numbers. Some of them settled down and formed states of their own, so that, in the course of time, there came to be two kinds of Fulani: 'cattle Fulani' who lived the old nomad life of the countryside, and 'town Fulani' who preferred to live in towns. Because of this, and because of their wandering habits, the Fulani have played a special and at times a leading part in the history of the Western Sudan.

What some of these Fulani did, soon after 1500, is told by traditions which may be accepted as truthful in outline, though not in detail. A group of Fulani cattle-breeders, ruled by a prince called Tenguella, was living at this time in the broad plains between Termes and Nioro, lands that were once the homeland of Ancient Ghana in the country between the upper Niger and the Sahara. This area had passed from the control of Ghana to the control of Mali, and was now under the authority of the emperor of Songhay whose capital lay at Gao. This emperor, as we shall see in Chapter 7, was the vigorous and efficient *Askia* Muhammad, afterwards called *Askia* the Great.

Tenguella Koli and the Denianke

Tenguella, the Fulani leader, revolted against the overlordship of *Askia*

60

Muhammad. No doubt he and his people wanted freedom of movement for their cattle. Perhaps they also objected to the taxes which they were supposed to pay their Songhay overlord or his officials. Tenguella led his warriors across the plains against Diara, one of the old successor-states of Ghana whose king was now a vassal (that is, a tax-paying under-king) of the Songhay emperor. There is reason to think that Tenguella was encouraged by the reigning emperor of Mali, who was now a declining rival of *Askia* Muhammad of Songhay.

Askia Muhammad's brother, Amar, led an army against this Fulani raider. The two armies met near Diara in 1512. Amar won, and Tenguella was killed. But this proved only the beginning of the Fulani adventure.

Tenguella had a son named Koli by a wife who belonged to the ruling family of Mali. Tenguella Koli led his father's warriors south-westward, crossed the upper Senegal River and arrived in Badiar, a region which lies to the north-west of the Futa Jallon Mountains.[1] Here he was joined by many Mandinka soldiers, who saw in him a bold leader as well as a relation of their own overlord, the emperor of Mali.

Seeking a new home, these Fulani and Mandinka allies marched north-westward into Senegal, passed round the fringe of the Wolof states, and fell upon the ancient state of Takrur in Futa Toro. This state was then ruled by a family of Soninke chiefs who owed loyalty to the king of Diara. Tenguella Koli and his Fulani-Mandinka army over-threw these Soninke chiefs in 1559 and set up a new line of kings.

These new rulers in Futa Toro were called the Denianke. They proved strong and capable, and remained in control of this country until 1776, more than two centuries.

Notice, here, three developments.

Firstly, these Fulani had changed their way of life. Those who had set out to invade Diara at the beginning of the century were little more than a raiding band of cattle nomads. They were after revenge for real or fancied hurts; even more, they were after loot in the settled lands of Diara. They behaved no differently from the nomad Tuareg of the southern Sahara, who often attacked the settled lands and cities of the Western Sudan. But the Fulani who conquered and settled in Futa Toro, some fifty years later, were a people ready to abandon their wandering ways and build a state of their own. It seems that this change was largely due to their long contact with Mandinka people who were not nomads.

The *second* development, flowing from the first, was that these Fulani

[1] In the modern Republic of Guinea, and not to be confused with Futa Toro.

had adopted new ways of living together. They had accepted the political authority of chiefs and ruling families settled in one place. They had adopted city manners, and acquired an interest in trade.

Thirdly, these Fulani-Mandinka state-builders in Futa Toro held fast to their own religions. They resisted Islam. And because they resisted Islam, the Muslim traders of Futa Toro (of old Takrur) began to quit the trading towns which had long existed there. This kind of thing, we may recall, had occurred before, when the non-Muslim rulers of old Takrur had attacked and taken Kumbi, Ghana's ancient capital. Then the Muslim traders of Kumbi had retreated northward and founded a new trading centre in the southern Sahara at Walata, a market that was still important in the sixteenth century.

There followed from this clash of religions a real decline in the commercial importance of Futa Toro, and one that was to last for some time. It was at this period, it seems, that ancient and famous markets like Takrur itself, Sila, and Berissa began to disappear from the map. The writers of North Africa had often mentioned these markets in the past. Today we do not even know exactly where they lay.

Thus the sixteenth century in Futa Toro may be seen as a period of both advance and retreat. The new rulers brought strong methods of government, but they also provoked a serious decline of trade.

The Gambia, Futa Jallon, Sierra Leone

Southward from the Wolof states and Sine-Salum,[1] along the Gambia River and the coast towards Sierra Leone, there lived small populations in the scrublands and forests. Like their neighbours, these peoples had long since entered their Iron Age by AD 1000. They developed their own methods of farming, fishing, metal-working and other skills, and their arts of dancing, music, and sculpture.

Little is known of their early development. Deep in their forests, safe in their valleys or along their remote river banks, they remained for a long time on the margin of the busy world of the inland country. Most of them lived at what was then the back door of West Africa, facing an empty ocean that was not yet crossed by ships from other continents. We may imagine that they lived quiet lives, keeping to their ancient ways, warring with one another from time to time for land to cultivate, but generally content with their ancient methods of social and political organisation in small family groups.

[1] See map on page 56.

After 1300 there came a change. Many of these peoples began to feel the influence of the growing empire of Mali, and of the expanding power of the southerly Wolof states. Some of them had valuable products to sell, among these being the wax, for example, of the Diola people as well as a great deal of dried sea-fish. The Dyula trading companies of the Mandinka of Mali began to link them with the Western Sudan. They found new and bigger markets. Their country also began to be penetrated by wanderers from the inland country.

New states emerged. Around 1400 the Susu people, for example, formed a state in the Futa Jallon, the hill region that lies in the centre of the modern republic of Guinea. Other Susu afterwards moved down to the coast where most of their descendants live now, while a branch of the Fulani won control of Futa Jallon, remaining there to the present.

Others took the same route. In Sierra Leone, partly by migration from outside the area, new states began to be formed by the Bulom, Temne and Mende peoples on either side of the Scarcies River. Most of these incoming groups mingled with the populations whom they found in the country, adding to their numbers, sometimes keeping their own language and sometimes adopting the language of the local people among whom they settled. So that while it is true that some of their distant ancestors undoubtedly came from the grassland country of the north, most were the descendants of peoples who had lived in Sierra Leone since distant Stone Age times.

The beginning of sea trade

Further changes began when European captains sailed in from Portugal and Spain, England and France. They brought the coastal peoples a new and previously undreamt-of chance of sharing in long-distance trade. But they also brought firearms and new forms of warfare, and, not much later, the beginnings of the Atlantic slave trade.

These visitors from Europe did a good service to history: they wrote many reports of what they found, saw, and heard along the coast. These reports confirm that contacts with Mali had brought many little states into existence, and that these states were deeply engaged in trade with the Western Sudan. Thus the same Cadamosto who had visited the Wolof empire, in 1455, came up the Gambia River a year later, and described what he found here. He made his base on an island in the estuary of the Gambia,[1] and got in touch with local rulers who included

[1] At first called St Andrew's Island, then James Island when the British made a base there in 1661.

the *mansas* or kings of Baddibu and Niumi (Barra).

After disputes and difficulties, European trade with these small river-side states of the Gambia became regular and peaceful. Portuguese ships now began coming here several times a year. In 1506 Duarte Pacheco Pereira wrote about the Gambian markets of his time. Far up the river, he wrote,

> there is a country called Cantor [probably between Basse and Yarbutenda]. It has four villages of which the biggest is called Sutucoo and has 4,000 inhabitants. The others are Jalancoo, Dobancoo and Jamnan Sura. They are surrounded by palisades of timber. . . At Sutucoo there is held a big market. Mandinka traders come there with many donkeys. And when times are peaceful, these traders visit our ships [in the river], and we sell them red, blue and green cloth of cheap manufacture, linen and coloured silks, brass rings, hats and beads and other goods. Here in peaceful times we can buy five to six thousand *dobras'* worth of good quality gold. These lands of Sutucoo and their neighbours are part of the Wolof kingdom, but the people speak the Mandinka language. . .

Such reports were made on most parts of the Guinea seaboard. They show how these coastal peoples, having long had trade with the inland country, now found new and useful partners from the sea. They also indicate that these peoples were well able to defend themselves. Pereira says that the Bulom of Sierra Leone, for example, were 'a warlike people', who dealt in gold, which they bought from the traders of the empire of Mali in exchange for salt, and which they now sold to the Portuguese for brass rings, large metal basins, and cotton goods. 'And in this country you can buy ivory necklaces that are carved better than anywhere else.' So greatly did the Portuguese admire the skills of West African ivory-carvers that rich traders and noblemen commissioned many beautiful objects, such as salt-cellars, for their own use at home.

Pereira explains how Sierra Leone, the Mountain of the Lion, got its name. 'Many people,' he wrote, 'think that the name was given to this country because there are lions here, but this is not true. It was Pero de Sintra, a knight of Prince Henry of Portugal, who first came to this mountain. And when he saw a country so steep and wild he named it the land of the Lion, and not for any other reason. There is no reason to doubt this, for he told me so himself.'

Behind the Bulom (or Sherbro, as they are sometimes called) was the kingdom of Loko, speaking a related language. To the north of them were the Temne; and behind these again, over the modern frontier of

Sierra Leone with the Republic of Guinea, were the Susu and the Fulani of the Futa Jallon, as well as other Mande-speaking peoples.

Methods of government

Another early Portuguese report, that of Valentim Fernandes written between 1506 and 1510, throws light on the political methods of these states. He mentions villages which had kings of their own, and explains that these kings also had councils of elders. 'If the king wants to go to war, he gathers the elders and holds his council. And if it appears to them that the war is unjust, or that the enemy is very strong, they tell the king that they cannot help him, and give orders for peace in spite of the king's disagreement.' It is also clear from this report that these councils of elders were already organised along lines very similar to those of the Poro and other 'secret' societies which continued to hold power in these lands.[1]

Not only were some people in these states more powerful than others, whether by their birth or their position in such associations as the Poro; they were also more prosperous. 'The houses of the poor are made of stakes stuck in the ground, hardened with mud and covered with thatch. [But] the houses of the rich are made of hardened clay and brick, well white-washed in the interior and outside covered with chalk or white clay, and the interior is very well adorned, and these are the best houses in all Guinea.' This dividing-up of society into people of differing power and wealth is a process to which we shall return.

It was from this time, too, that the little group of islands off the shore of modern Conakry, capital of the Republic of Guinea, were used by European sea-merchants as a base for trading expeditions, and were named the Ilhos dos Idolos (Islands of the Idols) from which they have their present name, the Islands of Los. Eastward again were the Kru and other coastal peoples, and the Mende and their neighbours who live in the lands behind the coast. All were now increasingly influenced by political events in the forest lands, and by the arrival of new openings for trade with sea-merchants.

SUMMARY

Causes of the rise of big states and empires

1 *Economic* A people who happened to control an important source of
<hr>
[1] See also Chapter 19: *Sierra Leone and the Poro Association*, page 254.

wealth found that they needed to defend it against rivals. Then they found that this wealth could give them the power to expand their control over the wealth of their neighbours. This led in turn towards the development of wider trading systems, and these, in turn, to wider political systems. Small states grew into big states. Big states grew into empires (into states, that is, which control the life of other peoples as well as their own peoples).

Example The Asante empire. In the beginning, around AD 1400, Asante was a group of very small states where there was gold in the ground and rivers. They began to export this gold to the north. For a long time they were weak, and had to pay tribute (taxes) to their neighbours. Then they found they could use the wealth they got from gold to build a strong army. They used this army against their neighbours. From about AD 1700 they went on to build a very big trading-system. They built the Asante empire.

2 *Military* A people who happened to occupy a good trading position found that they could become stronger, and make their trading system bigger, by getting control of their neighbours. They could do this by buying military supplies or equipment which they did not have or could not produce at home. Their good trading position enabled them to pay for these supplies.

Example The Oyo empire. In the beginning, when the northern Yoruba state of Oyo was founded, perhaps around AD 1300, the Yoruba of Oyo were farmers and craftsmen. Then their chiefs found that they occupied a key position in the long-distance trade between the southern Yoruba states and the states of the Hausa and others to the north of Oyo. This 'middleman' position gave them a good basis for expansion. They had wealth enough to buy horses from Hausaland and form an army of cavalry (horseriding soldiers), although, because of tse-tse fly, they could not breed horses themselves. This cavalry army made it possible for Oyo to expand into an empire.

3 *Political* A people who happened to occupy a bad position for defending themselves, or for developing their own political system, found that they could gain from going to war with their neighbours. If they won that war, then they also found that it would be wise to remain strong. But to remain strong they had to dominate their neighbours. This led them into building a bigger state than before.

Example The rise of the Fon state in Dahomey. After about AD 1600 the people who lived inland from the coast of Dahomey were the Fon. They had to pay tribute (taxes) to the Yoruba of Oyo. They were also raided for slaves by their small neighbours on the coast of Dahomey. These small coastal states could do this because they bought guns from the European sea-traders. So the Fon decided to invade these small states in order to win control of the trade with the Europeans. They did this in 1727 and after. This led to the rise of the military state of the Fon. In the end, after AD 1800, this Fon state helped towards the destruction of the empire of Oyo.

Of course, there were plenty of other reasons why small states grew into big states or empires. But the chief causes of this development were economic, military, and political.

CHAPTER SEVEN
The empire of Songhay

In this section we embark upon the early history of the peoples of the central or Middle Niger region of the Western Sudan and Guinea, remembering again that this is a geographical division made only for the convenience of study. Much of the central region was in fact part of the empires of Ghana and Mali, or felt their influence.

Gao and the Songhay

The Songhay are a people of the Middle Niger region. They too built a big empire in the past.

Not many years ago an important archaeological discovery was made at the village of Sané, near the ancient city of Gao on the middle reaches of the Niger River. There came to light some old tombstones of Spanish marble, with Arabic characters beautifully carved on them. When they had been cleaned and read, the inscriptions showed that these were the tombstones of kings who had ruled over Gao many centuries ago.

'Here lies the tomb of the king who defended God's religion, and who rests in God, Abu Abdallah Muhammad,' explains one of these inscriptions, adding that this king had died in the Muslim year 494, or AD 1100.

This was a valuable discovery. It provided the oldest examples of writing so far known in West Africa. It also provided the only certain knowledge so far available about the foundations of the state of Gao, later to become the heart of the famous empire of the Songhay people.

These tombstones reveal three interesting points. They show that:
1 Gao, by the eleventh century, was strong enough to have become a state ruled over by prosperous kings;
2 these kings had become Muslims;

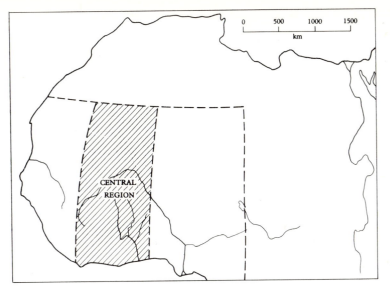

13 *The central region.*

3 they had extensive trading links with North Africa, and even had their
   tombstones brought from Muslim Spain.

The evidence of the early history of Gao, as it has come down to us
through the books of seventeenth-century writers in Timbuktu, does
not always agree with the evidence of the tombstones: the actual names
of the kings on the tombstones are not the same as the names recorded
from oral traditions. Otherwise the traditions greatly help to expand the
three certain points that are proved by the tombstones. They confirm
that Gao became a southern centre for trans-Saharan trade before AD
1000, and, secondly, that Gao had long since become a state on its own.[1]

The traditions also show that the Songhay people established them-
selves at Gao at the beginning of the seventh century, pushing out the
Sorko people who already lived there. But Gao was not yet their capital:
this was at Kukya, further to the east, where their *dias* or kings ruled.
These Songhay were enterprising traders and welcomed Lemtuna
(Berber) travelling merchants from the Adrar oases to the north of them.
Through these Saharan merchants the caravan trade with the Songhay
market-centres prospered and grew.

---

[1] Gao lies at the southern end of the route which caravans have followed through the central
Sahara for more than two thousand years.

An ancient tombstone, at Gao on the Middle Niger, such as described on page 68.

At the beginning of the eleventh century — and this is where the tombstones once again confirm the traditions — the ruling Songhay king, whose title and name were *Dia* Kossoi,[1] was converted to Islam. According to tradition, this happened in 1010. Soon after this, the capital of Songhay was transferred from Kukya to Gao, and Gao entered upon its period of growth.

Just why *Dia* Kossoi accepted Islam, and with how much sincerity, there is no means of knowing. But probably he saw in his conversion a useful way of gaining more influence with the Berber traders, who were

---

[1] The traditions say that Kossoi was the fifteenth of the *dia* line of kings.

all Muslims, upon whose caravan skills he and his people greatly relied for their trade. Like other Muslim kings in the Western Sudan, then and later, *Dia* Kossoi and his successors tried not to let their acceptance of Islam become offensive to their own people, who generally continued to believe in their local religions. *Dia* Kossoi even maintained court customs that were not Muslim: he tried, like many other rulers in the Sudan of those days, to combine his new position as a Muslim leader with his traditional position as a leader of Songhay religion.

Many *dias* ruled after Kossoi. Gao began to expand its power beyond the lands immediately round the city. One reason for this was that the value and size of the trans-Saharan trade were growing all the time. This growth increased the power and importance of Gao, whose position was very favourable for trade.

Three hundred years after *Dia* Kossoi's reign, Gao was so valuable that the great Mali ruler, *Mansa* Musa, sent out his generals and armies to bring it within the Mali empire. Apart from the wealth of Gao, *Mansa* Musa had other reasons for doing this. He and his governors already commanded the southern end of all the caravan routes across the western region of the Sahara. By securing Gao as well as Timbuktu, they could now command the southern end of the routes across the central region as well. This helped to strengthen the whole system of tax-collecting on which the government of Mali depended.

But this system, as we have noted, was too wide for Mali's strength. It

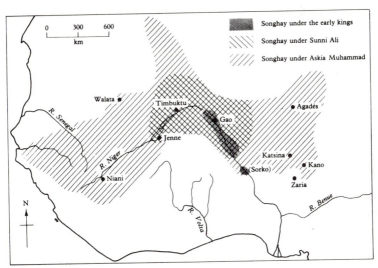

14 *The expansion of the empire of Songhay (very approximate frontiers).*

could not last. And Mali's overlordship of Gao lasted in fact only for some fifty years. In about 1335 the *dia* line of kings came to an end and gave way to a new line, whose title was *sunni* or *shi.* The second *sunni,* whose name is given in the traditions as Suleiman-Mar, won back Gao's independence from Mali in about 1375. Nearly a century of varying fortunes then followed for the people of Gao. After that they entered another period of expansion. Having defended themselves from their neighbours and rivals, they began to push far outward on the path of conquest.

This expansion was especially the work of a remarkable and far-seeing man whose title and name were *Sunni* Ali. Like other great rulers before and after him, *Sunni* Ali came to power in a time of confusion and set out to build a large and unified system of law and order, central government, and peaceful trade.

The growth of Songhay: *Sunni* Ali

The Songhay people of today number about 600,000, most of whom are farmers and fishermen along the banks of the Niger between the area of Timbuktu and the north-western borders of Nigeria. They play their part in the political life of the modern republics of Niger and Mali, but have long ceased to have a separate state of their own.

Yet their state in the sixteenth century was the largest in West Africa. The Songhay conquered many other peoples both north and south of the Niger; and their achievements hold a leading place in history. These achievements were to some extent due to their favourable position along the great river, which gave them good communications and chances of trade. But they were also the work of the Songhay or Songhay-controlled trading cities such as Gao, Timbuktu and Jenne. To the advantages of their position the Songhay repeatedly added vigour and intelligence in political ideas and organisational methods. *Sunni* Ali was their first outstanding leader after the *dia* line of kings of Gao.

Anyone who travels in the Songhay country today will find the name of *Sunni* Ali, better known as Ali Ber, or simply as the *Shi,* remembered still with honour and respect, although he died nearly five centuries ago. He is thought of as a great wizard, a man who understood a great deal about magic, but above all as a ruler of irresistible foresight, power and courage.

He became King of Gao and of the Songhay lands in about 1464. Mali was becoming weak and was in confusion. The Tuareg were raiding from the north, and Mossi from the south. Other people were claiming their independence along the banks of the Niger. The trade of great cities, Gao among them, was threatened by the insecurity of the times.

Sunni Ali was one of those great military captains whose energy and ambition kept him always in the saddle, always fighting, always at the head of one army or another. Knowing no other means of uniting the Western Sudan except by war, he made war often and with a ruthless skill. The early years of his reign read like a list of battles. He moved on swift horses from one campaign to the next, shifting his place of residence, reorganising his armies, refashioning his plans. In his long reign of thirty-five years he was never once defeated.

He began by fighting off the Mossi, who were attacking Timbuktu, the second city of the Songhay lands. He pursued them far into the west, then turned swiftly on the Dogon and the Fulani, who were also raiders, in the hills of Bandiagara. By 1468, four years after becoming emperor, he had cleared the country of immediate danger and at once attacked the Tuareg, who had held Timbuktu since 1433. Unbeatable, he drove the Tuareg out of Timbuktu. Their chief fled to distant Walata, while *Sunni* Ali set about punishing the leaders of a city who had done little to defend themselves against these nomad raiders.

Religious disputes were at work in this. The leading men of Timbuktu had been strictly Muslim for a long time now, and generally followed the beliefs of their trading partners from North Africa and the Saharan oases. Their *qadi*, or chief religious leader, tended to regard himself as the independent ruler of a Muslim city within the largely non-Muslim empire of Songhay. Here, as elsewhere, the coming of Islam to the Western Sudan gave rise to conflicts not only of religious belief, but even more of customs, laws, and political loyalties.

Faced with Tuareg occupation of their city, the leading men of Timbuktu do not seem to have fought very hard against it: both they and the Tuareg, after all, were Muslims interested in the trans-Saharan trade. They did not want to be occupied by the Tuareg, but they may have tried to use this occupation as a means to reassert their independence against their Songhay overlord.[1] *Sunni* Ali, at any rate, thought they had. He accused them of having acted disloyally to him, and treated them harshly. That is why the author of the *Tarikh as-Sudan*, himself a man of Timbuktu, afterwards described *Sunni* Ali as a tyrant and oppressor.[2]

---

[1] Later on, as we shall see, much the same thing happened when Timbuktu was occupied by Muslims from Morocco.

[2] See Chapter 13, *Law and Order* and *Clash of beliefs*, for more on this interesting subject.

With the recapture of Timbuktu, Ali had only begun his bold career. He now laid siege to Jenne, the vital market-centre for the trade in gold and kola and other goods from the southern forest lands. Jenne had never been taken by an invader, but Ali captured it after a siege of seven years. By 1476 he had the whole lake region of the middle Niger, west of Timbuktu, securely in his hands.

Through all these years of struggle, and through later years, Ali found means to fight back against a host of raiders. In 1480 the Mossi of Yatenga daringly sent cavalry to raid as far as Walata on the edge of the Sahara. Ali launched his cavalry after them, drove them back, pinned them down again in their own country in the south. He did the same with others of their raiding kind, Gurmanche, Dogon, Noromba, Fulani of Gurma: in short, with all those peoples who lived along the southern margins of the Niger Valley and envied the wealth of its towns and markets. Yet *Sunni* Ali was a skilful leader, as shown in Chapter 13 (*Clash of beliefs*) in peace as well as in war.

New methods of government: *Askia* the Great

Sunni Ali died in November 1492 while returning from an expedition against the Gurma, and his son, *Sunni* Baru, was named ruler of Songhay two months later. *Sunni* Baru reigned for only fourteen months. He was defeated in battle and deposed by a powerful rebel. This rebel was Muhammad Turay, who became *Askia* the Great.[1]

Here, once again, religious disputes were mingled with personal ambitions. In Songhay at this time the market cities were of growing wealth and importance. The leaders of these towns were mostly Muslims, and, because of this, Islam was now making great progress among the townspeople of the empire of Songhay, as indeed in other parts of the Western Sudan as well. While largely loyal to the traditional beliefs of the countryside, *Sunni* Ali had found it wise to make a good many concessions to Islam, although, as we have just seen in the case of Timbuktu, he did not hesitate to oppress Muslim leaders who failed in their political loyalty to him. *Sunni* Ali, in other words, set out to protect both the interests of the Muslim people of the towns and the interests of the non-Muslim people of the countryside. Always a skilful politician, he succeeded in holding the balance between these often opposing sets of interests.

Unlike his father, *Sunni* Baru refused to declare himself a Muslim

[1] The title of *Askia* came from a military rank in the Songhay army.

This is the outside of the tomb at Gao, of Askia the Great of Songhay, who died in 1538.

and at once made it clear that he was going to side entirely with the non-Muslim people of the countryside. Between the townsfolk and the country-folk — the traders and the farmers of Songhay — he chose the latter. But the people of the towns were too powerful to be treated in this way. They feared that they would lose power and influence, and that their trade would suffer. They found a rebellious leader in Muhammad Turay.

The consequences were far-reaching. With *Askia* Muhammad, the empire of Songhay entered on a new stage in its impressive political life. Becoming emperor at the age of fifty, he reigned from 1493 until 1528, and carried the political and commercial power of the empire of Songhay to its greatest point of expansion. He must be remembered for three main reasons.

In the first place, Askia Muhammad made a sharp break with the religious and family traditions of the *Sunni* line of rulers. He based his power firmly on the towns, and, in line with this, ruled as a strict Muslim. Although many traditional customs and practices were still observed at his court, his laws and methods were increasingly in accord

The inside of the tomb of Askia the Great at Gao.

with Muslim ideas. In this, clearly, he understood well the trend of power in Songhay. This is shown, among other things, by the fact that he could be absent on a pilgrimage to Mecca for two years (1494-97) without causing himself any trouble at home. During this pilgrimage the Sharif of Mecca, spiritual leader of the Muslims, named *Askia* Muhammad as his deputy or Kalif for the Western Sudan. Returning from Mecca, Muhammad set himself to remodel the laws and customs of his empire along more strictly Muslim lines.

Secondly, a point we shall come back to in Chapter 13, Muhammad took over the administrative changes made by *Sunni* Ali, and developed them still further. He built up a machinery of central government that was stronger and more detailed in its work than any known in the Western Sudan. He opened the way for men of talent, in the royal service, who were not necessarily members of leading descent-lines.

Thirdly, he used his talents as a political and military leader to continue with the imperial plans of *Sunni* Ali, and to carry them to a point where he successfully united the whole central region of the Western Sudan and even pushed his power, as Kankan Musa of Mali had done two centuries earlier, far northward among the oasis markets of the Sahara.

No people of the Western Sudan were free from the pressure of Songhay power. Their disciplined cavalry were everywhere. Like *Sunni* Ali, *Askia* Muhammad fought the Mossi of Yatenga and their raiding neighbours. In 1505 he even tackled Borgu (in what is north-western Nigeria today), though not with much success. In 1512 he mounted a big expedition against Diara. Successful there, he sent his troops still further westward, and attacked the Denianke king of Futa Toro in distant Senegal.

Then he turned his attention eastward again. His generals invaded the Hausa states, carrying all before them and meeting with serious resistance only at Kano. His distant frontiers now extended, at least in theory, as far as the borders of Bornu. Yet the addition of Katsina, and other Hausa states to the countries which paid tax and loyalty to Songhay, was worth little unless Songhay could also gain possession of the principal caravan-markets to the north. There, too, lay the Tuareg, ancient enemies of Songhay and of the cities of the Niger. So Muhammad sent out his generals once more. He ordered them to march north-eastward into the hot and thirsty lands of the oases of Aïr, far north of Hausaland in the southern Sahara.

Faced with the armies of Songhay, perhaps the best-organised troops that the Sudan had developed so far, the Tuareg could do nothing but turn about and retreat into their native desert. Muhammad ordered his generals to found a colony in Aïr. Many Songhay were settled in and around the ancient market of Agadès, where their descendants may be found to this day.

In 1528, by now over eighty, Muhammad became blind. He was deposed by his eldest son, Musa, and died ten years later.

The rulers of Songhay

As with Mali, the empire of Songhay went through three chief periods of expansion:

1 under *Sunni* Ali (1464-92).
2 under *Askia* the Great (1493-1528).
3 under *Askia* Dawud (1549-82).

Altogether, there were ten *askias*. Here are the dates of their reigns:

Askia Muhammad the Great	1493-1528
Musa	1528-31
Muhammad Bunkan	1531-37
Ismail	1537-39
Ishaq I	1539-49
Dawud	1549-82
Muhammad II	1582-86
Muhammad Bani	1586-88
Ishaq II	1588-91
Muhammad Gao	1591-?

Development of trade: Timbuktu and Jenne

As with other large states of this period, the strength and wealth of the Songhay government were based largely on the big trading cities. These became centres of a many-sided civilisation in which the laws and learning of Islam, as will be seen in Chapter 14, played a notable part. This is the place to consider briefly the history of two of the most important of these cities, Timbuktu and Jenne.

Timbuktu today is a small and dusty town of no distinction. No doubt it was small and dusty when it was founded about eight hundred years ago. But then its importance was very great. For Timbuktu became one of the wealthiest markets of West Africa, famous far and wide for its trade and for the learning of its scholars. Rising to importance a good deal later than its western sister-cities — Kumbi and Takrur, Audoghast and others — Timbuktu long outlived and outshone them.

By the fourteenth century, when Mansa Musa brought As-Saheli back from Mecca and ordered him to build new mosques and palaces, Timbuktu was well established as a trading city of great importance.

Yet Timbuktu never became the centre of an important state, much less of an empire. In this it differed from Gao. One main reason for this difference probably lay in its geographical position. Well placed for the caravan trade, it was badly situated to defend itself from the Tuareg raiders of the Sahara. These Tuareg were repeatedly hammering at the gates of Timbuktu, and often enough they burst them open with sad results for the inhabitants. Life here was never quite safe enough to make it a good place for the centre of a big state. Even in *Mansa* Musa's time, when peace and order spread widely across the Western Sudan,

The city of Timbuktu in the nineteenth century. It had not changed much since the fourteenth century.

Timbuktu never became a central point of government within the empire.

The political record underlines this special geographical weakness of Timbuktu. From 1325 until 1433 it was part of the Mali empire. Then the Tuareg had it for a few years. In 1458 it was enclosed within the growing Songhay empire, where it remained until Moroccans invaded Songhay in 1591. These Moroccans, whose invasion we shall consider in its proper place, ruled over Timbuktu until about 1780, although for most of this time they were no more than a weak ruling class within the city, half-merged with the local population and often cut off from their original homeland. Then the Tuareg again had command of the city for a time, being followed in their overlordship by Fulani rulers in 1826, who in turn were followed by Tucolor chiefs (1862-63), again by the Tuareg (1863-93), and finally by the French colonial invaders (1893-1960). Today, Timbuktu is part of the modern Republic of Mali.

But this political record would be misleading if it suggested that Timbuktu did not also enjoy long periods of peace and peaceful trade. On the contrary, the arts of peace and scholarship, of writing and theology, and the development of law, all flourished here, and flourished greatly. We shall discuss them in Chapters 12 and 13.

The Friday mosque at Jenne. Although rebuilt many times, the original mosque will have looked very like this.

Jenne was another of the great historical cities of the western Sudan. It seems to have been founded, like Timbuktu, soon after the eleventh century, although there was probably a trading settlement here in still earlier times. But the history of Jenne is not the same as that of Timbuktu. There is an important difference between them.

Both were big trading centres. Timbuktu, like Gao and ancient Kumbi and Takrur, were middleman cities between the traders of the Western Sudan and those of the Sahara and North Africa. But Jenne, by contrast, was a middleman city between the traders of the Western Sudan (especially of Timbuktu) and the traders of the forest lands to the south. It was through Jenne, at least after about 1400, that the gold and other goods of the forest lands passed increasingly to the caravan-traders who were waiting for these goods in Timbuktu and other trading centres. And it was through Jenne that the goods of North Africa increasingly reached southward into the forest lands.

This special importance of Jenne was associated with the spread and activities of the Mandinka traders of Mali, the Dyula or Wangara trading companies, who pushed down into the forest lands and settled there as buying-and-selling agents, just as the Berber traders of the Sahara, further north, had settled in towns like Kumbi and Timbuktu and Gao.

These Dyula traders, each group or company united under its Dyula-Mansa[1] by common language, Islam, and experience, were a vital link between the gold-producing forest lands and the whole wide trading network of the Western Sudan and North Africa. They dealt in many things besides gold, of course; notably in kola nuts. All their trade passed back and forth through markets such as Jenne. The long-established existence of this north-south trade within West Africa is one important reason why it is quite wrong to think of the forest lands as being cut off, in ancient times, from the grassland plains to the north of them. For the goods were carried by men, and were bought and sold by men; and all these men met and talked, discussed and exchanged ideas, and influenced one another through many centuries.

Unlike Timbuktu and Gao, Jenne retained its independence until taken by *Sunni* Ali in the 1470s, though without trying to become a large state or empire. One reason for its safety from conquest lay in its powerful defensive position. For much of every year, Jenne was encircled by the flood waters of the Niger River, as indeed it still is today. Its inhabitants also built high protecting walls round their city, somewhat like those that may still be seen at Kano, and proved able to

---

[1] Also known as Shehu-Wangara by Hausa-speaking people.

A street in Jenne.

defend them. They were helped by the fact that their southern neighbours were also independent.

Invasion of Songhay

After *Askia* Dawud, harsh times lay ahead. Troubles broke out at home.
The old enemies along the southern fringe of the empire — the Mossi
and their neighbours — were far from crushed. The Hausa states
revolted against Songhay overlordship during the reign of Muhammad
II. But in 1582, the year that Muhammad II succeeded Dawud, a new
note was struck, full of menace for the future of Songhay. The sultan of
Morocco sent a force of two hundred soldiers to seize the vital
salt-deposits of Taghaza far in the north of Songhay but a part of its
empire. These soldiers were armed with a weapon not seen before on the
battle-fields of the Western Sudan. This was the arquebus, an early form
of musket. Firearms had now appeared for the first time on any scale.

They were to have a profound and sometimes very destructive effect on the fortunes of West Africa.

This brief skirmish in a remote part of the Sahara was to open a war between Morocco and Songhay which proved disastrous for the men of Gao. Why did it happen? Let us pause for a moment to consider this question.

Briefly, there were two reasons, one military and the other commercial. In 1578, invaded by the Portuguese, the Moroccans had won a great victory at the battle of Al-Ksar al-Kabir. Historians have called this one of the decisive battles of the world. For many years it ended any idea of European conquest in North Africa. But it also encouraged the Moroccans to turn southward.

The Portuguese had invaded Morocco with an army of 25,000 men. At Al-Ksar al-Kabir they met with total defeat. It is said that only a few hundred Portuguese escaped to tell the tale of that day. The reigning sultan of Morocco died in the hour of victory and was succeeded by his younger brother, Mulay Ahmad, then aged twenty-nine. Mulay Ahmad was at once named *Mansur*, the Victorious. Skilfully, he made Morocco into a strong state again, and ended wars and rivalries both by the power of his armies and by generous gifts. But his purse was becoming empty. Soon he began to look round for new ways of filling it. Not surprisingly, he looked to the south, to the Western Sudan, as the Almoravids had done in earlier times. Under *Askia* Dawud, the riches of Songhay had acquired a great reputation throughout North Africa. Even the kings and merchants of distant Europe had begun to hear tempting tales of the wonders of the Western Sudan.

Sultan Mulay the Victorious began by nibbling at Songhay power. He raided Taghaza. But it brought him no good. He could seize the salt-deposits, but he could not keep an army in that thirsty place. He thought again. He decided to launch an army right across the Sahara and attack the men of Songhay in their own homeland. By this means, he believed, he could plunder the wealth of Songhay and vastly enrich himself with West African gold.

This army set out in December 1590. It was led by a soldier named Judar, by origin a Spanish Christian who had accepted Islam, and was composed of 4,600 picked men. Half of these were infantry armed with arquebuses, the most up-to-date weapon in the world of that time. Half of these arquebus-carriers were Spanish Muslims and the others were Portuguese or Spanish prisoners who had agreed to serve in the Moroccan armies, and accept Islam, rather than suffer death or long imprisonment. The invading army included a force of 500 horsemen armed with the arquebuses, and 1,500 light cavalry equipped with long

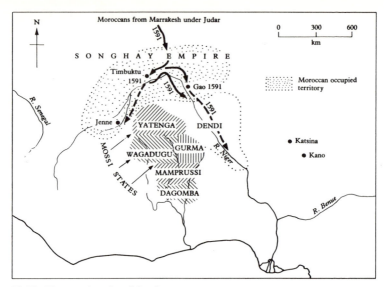

15 The Moroccan invasion of Songhay.

spears such as can be used from a horse. The army even carried half a dozen small cannon with them across the desert.

This force of mercenaries and ex-prisoners crossed the Sahara, taking many weeks from Marrakesh to the Niger, and fell upon the lands of Songhay with the fury of men who knew there could be no retreat. Gathering his troops, *Askia* Ishaq II tried to resist, but the armies of Songhay now met soldiers at Tondibi on 12 March 1591, who were even better armed and disciplined. They retired before the firearms of Judar's men. Weakened by trouble and revolts at home, the Songhay ruler lost battle after battle, often with heavy casualties. The Moroccans pushed into Timbuktu and then into Gao, hoping to find large stores of wealth ready to be collected up. In this they were at first not altogether disappointed. Much valuable loot was taken back to Marrakesh, where fine palaces were afterwards built on the profits of this piratical war.

Although routed in battle and driven from their trading cities, the Songhay did not give in. The towns were lost, but the country folk fell back on guerilla tactics. Unable to meet the Moroccans in pitched battle, they built up little raiding parties, attacked Moroccan posts and garrisons, harassed the Moroccans in every way they could, fighting to recover their land. They were never more than partially successful. Having lost the towns, Songhay proved unable to recover. Its central government was weakened from within and without.

The French soldier in this drawing shows the kind of gun which the Moroccans used when attacking Songhay.

Songhay's own subject peoples seized their chance to revolt on behalf of their own freedom. Many succeeded. And with this collapse the power of Islam dwindled or was lost for many years ahead. Another stage in the history of the Western Sudan began, in which the non-Muslim peoples of the countryside were once again to assert their power.[1]

---

[1] See Chapter 20.

CENTRAL REGION II

CHAPTER EIGHT

The Mossi, Akan and others

More than eight hundred kilometres, from north to south, separated the southern borders of Songhay power from the ocean waters of the Gulf of Guinea. Here in this large region, consisting of scrub and grassland in the upper part and forest in the lower, a number of other states were already in existence by the time of *Sunni* Ali and his successors.

The Mossi states

The nearest to Songhay of these southern neighbours were the Mossi who lived in a cluster of states between the great northward bend of the Niger River — the region of Jenne and Timbuktu — and the forest lands of Asante and Togo. They spoke the Mole-Dagbani languages, a 'sub-family' of the Gur group of languages.

These states were never brought within the imperial systems of Mali or Songhay. They conducted a vigorous and independent life of their own. Often they were a danger to their prosperous northern neighbours, for they raided northward and north-westward with strong forces of cavalry. After about 1400, too, they acted as intermediaries in the trade between the forest lands and the cities of the Niger.

Little is known about their origins. As in some other cases, the Mossi traditions speak of ancestors who came from the east, perhaps in the thirteenth century. There is some evidence for believing that these incoming ancestors were related to the Hausa peoples, and came from the region of Lake Chad. But they came a long time ago, if they came at all, and the Mossi of today are also the descendants of the Gur-speaking peoples who have lived in this country since ancient times.

In the course of time, five principal states were to emerge. These were

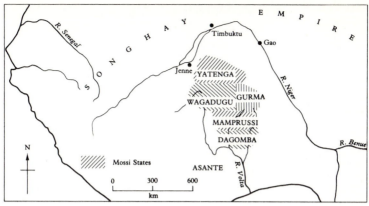

16 *The Mossi states.*

the states of Wagadugu, Yatenga, Fada-n-Gurma, Mamprussi and Dagomba. They all became strong before 1500. The territory of these states now lies within the modern republics of Upper Volta and Ghana.

The Mossi were not in the Mali empire, and they were a frequent peril to its wealth and safety. Their hard-riding horsemen took and looted Timbuktu in 1338, and continued such attacks far to the north until the armies of *Sunni* Ali of Songhay proved too strong for them. Even after that, the Mossi-Dagomba states (as historians usually call them) retained their independence until the French invasions of the late nineteenth century. Some of the rulers whom the French overpowered were the descendants of those who had founded these states many centuries earlier. The Mossi states were in fact outstanding examples of the *political stability* which West African peoples have often enjoyed in the past. They also illustrate the truth that West African states could enjoy stability over long periods without any dependence on Islam or on Muslim ways of thought and government. For the Mossi rejected all efforts to convert them to Islam, and remained true to their own religious beliefs.

Development of the central region of Guinea

We now turn away, for a moment, from the details of our story. We consider how the peoples of Guinea, of the forest and coastal lands of West Africa, grew and developed after AD 1000.

They evolved differently from their neighbours who lived in the open plains of the north. Their country has dense forests, much wider in

87

This fine Iron Age pot was found at Adwuku, Ghana. It is an excellent example of such work.

those times than they are today, steep hills, deep valleys, many rivers, heavy rainfull. These and other contrasts raised different problems for everyday life, politics and government.

The peoples of Guinea solved these problems. They learned how to grow food in dense forests. Even to this day their old farming methods have scarcely been improved, although the coming of cocoa and other new crops has greatly extended and developed these methods. They discovered how to find where metals lay in the earth. They found out how to mine and work these metals. They built up their own systems of community life and government, sometimes very different from the systems of the grassland plains, sometimes very much the same.

In about 1100-1200, central Guinea entered a new stage of development. This was a result of interplay between the peoples who already lived in Guinea and new ideas and influences moving in from the Sudan.

New states were formed. New alliances of states came into being.

There occurred a vast and complicated movement of peoples; although, as we have seen, the actual number of migrating groups may never have been large. It is to this obscure shifting round of population that we may trace the traditional beliefs of so many peoples in Guinea that their ancestors came from somewhere else.

At some point around 1200, it seems, the incoming ancestors of the Akan peoples of modern Ghana and the Ivory Coast began moving into their present homelands. They appear to have come from the north, from the grassland plains of the Western Sudan. Perhaps they moved in order to escape the chaos and confusion which had followed on the collapse of Ancient Ghana. Perhaps they were discontented with their treatment in the rising empire of Mali.

These incoming ancestors intermarried and merged with the peoples whom they found. By about 1200, if not before, the Akan were already beginning to settle in the lands to the north of the forest, in northern Asante and the grassland country beyond, while others had pushed further south. These others moved towards the coast along the banks of the Volta River, or, later on, directly through the tall forest. They were formed in different clans and groups and peoples. They were the founders of the later states of Denkyira, Adansi, Fante, Akwamu and others.

Much the same movement and settlement brought Ivory Coast peoples like the Senufu to their present homelands.

Bono-Manso and the new gold trade

Among early states, there was Bono in the Takyiman area. We know a little more about it than about the others. For it was through Bono that the principal trade with the states and empires of the Western Sudan — and thence, through many hands, with North Africa and Europe — became important. Here in Bono the Mandinka traders of Mali, the Dyula or Wangara, made their base in central Guinea.

Bono traditions indicate that it was founded by a strong chief or king called Asaman, and by his queen-mother Amayaa, who is said to have reigned between about 1297 and 1329. But scholars now believe that these traditional dates are wrong and that this new political system in the Takyiman region was founded not long before 1400.

Asaman and Amayaa built their first capital at Tutena,[1] not far from the present town of Nkoranza, but soon moved to a new capital a few

[1] In Twi, the language of this area, Tutena means 'a new settlement'.

kilometres further west. This they called Bono-Manso, the town of the land of Bono; and it was here that they settled. Other Akan states emerged in this region. Some of them came under the control of Bono-Manso. Thus the king of Bono became a king of kings. He became, even if in a small way, an emperor.

It is important to note why these early Akan states were small. They were formed in dense forest country. There was no chance of building big states and empires which could be controlled by fast-moving cavalry. Movement was difficult. Political authority could not stretch very far, at least in those early days. Later on, with the expansion of political ideas and trade, this would change. In the eighteenth century, the Asante empire would include nearly all of modern Ghana, together with some of the Ivory Coast and Togo as well. But this kind of big development was still in the future.

The traditions of early Bono also tell us something else. This is of importance. They say that gold was discovered in the Twi River and around Perembomase during Asaman's reign, and that this discovery led to a new prosperity and to social progress. The truth behind this particular tradition is no doubt rather different. Gold was almost certainly *discovered* in this area long before Asaman's reign, but it was probably not much *worked.* Now, soon after 1400, there came a greater demand for gold from the Western Sudan, itself responding to a bigger demand from North Africa and Europe. This led the Dyula traders to travel south in search of gold and it was offered to them in Bono. So the founding of Bono was partly the result of a growth in the gold trade. Once again, new ways of earning a livelihood went hand-in-hand with new ways of political organisation.

Bono continued to be an important state until much later times.

Along the coast of modern Ghana: early states

The earliest peoples whom we hear of along the coast of central Guinea are those who formed their states in the fifteenth and sixteenth centuries. These are the early states of the Fante and other Akan peoples, as well as of non-Akan peoples such as the Nzima to their west and the Ga-Adangme and Ewe to their east.

Although the coastal peoples of this early period were probably few in number, they were not without resources. They lived at what was then the backdoor of Guinea, faced with the empty ocean, but they evolved a stable way of life, and they also developed good relations with their inland neighbours. When Portuguese sailors first arrived on the coast of

Elmina Castle as a Dutch artist drew it in the seventeenth century.

Guinea in the 1470s, they found people who were quite ready to trade with them. What is more, they also found Mandinka traders who had come from the inland empire of Mali.

We have records of how the Portuguese were first received at Elmina. There, in 1482, they asked for permission to build a castle, and this permission was given them by the chief of the Elmina district, whom the Portuguese records call Caramansa. Some scholars have seen in this word Caramansa a sign of Mandinka-Dyula presence on the coast of modern Ghana in the fifteenth century. They point out that the second part of the word is the same as the Mandinka word *mansa,* king or chief. It seems more likely, however, that Caramansa is only a mistaken way of writing Kwamina Ansah, a name borne by several later rulers of Elmina.

Here is how the Portuguese of 1482 described their meeting with Kwamina Ansah at Elmina.

> He was seated on a high chair dressed in a jacket of brocade, with a golden collar of precious stones, and his chiefs were all dressed in silk. . . These noblemen wore rings and golden jewels on their heads and beards. Their king, Caramansa, came [towards the Portuguese] in their midst, his legs and arms covered with golden bracelets and rings, a collar round his neck, from which hung some small bells, and in his plaited beard golden bars, which

A high chair from Ghana, probably very like the one described by the Portuguese in 1482.

weighed down its untrimmed hair, so that instead of being twisted it was smooth. To show his dignity, he walked with very slow and light steps, never turning his face to either side.

The Portuguese went on to describe Kwamina Ansah as a man

of good understanding, both by nature and by his dealing with the crews of the trading ships, and he possessed a clear judgment. And as one who not only desired to understand what was proposed to him, who not only listened to the translation of the interpreter, but watched each gesture made by Diogo de Azambuja; and while this continued, both he and his men were completely silent; no one as much as spat, so perfectly disciplined were they . . .

These words tell us a good deal about the small states along the coast of central Guinea in the fifteenth century. They had chiefs and counsellors, orderly government, firm rules of public behaviour, trade with their neighbours and trade with the interior. Though distant from the great centres of political and economic development of those days, they were fully part of West African civilisation.

Growth of states and trade

In the sixteenth century the peoples of central Guinea — roughly, of modern Togo, Ghana and the Ivory Coast — further developed their methods of government.

Control of the gold mines brought the Akan peoples of Ghana fresh strength from the expansion of trade with the Western Sudan (and, through the Western Sudan, with North Africa). Equally helpful was their position near the coast, which brought them new opportunities of profitable trade with sea-merchants.

Bono continued in Takyiman as before. But now it had important rivals. Further south, about one hundred kilometres from the coast, Adansi was established some time before 1550 under a ruler whom tradition remembers as Opon Enim. To the west of them, along the valley of the Oda, there were the Denkyira. At first under Adansi overlordship, Denkyira became independent during the reign of Adansi's Ewurade Basa.

The Adansi, like the Asante, then had to pay tribute to Denkyira. So they moved eastward into Akim, where they made a new home. South-east of Denkyira, meanwhile, the Akwamu began to gather strength, although the rise of their empire came only after 1640. The Ga also grew in strength, and moved their capital from about twelve kilometres inland to the present site of Accra.

All these and similar movements must be seen against the background of the special problems, political and economic, which these peoples now faced. What was really happening was an effort to organise these forest and coastal lands into stronger states which could take full advantage of their commercial opportunities. Here, indeed, was the same underlying process of development as in the Western Sudan. Only here, because of the dense forest and broken nature of the country, divided by hills and rivers, the states were usually on a smaller scale.

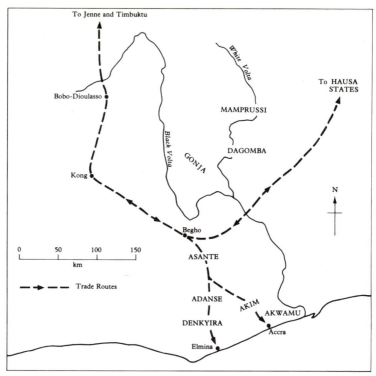

17 The trade routes of the Akan.

For a long while the trade with the north remained more valuable than the newly growing trade with sea-merchants along the
coast. Now, as before, the Dyula traders conducted their commerce
from a base at Begho on the north-western outskirts of the Akan forests
where the gold was mined. From Begho the main trading route went
northwestward through Dyula towns and little states, such as Kong and
Bobo-Dioulasso ('the house of the Dyula traders of Bobo'), that lay in
the northern part of the modern Ivory Coast, and then on to Jenne.
Another main route went north-eastward from the Akan forests to
Hausaland. Both were used for the export of gold, kola and other items,
and for the import of salt, copper, and manufactured products from the
north.

Coastal trade grew important during the sixteenth century. The gold
trade began to move southward as well as northward; not much at first,
yet in steadily growing volume. In 1554, for example, three English
ships bought no less than 400 lb of gold of fine quality on the coast of

modern Ghana (known to Europeans as the Gold Coast), as well as thirty-six barrels of peppercorns and about 250 elephants' tusks.

This shift in the movement of gold exports began to have political consequences. As coastal trade expanded, previously weak peoples along and near the seaboard began to evolve a new power of their own, helped by their control of the trade with Europeans. Chapter 18 will follow their story. Meanwhile we should note several other consequences.

Founding of Gonja: warriors and settlers

One of these consequences was the founding of Gonja. At some time between 1550 and 1575, *Askia* Dawud of Songhay found that his supplies of gold from the southern country were getting smaller. The main reason, as we have just seen, was that Akan gold-producers had begun selling some of their production to Portuguese and other

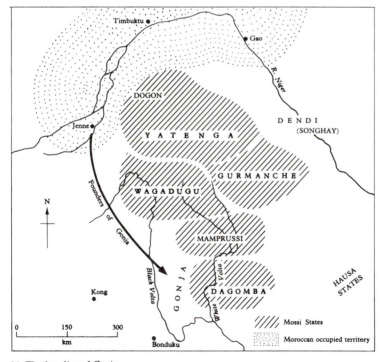

18 *The founding of Gonja.*

95

European traders along the seaboard. *Askia* Dawud accordingly despatched a force of Mandinka cavalry to see what could be done about stopping up this 'leak' in his supplies.

It soon turned out that nothing could be done. Dawud's armoured horsemen rode south from the neighbourhood of Jenne until they reached the scrub-and-grassland country of the Black Volta region of modern Ghana. But they got no farther. They discovered that cavalry could not operate in the dense forest country where the Akan lived and smelted gold.

Unable to affect the movement of the gold trade, Dawud's warriors settled in the Black Volta lands and founded there, in the course of time, no fewer than seven little states of their own. Dyula traders joined them and helped to turn these states into new trading centres. Of these the most important was Gonja. Two others which took shape around 1600, and were ruled by Dagomba chiefs, were Wa and Buna; and these, too, became centres of trade and Muslim learning.

EASTERN REGION I

CHAPTER NINE

The empire of Kanem-Bornu and the Hausa states

We have looked at the long record of political growth, between 1000 and 1600, in the western part of the Western Sudan and in Senegambia. Now we shall consider the same record in the eastern part of the Western Sudan — in what we may also call the Central Sudan — and especially in the empire of Kanem-Bornu and the Hausa states.

Not all the peoples of West Africa were drawn to the same extent into new forms of social life and government. Many peoples of the grassland country, like many people of the forest lands, went on living much as they had lived before, knowing and caring little of the world beyond the

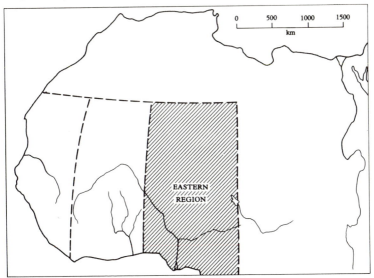

19 The eastern region.

97

reach of their pastures or farms, living as securely as they could in their villages and homesteads, content with what they had, and hoping, as we can imagine, that nobody would come and bother them.

This does not mean that these untroubled peoples were any less intelligent or sensible than their state-forming and empire-building neighbours. And they, too, were influenced by the big changes going on all around them. The whole of West Africa, during these centuries, was moving into new types of social and political organisation; and some outstanding examples of this occur in the history of the eastern region.

Early Kanem-Bornu: the Sefawa

The ancient and powerful empire of Kanem-Bornu became as important for this eastern part of the Western Sudan as were the empires of Ghana and Mali for the western and central regions.

Its earliest beginnings, like those of Ghana, are little known. Probably they occurred soon after AD 800. Then it was that four or five early states, including those of the Kanuri and Zaghawa peoples, appeared in the neighbourhood of Lake Chad.

Here, as with Ghana, the trade between West Africa and North Africa was important for political as well as for commercial reasons. For economics and politics always go hand in hand; and here, to the east and west of the great lake, there lay a vital crossroads of trade.

In these lands around Lake Chad were situated the southern market-centres of the trans-Saharan trade not only with Libya and Tunisia in the far north, but also with Nubia on the middle Nile and Egypt to the far north-east. These markets were valuable exchange centres for all goods going north from the lands of eastern Guinea that lie in southern Nigeria today.

So the little states of the Chad region, like the great empire into which they grew, faced southward towards eastern Guinea, north-eastward through the hills of Darfur to the distant Nile, and northward by way of the Bilma Oasis and the settlements of Aïr to Libya, Tunisia and Egypt. This key position did much to shape the fortunes of Kanem-Bornu. Its rulers were nearly always in touch with North Africa, with the peoples of the Nile, and with their neighbours in the south and west.

The royal traditions of Kanem-Bornu say a lot about early times. Like other royal traditions, they have two disadvantages. They are not exact. And they tell little or nothing of how ordinary folk lived and worked. All the same, they form a useful guide to the main political events.

The early state of Kanem, reaching some way to the east as well as to

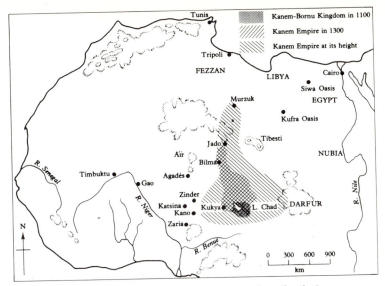

20 The expansion of the Kanem-Bornu empire (very approximate frontiers).

the west of Lake Chad, came into being under a line of kings belonging to the Sefawa family. This dynasty held power from about AD 850. Two centuries later, in 1086, there came an important change. A Sefawa king, called Hume, accepted Islam as his own religion and that of his court. From this time onwards the Sefawa kings and emperors of Kanem-Bornu, who continued to rule for another eight hundred years, were always Muslims.

This happened, we may recall, at about the same time as the Almoravid Muslims were battering at the cities of non-Muslim Ghana, and not long after *Dia* Kossoi of Gao had likewise accepted Islam.[1] So it was in the eleventh century that Islam made its first big advances in the grassland countries of West Africa, at least among their rulers and governors, and began to send trader-missionaries south toward the forest lands.

Growth of Kanem-Bornu: empire and rulers

Kanuri traditions say that there were sixteen kings of Kanem-Bornu down to *Mai* (king) Dunama Dibbelemi who ruled in about 1221-59.[2]

[1] See page 70.
[2] Note that all these dates are approximate. Not all historians agree about them.

We can distinguish two main periods of early expansion.

1 Under Dunama Dibbelemi, and the kings immediately before him.

By 1250 Kanem-Bornu had become an important empire. Its rulers were known throughout the Muslim world. One reason for this was that the kings had extended the empire's control of the northern trade-routes as far as the Fezzan (in southern Tunisia, on the northern side of the great desert). *Mai* Dunama Dibbelemi also got control of Adamawa, all of Bornu, and Kano, as well as of Wadai to the east of Lake Chad.

After *Mai* Dunama Dibbelemi there followed many kings in a period when this first empire of the Kanuri went through a time of troubles. Some of these were caused by disputes between leading men and their families. Others were the result of unsuccessful wars against their neighbours.

These troubles came to a head in the reign of *Mai* Daud (1377-86). Kanem's biggest rivals east of Lake Chad, the Bulala, drove the king and his court out of the old Kanuri capital of Nkimi (near Lake Chad). Another king, *Mai* Umar (1394-98) suffered worse defeats. At this time the capital of the empire was transferred to Bornu on the western side of Lake Chad. After this it is better to speak of the empire of Bornu, for that was now its permanent centre.

2 A second period of expansion began late in the fifteenth century, and especially under *Mai* Ali Gaji (1472-1504). His successful conquests were westward against some of the Hausa states, including Kano and eastward against the Bulala; while at the same time he regained control of the northern trade routes, and fought off raiders from the south (from the region of the middle Benue River).

These successes were continued under the next ruler, *Mai* Idris Katarkamabi (1504-26). He was able to liberate the old capital of Njimi from the Bulala, but the centre of the new empire stayed at the Bornu capital of Ngazargamu (founded by the king before him, *Mai* Ghaji). The Bulala once again became subjects of the empire.

Under *Mai* Muhammad (1526-45) the Bulala revolted but without success. *Mai* Muhammad followed this victory by marching north into Aïr, then under Songhay rule; and it seems that from this time onward the country of Aïr, vital for the northern trade from Bornu and Hausaland, came under the influence of Bornu.

Under *Mai* Ali (about 1545), Bornu clashed with Kebbi in the west of Hausaland. The reason appears to have been that the kingdom of Kebbi, eager for a bigger share in the northern caravan trade, had begun raiding the Tuareg and Songhay settlers of the Aïr oases. These appealed for help to *Mai* Ali. He marched a Bornu army northward round the Hausa

Ruins of the walls built by Mai Dunama (1548-63) to defend his palace at Ngazargamu in Bornu. This photo was taken a few years ago.

kingdoms (passing south of Zinder) and attacked the *Kanta* (king) of Kebbi in his fortress town of Surame, west of Katsina.

The Kebbi king pulled out of Surame, but Ali, for reasons not clear, turned back and made for home. The Kebbi army set out to chase him and his soldiers. They caught up with *Mai* Ali's soldiers near N'guru, and fought some battles. But the Kebbi men were out of luck. On the way home they were ambushed by the men of Katsina, and their king was killed.

The fortunes of Bornu now looked good, though more troubles lay immediately ahead. *Mai* Ali died in about 1546. His son, who had the right to become king, was very young. So his nephew, Dunama, took power. Dunama reigned from 1546-63. He was followed by *Mai* Dala (Abdullah), who reigned from about 1564 to 1570.

Bornu suffered at this time, especially from another Bulala revolt. Dunama even took the step of fortifying the capital, Ngazargamu, a sign of weakness absent in earlier times. Raiders threatened from many sides.

The new empire: *Mai* Idris Alooma

Meanwhile the little son of *Mai* Ali was growing to manhood. This

101

young prince, whose name was Idris, lived far away from Bornu in old Kanem, east of the lake, where the Bulala kings still ruled. No doubt he lived there because his mother was the daughter of a Bulala king, and had returned home on the death of *Mai* Ali. This woman, Queen Amsa, is said to have shown great courage in protecting the life of Idris against efforts by *Mai* Dunama and *Mai* Dala to kill him because he was the rightful heir to the imperial throne.

But Idris could not win his rights when *Mai* Dala died in 1570. The power in Bornu was seized by Dala's sister, the formidable Queen Aissa Kili; and it was only after several years of civil war that Idris at last succeeded to the throne. He reigned from about 1580 till 1617[1] and became one of the strongest and most successful of the kings of Kanem-Bornu. In a series of wars he revived the old empire and built a new one. He died at the head of his troops, and was buried in a marsh at Aloo, and so is remembered as *Mai* Idris Alooma.

His work, like that of other great leaders, was one of political reform. This took the shape of a reinforcement of Islamic beliefs and customs, just as it had in Songhay under *Askia* Muhammad. He placed much weight on obedience to the Islamic code of law, and tried hard to raise the prestige of his magistrates, even making it a habit, so it is said, to submit his own problems to their advice and decision. In the work and policies of Idris we may see emerging, once again, the old struggle between Islam and the religions of West Africa.

Now reunited with Kanem, east of the lake, Bornu prospered under *Mai* Idris. There was much trade with the north. There was regular contact with the rulers of Fezzan on the northern side of the Sahara. Diplomatic relations were opened with the Ottoman conquerors of Egypt. Idris even imported muskets from Tripoli and raised a company of musketeers. A Kanemi writer of those days, Ibn Fartua, had left us a description of the coming of ambassadors from the Sultan of the Ottoman empire, and of how they were received.

Mai Idris went out to receive the ambassadors at the head of companies of his quilt-armoured cavalry.

On the next day, all the soldiers mounted their horses after equipping themselves and their horses with armour, with breast-plates, shields and their best clothing. When we had all ridden a short distance we met the messengers of the lord of Stambul [the sultan of the then very powerful empire of the Ottoman Turks]... The troops of our lord were drawn up on the west in rank after

---

[1] Some historians think the true dates were 1571-1603.

rank, leaving enough space between their ranks for the wheeling of any restive horse. Then our troops charged [towards the Turkish messengers and their escort], and they galloped their horses towards us. This continued for a long time until the infantry were tired of standing still. After that our lord continued on his journey. . .

'O, my wise friends and companions!' continues Ibn Fartua. 'Have you ever seen a king who is equal to our lord at such a moment, when the lord of Stambul, the great Sultan of Turkey, sends messengers to him with favourable proposals?'

And so Kanem-Bornu, as in times past, stood firmly once more at the crossroads of trade and travel between West Africa and the valley of the Middle Nile, and between West Africa and Fezzan, Tripoli and Egypt. Strengthened and reunified by Idris Alooma, it helped to link the peoples of West Africa to the wide world beyond the desert.

Kanem-Bornu: methods of government

The actual size of the empire of Kanem-Bornu varied with time and fortune, as did all these empires. Its central people were the Kanuri, just as the Mandinka were the central people of Mali and the Songhay the central people of the empire of that name. The Kanuri lived then, as later, around Lake Chad. But they had, of course, no frontiers in the modern sense of the word. Their kings made alliances with neighbouring rulers. When the kings were strong enough to do so, they forced these neighbouring rulers to pay tax and obey their orders.

But like other kings of those times, the rulers of Kanem-Bornu were not dictators. They were not all-powerful. They had to listen to the advice and opinions of their lesser kings, chiefs and counsellors especially those of the Sefawa ruling family. Within Kanem-Bornu itself, they generally drew their power from a central council of leaders of the Sefawa family. This council consisted of about a dozen principal governors who reigned over different parts of the empire. These men had titles which were used for many centuries. Some of the titles, like *galadima* and *chiroma*, are still used in northern Nigeria.

Firmly based in Bornu and around Lake Chad, sometimes at war and sometimes at peace with the Hausa kingdoms to the west of them, the lords of this empire usually faced their greatest difficulties in the east. Here they met with energetic peoples, notably the Bulala, who resisted their rule, and the extent of the empire shrank or expanded according to

This figure in baked clay belongs to the civilisation of people called the Sao, who lived near lake Chad at the time of the early empire of Kanem.

their failure or success in mastering these easterly peoples by means of diplomacy or war.

But whether large or small, according to the way things turned out, the success of the empire can be compared to that of Ancient Ghana, while it was perhaps even bigger than the empires of Mali or Songhay, because it lasted longer. What the Kanuri and their allies and subjects were able to do, over a very long period and in a region of great importance, was to bring the advantages of a single system of law and order to a great many different peoples. And it was through this large empire that West Africa kept in regular touch with vital centres of civilisation beyond the Sahara, especially Egypt. It was through Kanem-Bornu that the goods of Egypt and other northern lands; horses and fine metalware, salt and copper, came into West Africa by way of the eastern Sahara; and it was often by the same route that the goods of West Africa, notably kola and ivory, were taken in exchange to those northern lands. In this respect the markets of Bornu and Kanem were as important as the markets of Hausaland, or as those of the central and western regions of the Western Sudan.

Often, of course, the Kanuri and their allies achieved their successes by invasion and conquest; and their successes were sometimes threatened, like those of other large states, with rebellion by subject peoples. These were the peoples who had to pay for the progress that Kanem achieved. And they, we may be sure, did not think that Kanem was a progressive state and empire. Can we speak, then, of progress in this connection? There is a general rule we may apply in trying to answer this difficult question. Where states and empires in the past have generally helped the expansion of production and trade, opened new ways of livelihood, found wealth for the enlargement of the arts of peace, and brought security from everyday perils and fears to large numbers of their people, then we may reasonably speak of progress in the growth of civilisation.

Kanem-Bornu achieved these things. Not all the time, of course. As elsewhere, there were bad governments and foolish kings; cruel and greedy, self-seeking, oppressive. Then life became unbearable and brave men took arms and tried to change it. But there were also long periods of peace and security, when men could expand their work and develop their skills. Because of this, Kanem-Bornu became one of the great builders of civilisation in West Africa.

Origins of the Hausa states: security and trade

The traditions of the Hausa states, situated in the lands of northern Nigeria, go back to their kings of the eleventh century AD.

According to the *Kano Chronicle*, a collection of Hausa traditions

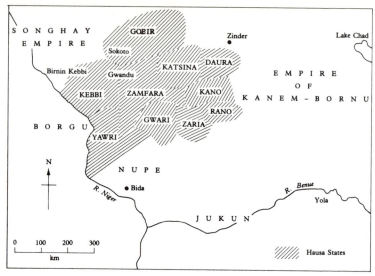

21 *The Hausa states and their neighbours in about* AD *1400.*

written down many centuries later, and whose dates, of course, are not exact, the first *Sarki*, or king of Kano, was Bogoda, who came to power as early as AD 999. Other Hausa communities, each dependent on its main settlement or *birni*, also began to turn themselves into states with kings towards the end of the thirteenth century. By about 1350 this state-forming process had gone quite a long way. The stronger Hausa states had pushed their power across the neighbouring countryside, and were beginning to form frontiers between each other. Many wars followed. These did not last long or destroy much, but were designed to win this or that local advantage or to bring home plunder from neighbouring towns and markets.[1]

These Hausa states had three main reasons for existence. These reasons were to be found in their cities. Each main Hausa city or town (for these settlements were at first quite small) was a place for government and military defence. Neighbouring farmers could take refuge there when threatened by invaders or raiders. In exchange for this protection, they paid taxes to the men who ruled the city, who in turn paid the soldiers and kept law and order. These men were in turn ruled by a *sarki* or king, a member of one or other leading family.

---

[1] There were to be seven true Hausa states, or Hausa *bokwoi* (Biram, Daura, Gobir, Kano, Katsina, Rano and Zaria (Zazzau)); and seven outliers, the *banza bokwoi* (Gwari, Kebbi, Kwororafa (Jukun), Nupe, Yawri, Yoruba, and Zamfara).

Secondly, each Hausa city was a market place for the nearby countryside. Here country people could exchange their products for the goods that town craftsmen made in leather and other materials.

Thirdly, each Hausa city became gradually a centre of long-distance trade. It became a place for the exchange not only of locally-produced goods but also of goods brought from North Africa and Egypt, from the rest of the Sudan, and from Guinea.

This prosperity was the result of much development. In the beginning, the Hausa states had difficult problems to solve. Before they could grow strong and wealthy, they had to build the power of their cities and extend this power over the neighbouring peoples of the countryside. Many of these peoples had their own ways, their own religious customs and beliefs.

Should the new Hausa rulers impose their own customs and beliefs on the peoples of the countryside, or should they tolerantly let these people believe as they wished? The question was certainly much discussed in towns like Kano. The *Kano Chronicle* offers a vividly clear illustration of this kind of problem. According to tradition, the *sarki* in AD 1290 was a certain Shekkarau. One day Shekkarau's counsellors came to him and complained of the disloyal talk they had heard among country people coming into town. Shekkarau replied that he thought such discontent could be settled without fighting. But Shekkarau's counsellors were not sure that he was right. 'If you try to make peace with these people,' the counsellors argued with him, 'they will only say that you are afraid of them.' And they advised the *sarki* not to listen to the delegates of these discontented folk.

But when the delegates came to Shekkarau, and entered his palace, and stood before him, they begged him to let them keep their customs and beliefs. For 'if the lands of a ruler are wide,' they argued, 'then he should be patient. But if his lands are not wide, he will certainly not be able to gain possession of the whole countryside by impatience.' And the *sarki* agreed with them. As the Kano Chronicle explains, 'he left them their power and their own religious customs.'

Behind this little story, nearly seven hundred years old, we may see how hard it was for the chiefs of the towns and the chiefs of the countryside to reach agreement and settle down together for their common benefit. We may also see that while there was warfare among these states, there was also diplomacy — the effort to end disputes by compromise and peaceful give-and-take.

There were many Hausa cities engaged in trade and politics. Daura and Gobir, Katsina, Kano and Zaria — these are only five of the better-known names. Sometimes these states cooperated for their common good. Often they quarrelled. They never had a single government that ruled them all. They did not form a Hausa empire. Yet the Hausa states, generally more friendly with each other than with their non-Hausa neighbours, had influence and commercial power over a wide area of the eastern region.

These states were in close and constant touch, sometimes by war but more often by peaceful trade, with the peoples of the forest lands of eastern Guinea, notably with the Yoruba and their neighbours. It was largely through Hausaland that the goods of the Yoruba country, especially kola nuts, went northward into the Western Sudan and across the Sahara to North Africa; and it was largely through Hausaland that the peoples of eastern Guinea could import the North African goods they needed.

The Hausa states were a necessary and therefore prosperous link between Guinea and the far north. Partly it was for this reason that the Songhay rulers, as already noted in Chapter 7, wished to gain control of Hausaland, and succeeded for a short time in doing so. Some of the Bornu rulers also tried to control the Hausa states. Kano became a vassal state of Bornu for part of the fifteenth century. But most of the Hausa states remained independent until the Fulani conquest of 1804-11.

The Hausa achievement

Built in a fertile land, rich in skilled farmers and determined traders, the Hausa cities and states became a strong and stable part of the West African scene.

They were deeply influenced by Muslim methods of government as practised in the neighbouring empires of Songhay and Kanem-Bornu. These methods tended to strengthen the power of kings at the cost of ordinary folk. Government taxes and tolls grew heavier. The needs of courts and armies weighed down on tax-paying citizens and the farmers of the countryside. Armouries glinted with the metal of expensive coats of chain-mail and fine helmets.

By the 1440s there were even a few muskets in Hausaland, brought in by traders from Bornu who had got them from Egypt. And now the Muslim rulers began to use slave labour on a large scale. In 1450, for instance, the then ruler of Kano, Abdullahi Burja, a tributary vassal or under-king of the empire of Kanem-Bornu, sent out soldiers on raids for captives which are said to have brought him as many as one thousand slaves a month. He is reported to have established no fewer than twenty-one settlements of royal slaves, each with a thousand men.[1]

These new methods called for changes in the administration. Kings like Muhammad Rumfa, who reigned in Kano from 1465 to 1499, borrowed ideas from Kanem and Songhay. They formed troops of fulltime soldiers, often from captives whom they had turned into slaves, built luxurious palaces, and owned large areas of land. As was the rule in those days, the wealth of the privileged few had to be paid for by the labour of the many. Yet the prosperity of the cities remained impressive. Expansion of long-distance trade using currency and credit went hand-in-hand with the growth of learning, and with valuable advances in the handicraft industry.

Travellers from distant lands did not fail to notice this bustling city progress. One such visitor, the North African trade-traveller Hassan ibn Muhammad[2] has left colourful descriptions of Hausaland as he or his friends saw it at the beginning of the sixteenth century.

Gobir in the west was rich in people and in cattle. 'The people are in general very civilised. They have very many weavers and shoe-makers who make shoes like those that the Romans used to wear; and these they export to Timbuktu and Gao.' Probably Leo Africanus was thinking of sandals of the Tuareg fashion. The Gobir town of Madawa made such sandals for long afterwards.

Of the state of Guangara, later absorbed by Katsina, he wrote that it was 'inhabited by a great number of people who are goverened by a king with more than 7,000 infantry armed with bows, and 500 foreign cavalry on call. He draws a great revenue from dealing in goods and from commercial taxes. . .'

Kano, he found, was 'encircled by a wall made of beams of wood and baked clay; and its houses are constructed of the same materials. Its inhabitants are civilised handicraft-workers and rich merchants. . .' Like some other Hausa cities, Kano was an important place for Muslim learning.

But all this prosperity, whether from trade or taxation, had its disadvantage. It attracted raiders. Thus Guangara, whose king had such great revenue from trade and taxes, was menaced by both Songhay on the west and Bornu on the east. After a long siege Kano had already

---

[1] These methods by which kings strengthened their power occurred in other kingdoms, and are discussed at several places in this book. See for example Chapter 18 and the reforms of King Osei Kwadwo of Asante, and Chapter 21 for the further story of kingly rule in Hausaland.

[2] Captured by Christian pirates during a voyage in the Mediterranean, Hassan ibn Muhammad was taken to Rome. There he took the name of Leo Africanus, and in 1525 completed a famous book in Italian about the Western Sudan. It was first published in 1550.

An old house in Kano.

fallen to the armies of the Songhay emperor, *Askia* Muhammad, who obliged its ruler to pay him one-third of all the annual revenues of Kano. Other Hausa states suffered in the same way. Gobir and Katsina, for instance, were attacked by Kebbi as soon as the latter had regained its independence of Songhay in 1517.

In the south, Zaria flourished. For much of the sixteenth century this was the strongest state in Hausaland, making vassals, or subject-states, both in the east and west, and even for a while having control of Nupe and the Jukun kingdom in the south.[1] This brief though brilliant rise to supremacy is said to have been the work of a remarkable queen called Barkwa Turunda and even more of her forceful daughter, Queen Amina, who is said to have reigned for thirty-four years, subduing Nupe and the Jukun. Amina became famous for building Zaria's first city wall.

Little is certain about these events in Zaria. Yet two points seem clear. The first is that Zaria, like Kano, held a key position in the trade

[1] The Hausa name for Jukun was Kwororafa.

110

between the lands of what is now southern Nigeria and the caravan markets of Hausaland and Bornu. Further to the south, so did Nupe and the Jukun, which is no doubt why these two states were often at war with Zaria. Each will have wanted to secure a greater control of the north-south trade. The second point is that Zaria, in having female rulers, had made a compromise between Islam and West African religion, and was therefore able, at least for a while, to make the best of both worlds — to appeal for loyalty, that is, from both Muslims and non-Muslims.

Towards the end of the century the Jukun turned the tables on Zaria. They began pushing northward. By 1600, according to tradition, they had conquered Bauchi and Gombe, and had possibly brought Zaria itself under their temporary control. Even Kano felt the shock of their raids.[1]

Here as elsewhere (in Songhay, Kanem, or the lands of Guinea), the bare record speaks much of raids and wars, quarrels and miseries. Rulers strove with one another for power and wealth, competing for the taxes without which they could maintain neither governments nor armies, battling for the trade routes that guaranteed the taxes, struggling for the cities where the craftsmen lived and the treasuries lay.

Yet this bare record has little or nothing to say of the life of the majority of people. They suffered in the wars and raids, but certainly less than the record suggests. The raids were painful, but they were brief. The wars were harsh, but they were small. Soldiers did not and could not occupy the land as modern armies do. Even the new firearms that were beginning to be used were harmless at a range of more than a hundred metres or so. So that although upheavals appear very important in the bare record of events, Hausaland became rich and often peaceful. Farmers prospered; craftsmen multiplied; traders flourished; and cities grew in wealth and civilisation.

[1] See also Chapter 10, *Nupe and Jukun*, page 135.

CHAPTER TEN

The Igbo, Yoruba, Edo and others

In eastern Guinea, the large and fertile region of the Lower Niger and its immediately neighbouring lands to west and east, the earliest political events which we know about with any certainty were the work of the peoples who live in that region today. They were the work of the Igbo, Ibibio, Efik and their neighbours, of the Edo-speaking peoples, and of the Yoruba and their neighbours. These events can to some extent be traced back, through European reports, to the fifteenth century; but before that, because these people did not use the art of writing, we know this history only from archaeology, the study of languages, and oral tradition.

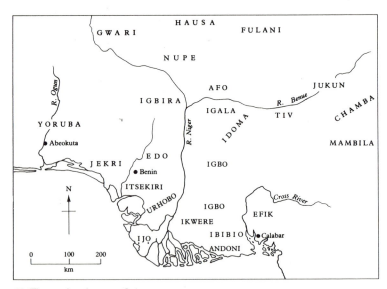

22 *The peoples of eastern Guinea.*

This rich belt of forest country between the ocean and the grassland plains was the scene of many important developments in the distant past. Today the region has some of the densest countryside populations in any part of Africa, and this appears to have been the case in much earlier periods as well. Archaeology and the study of languages support the opinion that it was from this region that pioneering groups of early Iron Age people carried the knowledge of iron-working into distant lands of the Congo basin. Even local tradition has a little to say on this. The Yoruba, for example, have an interesting legend about the creation of man. According to tradition, it was at their holy place of Ile-Ife that the gods first created men and women, and it was from here that men and women spread out to populate the earth.

As time went on, the peoples of eastern Guinea, as in other parts of Guinea, changed their ways. They learned new methods of earning a living. They developed new systems of keeping law and order.

The Igbo and their neighbours

Many political systems of Africa did not develop into states or empires. A lot of peoples found it better to do without kings or emperors. They continued to live peacefully together, to defend themselves and enlarge their wealth, with the help of very little central government.

Does this mean that peoples without chiefs or kings were any less successful than the peoples who formed themselves into states with central governments? Far from it. Some of these peoples without kings were to be among the most go-ahead of all the peoples of Africa: very active in trade, very skilful in politics, very shrewd in dealing with their neighbours.

Prominent among them were the Igbo who have lived, since times beyond the reach of history, in the fertile lands to the east of the lower part of the Niger. Here the common man was his own ruler, though within a complex pattern of community life.

In historical times the Igbo have always been divided into five large groups who have somewhat differed from one another in language, customs, ways of work, and religion.[1] These differences are certainly very old. So are the various types of Igbo government. Most Igbo have governed themselves without giving power to chiefs. Some, however, like those of Nri Awka towards the Niger, have had kings of their own;

[1] Northern or Onitsha (and Nri Awka) Igbo; southern or Owerri Igbo; western Igbo, eastern or Cross River Igbo; north-eastern or Ogoja Igbo.

A bronze bowl found at Igbo-Awka in present-day Anambra State, Nigeria. Every bit of the pot is made of bronze.

while their Cross River neighbours of the eastern Delta have made much use of political associations such as Ekpe.[1] Nearly all Igbo have divided themselves into regular 'age-sets', with each set having its own special rights, duties and responsibilities.

Some of these differences have been in response to varying natural conditions and problems of everyday life. The Nri-Awka Igbo were influenced by what happened along the Niger, and perhaps by the centralised methods of rule adopted by the Edo of Benin even before 1400. Other Igbo, notably those of the Cross River, were far more concerned with local activities in the eastern Delta, and afterwards with the specialised challenge of the ocean trade. All had skilled craftsmen in weaving, metal-working and other activities, and were interested in local trade. But the great formative influence on Igbo politics has undoubtedly been their forest life. They have lived in forest villages and practised forest agriculture with outstanding success. As long ago as 1789 an Igbo writer published an excellent description of his country that was also true for still earlier times:

> Our land is uncommonly rich and fruitful, and produces all kinds of vegetables in great abundance. We have plenty of Indian corn (maize), and vast quantities of cotton and tobacco. . . We have spices of different kinds, particularly pepper; and a variety of delicious fruits that I have never seen in Europe, together with gums and various kinds and honey in great abundance.
>
> All our work is exerted to improve these blessings of nature. Agriculture is our chief employment; and everyone, even the children and women, are engaged in it. . . The benefits of such a way of living are obvious. . . Those benefits are felt by us in the general healthiness of the people, and in their vigour and activity.[2]

Government without kings: the Igbo achievement

This emphasis on farming helps to explain why nearly all Igbo, though divided into several cultural groups, were united in more basic ways. Like many other peoples in Guinea and elsewhere, they ran their affairs

---

[1] For more discussion about political associations, and their importance for everyday life in historical Africa, see Chapter 19: *Sierra Leone and the Poro Association*, page 254.

[2] Olaudah Equiano, *The Interesting Narrative of. . .*London 1789, page 20. This remarkable Igbo was born in about 1745, sold into slavery, but was able to win his freedom and escape to England. There he took a leading part in the great campaign against the slave trade. In 1792 he married the daughter of James and Ann Cullen of Cambridge.

on what is called a segmentary pattern. Many readers will be familiar with the laws and customs which go with segmentary organisation. But it will be useful to discuss, at least briefly, the principal ways in which segmentary systems worked, because they made up a significant aspect of historical politics in West Africa, and in other parts of Africa as well.

Segmentary government is a kind of 'government without rulers'. The best way to understand it is to begin by thinking of one big family, from grandparents to grandchildren, who start a village and farm the land nearby. As time goes by, this family grows bigger. Sons become fathers, and grandchildren become grandparents. As this happens, the original family unit breaks up into a number of self-governing parts, or segments, led by heads of new families within the group. But all the parts stay held together in common loyalty to their ancestors. This loyalty is maintained by the group's religious beliefs, by their prayers at the shrines of their ancestors, and by their understanding of how their ancestors wished them to behave. These beliefs give force to the laws of the village. So this kind of village government is held together by family and religious ties.[1]

Village governments of this kind had two main problems in their political life. The first was to know how to change their rules, from time to time, so as to take account of the rise of new families as the population grew bigger. The second problem was to make sure that separate loyalties to different descent-lines, or 'big families', were balanced by a common loyalty to the group as a whole. These two problems were solved in ways which differed much in detail, but were basically the same.

The solution to the first problem was to enable junior branches of a family to split away peacefully from senior branches, acquire their own land, find a place of honour for their own (but now separate) line of ancestors, and generally fit quietly into the life of their neighbourhood. This was done, essentially, by ceremonies which transferred authority from the heads of senior branches to the heads of junior branches who wanted to start a new and semi-independent life of their own. Other ceremonies allowed different 'big families' to band together if they wished. In short, there were laws and customs which allowed for splitting-away or *fission*, and also for joining-together or *fusion*.

The main solution to the second problem, of making sure that separate family loyalties were balanced by common loyalties, was found in religious ties which joined these families in respect for their common ancestors. But these ties were reinforced in various ways. They might be

[1] For more discussion, see Chapter 12, *The value of religion*, page 163.

116

reinforced through the formation of 'age sets' to which all men and women belonged, or by special political associations whose leaders had power throughout the area of the government in question. Many village governments might also join together, through religious ties and ceremonies, in respect for the ancestors of still bigger units, usually called 'clans'. Igboland had many hundreds of clans, the product of a few village governments which had grown in size, and which had split up, during the distant past, into many governments.

For the affairs of everyday life, however, fairly small numbers of people worked together in separate village governments. This could be a disadvantage to them in times of danger from invaders: unlike peoples organised in big units under kings, they could not rely on big armies. But it also had an important advantage. It was extremely democratic. The village governments of the Igbo, and others like them, were popular governments. Every grown-up man could and did have his say at village assemblies where matters of common interest were decided. Governments like these were good for individual development. People accustomed to a great deal of everyday democracy are people with a great deal of individual self-confidence: they tend to be enterprising, always ready to deal with new problems, easily adaptable to new conditions.

Of course the amount of democracy varied. Some of the Igbo, like the Tiv, Konkomba, Tallensi and other peoples with village governments, had much democracy. There was less among the Igbo who developed 'title societies', such as those of Ama at Nsukka and Ozo at Awka. These were run by a minority of men who were rich enough to pay high fees for the privilege. The same was true among the Cross River Igbo whose Ekpe association worked on the same principle. Yet a man's own skills and ambitions were still the important things. Systems with 'title societies' might be dominated by a handful of rich men. But it was always possible for other men to enter the ruling group by hard work, and not, as in most governments with kings, simply because they had been born into one or other ruling family. Promotion, in other words, was by *achievement* and not by *ascription*.[1] In this way, if not in others, village governments of this type were very much in line with the democratic habits of the modern world. All this helps to explain why the peoples of the Igbo country, most of whom had segmentary governments of one kind or another, acquired a well-founded reputation for enterprise in trade.

[1] For a further explanation of these terms, see Chapter 18, *The Asante empire* and the reforms of King Osei Kwadwo, page 247 and also Chapter 13, *Kings, nobles, governors*, page 184.

The Niger Delta and its peoples

The history of the Delta peoples; that is of all these most southerly lands that are watered and divided by the many out-flow channels of the great River Niger, may be said to have begun in the sixteenth century. Groups of Ịjọ fisherfolk and saltmakers had lived here since early times. Their ancestors had probably come from the region of Benin and Igboland. Pressures of population in Igboland, always fertile in people, now combined with the new attraction of coastal trade with European sea-merchants to carry more people into the delta lands. These newcomers were of many origins, Ịjọ, Igbo, Edo, Jekri, Ibibio, Efik, and even some Tiv and Fulani from the distant north.

These delta peoples lived on islands in the swamps and along the banks of their creeks and rivers, and relied greatly on canoe-transport. Facing special problems of their own, they became a population with notably different ideas and ways of life from their neighbours of the inland country. They were called *Ndu Mili Nnu*, the People of the Salt Water, by the inland Igbo; and it was they who dominated the trade of the whole Niger Delta from the Cross River to the River of Benin, along a coastline of more than five hundred kilometres from east to west. They it was, too, who opened the channels of sea trade to the Igbo of the inland country.

The People of the Salt Water were all organised on segmentary lines, even though some of them, in later times, had kings of their own. As time went by, they found special and often very interesting solutions to the problems of living together in the Delta, a land of creeks and islands, dense vegetation, and many other natural difficulties. These Delta institutions took their rise in the seventeenth century, though they flowered fully only in the nineteenth, and will be discussed in Chapter 16.

Early Yoruba history

West of the Lower Niger, in ancient times just as today, lay the home of the Yoruba, another large people who took shape long before AD 1000 and whose political development followed distinctive patterns of its own.

The Yoruba have several traditions about how their people began life. One of them says that it was at Ile-Ife, which the Yoruba regard as the birthplace of their nation, that mankind was first created. Another tradition tells the story of a great ancestor and hero called Oduduwa. He

118

is said to have come from far in the east and settled at Ile-Ife, and it was from here that his descendant went out to rule the various branches of the Yoruba. One of his sons, for example, is said to have become the first *Alafin* of Oyo, as well as being the father of the first *Oba* of Benin, while another was the first *Onisabe* of Sabe; his eldest daughter is remembered as the mother of the first *Alaketu* of Ketu (in modern Dahomey), while another daughter gave birth to the first *Olowu* of Owu.

What historical truth lies behind these beliefs? They point to the early arrival of newcomers who settled in Yorubaland and merged with the more numerous people whom they found there. These people who were already living in Yorubaland had certainly been there since distant Stone Age times. Archaeological evidence suggests that they were pioneering metal-workers and fine artists in baked clay, and that they were possibly related to the people of the Nok Culture.[1] Experts in language explain that the Yoruba language (like other languages nearby) probably came into existence several thousand years ago.

Then who were the ancestors, personified by Oduduwa in the traditions, who joined these people and built the Yoruba civilisation of historical times? Here again, modern experts in the study of language have something useful to say. They think that there were two main movements of incoming ancestors, one towards Ekiti, Ife and Ijebu in the zone of dense tropical forest, and the other towards Oyo in the much more open country to the north of the forest. The earliest of these migrations probably started soon after about AD 700.

Where did these incoming ancestors come from? Some Yoruba legends say that they came from Arabia, and quite a few Yoruba customs seem to reflect the ideas of ancient peoples who lived along the Middle Nile, notably the people of the ancient empire of Kush. No doubt the truth about where the incoming ancestors came from, however, is that they came from the Central Sudan, or more probably from a little way to the north of Yorubaland, and had felt some influence of Nile civilisations which had sent out traders and travellers in ancient times. Entering Yorubaland, they brought new political ideas and methods with them. They introduced or developed new types of government. We may see the reflection of this in the story of how Oduduwa sent out his children to rule the various branches of the Yoruba in new ways.

Yorubaland, in any case, entered on a new stage of development about AD 1000; and this development, partly because of these influences, launched the people of Yorubaland into forms of political life that were different from those of the Igbo.

---

[1] See map on page 18.

Like the Igbo, the Yoruba relied on forest farming for their livelihood. Unlike the Igbo, their political life was dominated by town government and not by village government. Many towns were founded in the forest lands to the west of the Niger and, somewhat later, in the more open country north of the dense forest. These towns varied in size, power and wealth.

Yoruba achievement: the growth of towns

Yoruba towns evolved from the rich complexity of Yoruba ways of life. In many fields the Yoruba shared the skills of their neighbours in forest farming, iron-smelting, brass-work, cotton-weaving and other valuable handicrafts. Yet their special contribution to West African civilisation, as a modern Yoruba writer has rightly claimed, consisted in 'their remarkable urban centres, unparalleled anywhere else in tropical Africa'.[1] They had, of course, many villages and small settlements: *abúlé* (hamlet), *iletò* (village), *ilú ọlójà* (small market town); but it was in their big towns, their *ilú aládé*, that their urban achievements were greatest.

The *ìlú aládé*, of which Ife was the most important in ancient times, were the seat of powerful rulers: of *obas* whose ancestors were believed to be descended from Oduduwa, and who had the right to wear crowns with bearded fringes as a symbol of authority. Little is known of the size of these 'crowned' or capital towns in the distant past, but they certainly had large populations. They were usually surrounded by a defensive wall. The wall round Old Oyo, once the capital of the Oyo empire, was as much as forty kilometres round, and seven metres high, at the beginning of the nineteenth century. Other such walls were not much smaller.

Yoruba methods of government

Externally, the capital towns of Yoruba states were linked together during ancient times in a confederation under the spiritual and political leadership of the senior Yoruba ruler, the *Oni* of Ife, and by arrangements between ruling families.

This confederal system left each state to run its own affairs, while

---

[1] G. J. Afolabi Ojo, *Yoruba Culture*, London 1966, page 104.

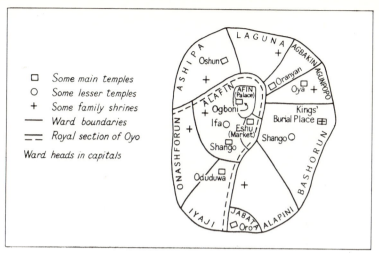

Plan of the city of old Oyo.

providing means for keeping the peace between them. Only with the rise of Oyo in northern Yorubaland, during the sixteenth century, did the central influence if Ife begin to decline. Even then, the arrangements between ruling families continued.

'All these kingdoms', wrote a Yoruba historian, 'believed in and practised the *Ebi* system of government. Under this system, a kingdom was regarded as a larger version of a family, and a country as a collection of kingdoms whose rulers look on one another as relations'. Seniority was based on the believed ages of the various kingdoms. To some extent, the Oyo empire cut across these arrangements by asserting the leadership of Oyo, historically a 'junior' kingdom.[1] The Oyo empire and the *Ebi* system were thus in conflict.

Internally, these populous and busy capitals were organised in a way which combined segmentary patterns of authority, such as those we have noted for the Igbo and others, with government by ruling families and *obas* (kings). This combination of different types of self-rule was reflected in the architecture of the towns, whether they were capitals or not. At first sight these might appear as a mere confusion of dwellings, densely packed together and divided only by narrow roads. But the apparent confusion had an order of its own. Each family — each 'extended family', that is, of grandparents to grandchildren — lived in

---

[1] I. A. Akinjogbin, 'The Oyo Empire in the 18th century', *Journal of the Historical Society of Nigeria*, December 1966, page 451.

A baked clay (terra cotta) head from Ancient Ife (Yoruba).

its own cluster of homes, its compound or *agbo'le*. Each *agbo'le* was gathered round the house of the head of its *agba ile* or descent-line (in this case a descent-line through fathers and not, as in Asante, through mothers). At the centre of the town, if it was a capital, stood the *afin* or *oba's* palace, often a big building.

Government and religion

Political organisation developed in the same way. Each head of a descent-line or 'big family' was in charge of his own quarter of the town. All the descent-lines sent representatives to sit on a council of chiefs who owed their positions to their birth. These chiefs, usually known as the *iwarefa*, had important political powers of decision. Often these included the right to choose the man who should be *oba*.

But it was seldom the work of the *iwarefa* to take action on decisions. Political action, as distinct from political decision, was the duty of the *oba* and his officials (civil servants). This formed another aspect of the Yoruba system. So the *oba's* government consisted mostly of the servants and messengers of the *oba*. These might be very numerous in wealthy states. They took their orders only from the king. It could also consist of men who belonged to one or other of the special societies who were in charge of the various age-sets of the Yoruba. One or other of these age-sets carried out public works and performed services of value to the whole community. Inside the towns the various heads of descent-lines looked after purely local affairs.

In practice, the system was more complicated than any brief description could show. Though democratic in small matters, Yoruba government differed from Igbo government in being aristocratic wherever important decisions were concerned: power in big matters, that is, always rested in the hands of a minority of nobles.[1]

Government by kings and nobles make it possible to unite the people of each main town firmly together, but difficult or impossible to unite the different towns. Each town's nobles tended to feel themselves in rivalry with those of neighbouring towns, even though the *Ebi* 'family system', as mentioned above, made all the towns part of the same big Yoruba 'family'.

Politics was mixed up with religion, even more than among other West African peoples. The Yoruba system of government in this respect, like other systems, rested on the political power of appointed

---

[1] The same aristocratic pattern has been noted in the Wolof empire: see Chapter 6, page 56.

rulers among leading families, but also on their religious power. In the distant past all the Yoruba states felt strong loyalty to the ancestors of Oduduwa, and so to the *Oni* of Ife who was the senior living representative of those ancestors. But as civilisation grew, and Yoruba populations became more numerous, this common loyalty to Ife proved difficult to maintain. Each state tended to develop its own separate loyalties, and to worship the spirits and gods in its own separate ways. This is one reason why some of the leading Yoruba spirits and gods have taken different forms. In some places, for example, Oduduwa is thought of as a man and in other places as a woman.

'The real keynote of the life of the Yoruba', according to a modern writer, 'is neither in their noble ancestry nor in the past deeds of their heroes. The keynote of their life is their religion. In all things, they are religious. . . As far as they are concerned, the full responsibility of all the affairs of life belongs to the Deity; their own part in the matter is to do as they are ordered through the priests or diviners whom they believe to be the interpreters of the will of the Deity. . .'[1]

This emphasis on the religious powers of their rulers was reflected in Yoruba life by the beauty and excellence of Yoruba sculpture in wood and brass, clay and ivory. The 'home-city' of the Yoruba people, Ife, has yielded many splendid things that were made long ago in honour of Yoruba beliefs and rulers. At Ife, for instance, Yoruba artists were called on to celebrate the *Oni* of Ife and his kinsmen, and evolved one of the greatest schools of sculpture that the world has known. They modelled works in clay and brass that are of great power and beauty. Here, too, we find an interesting thing. For a study of these sculptures shows that some of their features are like those of the baked clay sculptures of the Nok Culture people in earlier times. On the other hand, the Ife brass sculptures were made by a special method, using wax, which was certainly used by the sculptors of the ancient civilisations of the Nile. Yoruba civilisation was thus a creative combination of many ideas, customs and beliefs that were born in Guinea as well as in other parts of Africa.

Later Yoruba history: the growth of Oyo

It seems likely that Ife reached the height of its brilliance soon after AD 1300. By this period, there were many Yoruba towns and a much larger Yoruba-speaking population than in earlier times, while the language

[1] E. Bolaji Idowu, *Olúdùmarè: God in Yoruba Belief*, London 1962, page 5.

A bronze head from Ife. These sculptures, made by Yoruba artists, have become world famous.

they spoke varied from place to place. Yoruba states existed far westward in Dahomey and northward through the rolling country beyond the edge of the forest, as far as the Niger above its confluence with the Benue. Here in the north there was Oyo, founded after most of the forest towns to the south but now destined, because of its favourable trading position and its local wealth, to become the strongest of them all, and the capital of a powerful empire.

Early in the sixteenth century, Oyo was still a small state scarcely able to hold its own against two strong neighbours, Borgu to the north and Nupe to the north-east. Nupe even conquered Oyo in about 1550. The king (*alafin*) of Oyo and his senior chiefs retired into Borgu, but soon returned south again and built a new capital at Igbohu. But now they began to consider ways of making themselves strong enough to prevent further defeats. One solution, it was clear, would be to build a strong cavalry army such as was repeatedly used by Borgu and Nupe.

Yet here there was a difficulty. Northern Yorubaland, like some other parts of West Africa, harboured two types of tse-tse fly that were very harmful to horses. The northern Yoruba could keep horses, but they could not breed them. The answer, then, was to buy steady supplies of horses from north of the Niger, and to train soldiers in the tactics of cavalry warfare. This was the policy adopted by *Alafin* Orompoto who, it is said, raised a corps of one thousand cavalrymen and laid the foundations for Oyo power towards the end of the sixteenth century.

Fortunately for Oyo, it was able to pay for the needs of this policy. Its wealth came from two economic facts. In the first place, the Oyo Yoruba were particularly well placed to win success in the long distance trade. Living not far south of the Middle Niger, they were linked to the whole trade of the Western Sudan by grassland routes running northward to the markets of Hausaland in one direction and to those of Gao, Timbuktu and Jenne in another. They could feed these markets with the export goods of all Yorubaland, for, as Professor Ajayi tells us, 'Oyo traded with all parts of the Yoruba country', and became 'an important centre for gathering the produce of the rain forests to sell to people of the drier savannahs'.[1]

But the Oyo were not only fortunate traders: they were also valuable producers on their own account. They were skilled in the spinning, dyeing, and weaving of cotton, and their cloths were prized in many lands. Their iron smelters and blacksmiths were famous, as were their makers of calabash bowls and jugs. They traded in these goods with the

---

[1] J. F. Ade Ajayi (with Robert Smith): *Yoruba Warfare in the Nineteenth Century*, Ibadan/Cambridge 1964, page 3.

peoples of the north and were able to import 'such articles as salt, leather goods, antimony and glass ware. But the most significant imports were horses which formed the basis of the political power of Oyo'.[1] By the seventeenth century, as we shall see in Chapter 16, Oyo had used this power to build a large empire west of the Niger.

The Edo and Benin

The beginnings of the state of Benin, like those of the Yoruba states, lie deep in the forgotten past. It seems that the first rulers of Benin, a trading settlement and afterwards a city of the Niger Delta, acquired their power soon after the forming of the first Yoruba states, or soon after about AD 1000. Tradition knows them as the Ogiso dynasty or line of kings.

There is no doubt that the Edo people of Benin took some of their political ideas from their Yoruba neighbours. Tradition says that hundreds of years ago the Edo of Benin became dissatisfied with their own kings. They accordingly sent to Ife and asked Oduduwa for one of his sons to rule over them. He sent them Prince Oranmiyan (or Oronyon); and Oranmiyan started a new period in the political life of the Benin state.

This does not mean, of course, that the Edo took over Yoruba ideas completely. In fact, this change probably happened long after the time when Oduduwa is supposed to have lived; perhaps as late as AD 1400. Even if there was a close connection between some of the rulers of Benin and those of the Yoruba states, the Edo were very much a people with ideas of their own. We can see this in many ways. Their artists, whether at Benin itself or in other Edo towns, were especially brilliant in the skills of working metal, and developed many styles of much distinction.

Edo expansion at Benin dates back to a period long before the first European written reports were made, and was no doubt linked to Benin's strong trading position on the Niger Delta. Tradition suggests that the political system and customs of Benin were already well established by the fourteenth century. By the fifteenth century Benin had become an important power in the land. It was at this time that the artists of Benin, like those of Ife before them, were called on to celebrate the power and authority of their rulers. In doing so, they developed a

[1] Ajayi, page 3.

Part of a metal plaque from Benin showing a soldier with an early kind of gun.

A Benin ivory leopard decorated with bronze studs.

special style of royal sculpture that was different from the more popular (and often more beautiful) styles which were liked by ordinary folk. As well as producing many fine heads and figures, the royal artists also designed and made many splendid brass plaques, or large rectangular pictures in metal, which were used to decorate the *Oba's* palace. Many of these fine old sculptures, whether in the royal style or in other styles, have survived and become famous throughout the world.

Here again we find an interesting point. The sculpture of Benin was mainly in brass. Yet brass cannot be made without copper, and there is no copper in southern Nigeria. So the copper must have come from

129

somewhere else, and it must have come in exchange for goods produced or sold by the Edo of Benin. Benin, in other words, was deeply concerned with foreign trade. This trade seems to have consisted of buying copper and other goods from the Western Sudan in exchange for Edo cotton stuffs and other goods. Once again we see how the rise of states and empires was linked to the *production* of goods and the *exchange* of goods. The power of the empire of Benin, like that of other big states and empires, was built on economic foundations of this kind.

By the middle of the sixteenth century, perhaps earlier, the *Oba* of Benin ruled over an area which spread from the region of modern Lagos to the Niger Delta. Even when the Portuguese first came in touch with Benin in 1486, they were impressed by the large size of the empire

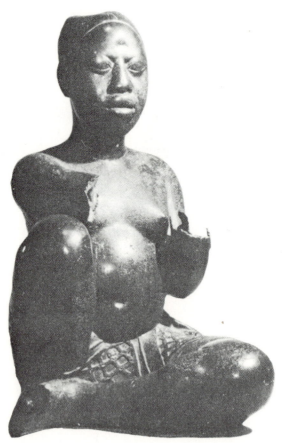

One of the most famous sculptures of old Nigeria, from Tada.

and the strong power of its ruler. Benin soon became the largest of the political systems of Guinea. It traded far and wide. It received ambassadors from Portugal and sent ambassadors to Europe.

Those were the days when Portugal was glad to find friends among the strong rulers of Africa. A Portuguese report of the early sixteenth century tells us how the *Oba* of Benin wanted to learn more about Europe than his Portuguese visitors could tell him. So he sent one of his chiefs to Portugal. 'This ambassador was a man of good speech and natural wisdom. Great feasts were held in Portugal in his honour. He was shown many of the good things of Portugal. He returned to his own land [as he had come] in a Portuguese ship. When he left, the king of Portugal made him a gift of rich clothes for himself and his wife, and also sent a rich present to the king of Benin. . .'

The Benin empire

Written down not long ago by Chief Jacob Egharevba, the royal traditions of Benin speak vividly of this period. One of the most famous *Obas* of this time of expansion was Ewuare, who came to the throne in about 1440. He is said to have travelled widely in Guinea and to have visited the Congo.

Ewuare was 'powerful, courageous and wise', say the traditions.

> He fought against and captured 201 towns and villages in Ekiti, Ikare, Kukuruku, Eka and Igbo country. He took their rulers captive, and he caused the people to pay tribute to him.
>
> He made good roads in Benin City. . . In fact the town rose to importance and gained the name of city during his reign. . . It was he who had the innermost and greatest of the walls and ditches made round the city, and he also made powerful charms and had them buried at each of the nine gateways of the city so as to ward against any evil charms which might be brought by people of other countries in order to injure his subjects.[1]

It was under Ewuare, too, that the people of Benin had their first contact with Europeans. in 1472 the Portuguese captain Ruy de Siqueira brought a sailing ship as far as the Bight of Benin.

But Ewuare is remembered as an outstanding ruler not only for his conquests and breadth of contact with the world. He also presided over important political changes. For it was under Ewuare, according to

[1] J. Egharevba, *A Short History of Benin*, Ibadan. Third edition 1960, page 14.

tradition, that the State Council of Benin was formed, together with other new political bodies. And it was from this time that the empire of Benin acquired not only a central ruler but also a central government, with officials and departments and regular means of ruling the empire.

New links with Europe: *Oba* Esigie

These changes were carried further under Esigie who came to power in about 1504 and added to the empire the state of Idah, lying between Benin and the Benue. Esigie is especially remembered for having taken several important steps in changing political power in Benin from the bases of ascription to that of achievement: from men who wielded power, that is, simply because they were members of noble families, to 'commoners' who were appointed to positions of power as servants of the king.[1]

Esigie is also remembered as the *oba* who entered upon good relations with Portuguese envoys who were now arriving more frequently on his coasts. Missionaries also came from Portugal and were well received. One of them, Duarte Pires, wrote to the Portuguese king in 1516, telling how generously the *oba* had shown them hospitality, and how he had 'sat them at table to dine with his son'. This *oba* is remembered as a man of learning, and as having practised astrology (*Iwe-Uki*), forerunner of the science of astronomy, the study of the stars. He could speak and read Portuguese. He is said to have reigned for nearly half a century. Benin was now a city of great size and wealth.

Orhogbua followed Esigie in about 1550, Ehengbuda in about 1578, and Ahuan in about 1606. All three are praised in the royal traditions as sensible and forward-looking rulers, the memory of *Oba* Ahuan being especially honoured as a herbalist and skilful maker of charms.

The first Englishmen to reach this powerful Edo empire arrived at Gwato, the port of Benin, in 1553 during *Oba* Orhogbua's reign. A Portuguese who was with them wrote afterwards that the *oba* (like Esigie before him) could speak, read and write Portuguese. These Englishmen bought a cargo of Benin peppercorns in exchange for English metal pots and other goods.

Westward of Nigeria, in what is modern Dahomey,[2] the states of the Yoruba, notably Ketu, and the empire of Benin shared control over

[1] For more details about this, see Chapter 13, *Kings, nobles, governors*: Esigie's dealings with the Uzama nobles of Benin.

[2] Now renamed Benin.

132

much of the inland country and over the little states along the coast. The Fon people had yet to make their successful bid for independence. The Ewe were already well established in the southern country of what is modern Togo.

This small ivory head from Old Benin was made as a pendant to be worn with the chief's dress.

This sculpture was made long ago for the founders of Nupe.

Nupe and Jukun

North of Oyo and Benin, other states developed along the Middle Niger and Benue Rivers, Nupe and Jukun were two of these.

The Nupe today number about a million people. Their early state began a very long time ago, perhaps as early as the eleventh century. But it took historical shape only around 1400. One story, which we cannot be certain is true, is that a great Nupe leader called Tsoede or Edigi united several small Nupe states into a single and much stronger state at about this time.

The Nupe gained from their position along the River Niger because they became middlemen in trade between the south and the north: between southern Nigeria, that is, and the Hausa states. But they also lost from this position, because they were often brought under the control of Oyo or of the Hausa states, and had to pay tribute to these stronger states.

In about 1750 the ruler of Nupe accepted Islam. Later again, Nupe was ruled by one of the Fulani 'big families'.

The history of the Jukun kingdom, lying east of Nupe, is much the same. The Jukun became middlemen in the south-north trade. But this attracted the interest of their rivals. The Jukun were often at war with Zaria, to the north of them.

Between 1500-1600, Zaria had the upper hand and made Jukun pay tribute to its strong rulers. After about 1600 the Jukun rulers reversed this position. They invaded to the north, and are even said to have brought Bauchi and Gombe under their control for a while, and to have raided as far as Kano. After 1800, the Fulani also brought Jukun under their control.

TWO SUMMARIES
AD *1000-1600*

1 What does all this mean?

We see in these centuries how the peoples of West Africa grew from being very few, very backward in their way of life, cut off from the rest of the world, without any foreign trade, into large, and go-ahead peoples.

Soon after 300 BC they began to move out of their Stone Age into an Iron Age. That opened the way for all kinds of progress: the use of better tools, the growing of more food, the development of foreign trade, and bigger populations.

This Early Iron Age came to an end around AD 1000. There followed six centuries of further development and expansion. These built the civilisation of West Africa that is the parent of our own civilisation of today.

West Africa today is inhabited by the descendants of the same peoples who built that civilisation. Although West Africa today is a much wealthier region for its peoples to live in and has many things, such as good roads and railways, that did not exist then, the foundations of West Africa's modern wealth and way of life were laid in these six centuries of expansion between 1000-1600.

2 Islam and West Africa

Islam is one of the great religions of the world, uniting many peoples. It began when the Prophet Muhammad and three companions proclaimed the new Faith in AD 622, which is Year 1 of Islam.

By AD 700 the followers of Muhammad had won control of most of North Africa. They founded new states there. Some of these states became active in the trade across the Sahara with the states of the Sudan.

In this way, Islam reached old Sudanese towns, such as Gao, long before AD 1000. It also came to West Africa by way of Mauretania and Senegal. This too was long before AD 1000.

Soon after AD 1000, some of the rulers of the Western Sudan became Muslims: that is, they were converted to Islam. Gradually, the new religion spread among West Africans. But in these centuries, down to 1600 and after, Islam was a religion of the peoples of the towns of the Sudan. Outside the towns, nearly all West Africans of the Sudan remained loyal to their own religions until after 1700.

Islam became important for West Africa in three chief areas of everyday life:

1 *In religion and education:* Islam came to West Africa — at first to the towns of the Western Sudan, then gradually to other places and countries — as a worldwide religion (just as Christianity did later). Islam was and is 'for everybody'. So Islam could be a means of uniting peoples who had previously believed in their own separate or national religions. All who joined Islam belonged to the *umma,* the worldwide 'family' of Islam, even if they were not united in other ways. This gave West African Muslims (believers in Islam) new and valuable links with each other, and with Muslim peoples in other parts of the world.

Islam is based on a book, the Koran, just as Christianity is based on the Bible. So Islam called on West Africans to learn how to read and write. Muslim teachers set up schools where students read the Koran, and learned to recite passages from it by heart. They also founded centres of advanced learning where books written by Muslim scholars were studied and discussed, and new books were written.

So it came about that important centres of book-learning arose in West Africa, the first of their kind: after 1300 at Niani, the capital of the Mali empire; after 1400 at Timbuktu, which became a city of the Songhay empire; and elsewhere. The Muslim schools of Timbuktu became especially famous; they formed an early kind of university.

Different branches of learning were taught and studied. One was *tawhid,* the study of the unity of God. Another was *tafsir,* the study of the Koran. A third was *fiqh,* the study of law and administration. History and geography were also taught.

All Muslims have a code of basic rules for behaviour. This is the *sharia.* In West Africa, after about AD 1000 (or 391 in the Muslim calendar, which begins in AD 622 and has a slightly shorter year), the *sharia* was taught according to the ideas of the Maliki school of religious teachers.

2 *In politics and law:* the ideas and beliefs of Islam helped the rulers of the Sudan to build larger states than before. One reason for this was that when people became Muslims they could join together more easily than before: Islam was a means of creating unity between

them. Another reason was that Islam provided the kind of laws that were useful to bigger states and larger market-towns. Such laws were about the administration of justice, the inheritance of property, the improvement of market organisation, and other matters that became important as civilisation developed.

Famous scholars taught these things. One of them was al-Maghili, a North African who wrote a book of advice about new methods of government for the benefit of King Muhammad Rumfa of the Hausa state of Kano in about 1490. He called his book *The Duties of Kings*. Afterwards, in about 1500, al-Maghili went on to Gao, the capital of the Songhay empire, where he gave advice of the same kind to the Songhay emperor, *Askia* Muhammad the Great.

3 *In long-distance trade:* when long-distance trade with North Africa, across the Sahara, became important for West Africans (especially for West Africans of the Sudan), new methods of conducting this trade were required. North African Muslims had already developed useful techniques for credit and exchange, for reckoning in values based on coins, when they were trading with other peoples who lived far away. These techniques began to be adopted by West African traders as well; and many of these West African traders became Muslims.

After about AD 900 the standard measure of value in North Africa became the Almoravid *dinar*, sometimes in West Africa called the *mitcal*. Although West Africans continued to use their own standards for measuring value — the cowrie shell became the most important of these — they also began measuring in dinars or mitcals when they were trading with North Africans. Such developments encouraged long-distance trade and also helped to spread Islam.

All this means that the study of West African Islam has become a complex subject. West African Muslims have belonged to several important Muslim brotherhood communities, or *tariqas*. After 1600, the two chief *tariqas* became the Qadiriyya and the Tijaniyya. (The Ahmadiyya, important today, took shape early in the present century).

And all these were positive effects which helped human and social development. Other effects could be negative, and one of these was that the people of the big trading cities of the Sudan, becoming Muslims, came into conflict with peoples of the countryside who continued to believe in their own religions and follow their own religious rules. We have seen this especially in the history of the Songhay empire, but it was also true of other big states whose power was based on Muslim cities.

Another negative effect, for peoples who were relatively weak in military power and could easily be raided by stronger neighbours, was the growth of the trans-Saharan slave trade, as well as of new forms of servitude in West Africa itself.

Especially after 1700, religious wars developed. Islam has always divided the world into two parts: the *Dar al-Islam,* the Home of Islam where all people are Muslim, and the *Dar al-Harb,* or Home of War, where most people are non-Muslims. (Christianity also divided the world into two parts: Christendom and Heathendom). The Muslims of Dar al-Islam had a duty to make war on the people of the Dar al-Harb to convert them to Islam. Often, such wars were also made in order to capture non-Muslims and turn them into slaves.

Some useful dates about Islam in West Africa

AD

622	Foundation of Islam in Arabia. Year One of Muslim Calendar.
641	Muslim Arabs capture Babylon, then the (Christian) capital of Egypt.
670	Muslim Arabs, under Uqba ibn Nafi, occupy Ifriqiya (Tunisia). In 711 a Muslim Arab army under Tariq crosses into Spain at Gibraltar (Jebel al-Tariq: the Hill of Tariq). They conquer most of Spain and Portugal, and go raiding into France. This leads to the rise of a brilliant North African Muslim state in Spain, with its capital at Cordoba (756-1031).
about 750	Small Muslim trading states in North Africa (especially Tāhert in Algeria) are active in the trade with West Africa across the Sahara.
773	Muslim Arab geographer, al-Fazari, writes of ancient Ghana as 'the land of gold'. Muslim traders from North Africa become active in cities of the Western Sudan: Takrur, Audoghast, Gao.
about 1010	King of Gao becomes a Muslim. So do some other kings of the Western Sudan, including the king of Mali (Barmandana) and of Kanem-Bornu (Hume).
1054	Southern wing of Almoravid (Mauretanian Berber) Muslims invade Ancient Ghana.
1076	Almoravids capture capital of Ancient Ghana.
1324	Famous pilgrimage of *Mansa* Kankan Musa of Mali.
1335	*Sunni* line of Songhay kings begins at Gao. They are Muslims.
1400	Rise of Timbuktu and Jenne as centres of Muslim learning and of trade in gold with the Akan people of central (modern) Ghana.
1490	Al-Maghili writes *The Duties of Kings.*

about 1550	Kings of Kanem-Bornu enter into good relations with the great Muslim empire of the Ottoman Turks. (In 1517 the Ottoman Turks completed their conquest of Egypt. In 1529 they dominated Algeria. In 1534 they set up a new (Ottoman) state in Tunisia).
1665	The writers of Timbuktu complete two important histories of the Western Sudan, the *Tarikh al-Sudan* (History of the Sudan), and the *Tariqh al-Fattash* (History of the Seeker for Knowledge).
1725	Fulani Muslims of Futa Jallon (modern Republic of Guinea) form new religious state. Beginning of the Revival of Islam in the Western Sudan during the eighteenth century. This also continues after 1800.
about. 1775	Foundation of Muslim state of Futa Toro (in the north of modern Senegal).
1804- 1811	Muslim Fulani conquer Hausaland. Origins of the caliphate of Sokoto.

PART TWO

Character of West African civilisation up to the sixteenth century

Some different questions

West Africans by 1500-1600 had many different achievements to their credit. Their 'cloth of history' was now woven in many different patterns. Many different ways of life were being followed. Farmers cultivated a great variety of seeds, plants and trees for food and trade and manufacture. Craftsmen worked in a wide range of skills. Traders extended their business. Outstanding men governed and taught, made war or pursued the arts of peace, wrote books or spoke poetry, composed music or carved in wood and ivory or made fine sculpture in clay and metal.

But now it was, too, that other ideas, inventions, and invaders from outside West Africa began to appear on the scene. Entirely new designs and patterns took their place on history's cloth.

Earlier chapters have followed the political record. What needs to be asked now is a different set of questions. What was the civilisation of West Africa really like in the sixteenth century? How did people live in those days? How did they work and produce goods, and conduct their trade? What were their main successes and failures? Chapters 11, 12 and 13 discuss such questions as these, concerned with economic and social history rather than with the political record of events.

Then comes another aspect of the sixteenth century, dealt with in Chapter 14. This was the impact of new pressures and influences from outside West Africa. It was during this century that ships of several European nations began sailing frequently to the coasts of Africa and India, started conquering and plundering the islands of the Caribbean Sea and the mainland of Central and South America, and, in doing so, opened a fresh range of adventure and ambition. Much of this shaped a new pattern of power in Western Europe: and this made itself increasingly felt along the coast of West Africa. Other big changes occurred in Egypt and North Africa. These formed a new pattern of power; and this affected many of the inland countries of West Africa. All these outside changes were important in African history.

CHAPTER ELEVEN

The general economy of West Africa

Unity and variety

Big events and useful dates are the skeleton of history: the rise and fall of states and empires, the reigns of kings and queens, conquests and invasions, victories and defeats. It is necessary to understand the skeleton, for this is the way to understand how the bones and body of daily life, of civilisation, were built up and put together.

But the skeleton by itself is a lifeless thing. To enjoy the living reality of the past, another thing is necessary. We must put the flesh of life on these bare bones. We must turn to vital questions about how people lived and worked, believed and thought, built and evolved the historical civilisation of West Africa four centuries ago.

The people of West Africa lived and worked in many different ways, spoke many different languages, created many different gods, served many different rulers. All this, and much else besides, was part of their civilisation. It was therefore a civilisation of great *variety*. Some peoples lived well; others lived badly. Some made much progress in finding better ways of working and of governing themselves; others did not. With some, power and wealth grew; with others, they declined.

But it was also a civilisation, however varied in appearance and in detail, of great underlying *unity*. This underlying unity came from the common origins and formation of nearly all West African peoples. They were all, or nearly all, shaped and influenced by the same general conditions and opportunities, by the same kind of handicaps and advantages, by the same West African land and life.

In many ways it is impossible to distinguish the civilisation of West Africa during the sixteenth century, as at other periods, from the civilisation of a much larger part of Africa. The peoples of central and southern Africa, of eastern and even to a large extent of northern Africa, have all built their ways of life on the same deep foundations.

West Africa can therefore be regarded as a separate historical unit only for purposes of study. Yet the achievements and experience of West African peoples have been so rich and interesting, so fertile and full of meaning for the future, that it is reasonable to speak of West African civilisation on its own, so long as one remembers that this civilisation was always a part of the wider unity of African civilisation as a whole.

Continued growth

There is a third important point we must note. West African civilisation enjoyed great *continuity:* it was a process, in other words, of continual change, development and growth. It is easy to see why. For many centuries, because of the wasteland of the Sahara on one side and central Africa's vast forests on the other, West Africans were left to work out their own problems in their own way.

They suffered very few invasions from outside. Of major importance we can count only three: the Berber invasion of the eleventh century, aimed at the wealth of Ancient Ghana; the Moroccan invasion of the late sixteenth century, aimed at the wealth of Songhay; and the nineteenth-century conquest by the Europeans, aimed at the wealth of the whole continent. Yet the first two of these invasions were soon over. They were painful, even disastrous, to the West African countries which they touched; but these countries were few. Safe behind their seas of sand and water, most West Africans were unaware of or barely disturbed by these invasions.

This safety from outside interference was often helpful to West Africans, but it had a big disadvantage. For while the seas of sand and water certainly protected West Africa from many dangers, they also cut off West Africans from close contact with the outside world. This meant that they had no share in the great advances of scientific thought, and in the new uses of machinery, which began to appear in Europe long before the sixteenth century. While Europe discovered ever more profitable and skilful ways of producing goods and of mastering nature, West Africa largely remained in the age before mechanical science. This scientific backwardness was to prove a very great handicap.

West Africa's isolation was not complete. Many links with North and Central Africa were never broken. On the contrary, as we have seen at many points in this book, trade between North and West Africa was often of great value to both. New kinds of useful plants also came into West Africa in this way, notably cotton. So did new ideas about religion and government, those of Islam being the most obvious example, and the arts of writing and scholarship. By 1500, West African civilisation had absorbed many ideas from North Africa. It had taken over these

A forest farm in central Guinea.

ideas, and put them to West African use. In all this we can see the mixture of unity and continuity.

How the people lived

West Africa has more than 100 million people today. In the sixteenth century there were far fewer. (This is true of nearly all countries everywhere: the population of England or France in the sixteenth century was only a small part of what it is today.)

There were fewer kinds of food. But more were now added. Valuable plants and fruits like maize and pineapples were brought from Central and South America in the ships of Portugal, after about 1500, and cultivated in West Africa for the first time. These new crops were eagerly accepted, and they spread rapidly.

Though without any knowledge of modern science, West Africans had already solved many hard problems about living in their vast and often difficult region. They had learnt the secret of many medicinal herbs and how to use them to cure sickness. They had discovered how to look after cattle in very dry weather. They had become experts at growing food in the forest. They had found out how to recognise minerals in rocks, how to sink mines, how to get the ore and smelt and work it. They had developed a wide range of hand-manufacture in many materials. They had formed religions of their own. They had evolved effective methods of government, though mostly without the use of writing.

These skills impressed foreign visitors. A Portuguese report of 1506, that of Duarte Pacheco Pereira, tells how high-quality cotton goods could be purchased at many points along the Guinea coast. An English captain called William Towerson wrote in 1556 of the 'fine iron goods' that were hand-made in Guinea: 'spears, fish-hooks, farming tools, and swords that are very sharp on both edges'.

Of all their material skills, *tropical farming* and *mining* were the most important. In both these fields, West Africans were far advanced among all the peoples of the sixteenth century. They were so far advanced, indeed, that it was Africans (even though working as slaves) who later pioneered the development of tropical farming and mining in South America.

There was one great difference, between then and now, in the way people obtained the goods they needed. Today most people work partly or entirely for money, for wages or salaries or business profits. With this money they buy the goods they need or can afford. This is what we call a *money economy*. In the distant past, however, very few West Africans worked for money. They did not have a money economy. They had what we call a *subsistence economy*. This means that most West Africans worked in order to grow or make the goods they *personally* needed, and not in order to earn money with which to buy such goods.

A farmer then would grow enough food for his family's needs, but little or no more. A blacksmith would make enough hoes or spears to be sure that he could get what he and his family needed in exchange; but he seldom exchanged these for any kind of money. He took them to market and exchanged them *directly* for the goods he wanted. This kind of economy was a stage of development which occurred nearly everywhere in the world. In later times, with steady progress in production, West Africans increasingly entered a money economy, the way of living that depends on earning cash, in which most of us live and work today.

Of course the detailed picture is far from simple. There was a growing

Cattle and their herdsman in Northern Nigeria.

quantity of internal and external trade in the sixteenth century; and this trade was carried on in foods that were grown, and goods that were manufactured, with the idea of exchanging them for other goods or for various kinds of money. The beginnings of a money economy did indeed develop wherever traders gathered in markets and began to deal in goods for sale. We shall discuss this development in the next section.

The fact remains that nearly all West Africans still lived outside the centres of this small though steadily expanding money economy of the towns and big markets. Even inside these centres the idea of employing men and women in exchange for wages or salaries was still in the future. The only form of city employment that was known then was a kind of servitude, which historians call domestic or household slavery, in which wages played no part. Employment outside the towns and market-centres was also in the same form of slavery, or else, as in the forest areas, in work provided by customary duties and age-grade organisations. Once again money and wages played no part.

This is not the place to discuss the full effects of this absence of wages

Left: *Old types of metal hoes used by West Africans in the past.* Right: *Another old West African farming tool.*

149

and of the habit of working for money. One main effect, though, was to keep the production of goods at the same general level as before. Most people were content to live as they had always lived. They felt no need for the invention or use of machinery which would enable them to produce more goods, or at a much cheaper price. All the goods that were required for a normal everyday life could be well enough grown or made with the equipment that was already known.

Making goods and trading in goods

Other West Africans, mostly those who lived in or near towns and big market-centres, were busy making goods for local and long-distance trade, as well as trading in these goods with their neighbours or with North African traders.

Even before 1600, many were producing goods for trade, and not because they needed these goods for their own use. By 1600 this local and long-distance trade was very large and had become an important part of West African life.

People on the sea coast caught and dried fish for sale to inland

Two weavers using traditional methods.

peoples. Forest peoples traded in kola nuts and other items. Grassland peoples traded in cattle and skins.

They also traded in manufactured goods: goods produced by turning raw materials into useful things. Two such raw materials became very important. One was cotton. The other was gold.

Cotton was widely grown in West Africa before AD 1000. Many West African peoples — for example, the Yoruba of southern Nigeria, the Akan of Ghana — became expert in the spinning and dyeing of cotton for clothing. When the European sea-merchants came to West Africa, after about 1450, they found that some of this West African dyed cloth was better than any that was made in Europe.

More and more cotton cloth was made. We can get some idea of the amount from the writings of a German traveller called Henry Barth. He wrote about the cotton-cloth production of the busy Hausa city of Kano in northern Nigeria during the 1850s. But what he said about Kano then was also true of cotton-producing towns in earlier times.

> The great advantage of Kano is that trade and manufacture go hand in hand. Almost every family has a share in them. There is something grand about this kind of industry. It spreads to the north as far as Murzuk, Ghat and even Tripoli (on the coast of the Mediterranean Sea). It spreads to the west not only to Timbuktu, but in some degree even as far as the shores of the Atlantic, the very inhabitants of Arquin (on the coast of Mauretania) dressing in the cloth that is woven and dyed in Kano. It spreads to the east all over Bornu. . .

And it also spread to the south.

So cotton cloth was a big part of the long-distance trade, as well as of local trade.

What about *gold*?

The prosperity of several states and large empires of the Western Sudan, during 1000-1600, depended largely on the mining of gold ore, and the sale of gold. How much gold did West Africa produce?

West Africa today can still show many thousands of old gold-workings, especially in Asante and the northern part of the modern Republic of Guinea. Gold was also 'panned' from rivers in those two regions. Men stood in the water and sieved the gravel of the river-bed for the little bits of gold that it contained. Professor Raymond Mauny, who has studied this question, believes that West African miners and 'panners' got about nine tonnes of gold every year during the sixteenth century. He thinks they had been doing this for a long time by then.

Of these nine tonnes of gold produced every year, about four tonnes

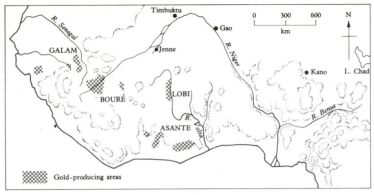

23 The gold-producing areas of West Africa.

English gold coin of Charles II, 1663. The little elephant under the King's head shows that these coins were made from African gold.

came from the goldfields of Asante, and about four tonnes from the (modern republic of) Guinea. 'The total amount of gold produced in West Africa from ancient times till 1500', Mauny estimates, 'may be placed at several thousand tons (tonnes); with an amount of about the same size, perhaps 3,500 tons (tonnes), for the period between 1500 and 1900'[1]. Some historians think this estimate is too big, but all agree that the total was large.

It was hard to produce this gold. West Africa's miners had to be able to

[1] R. Mauny, *Tableau Géographique l'Ouest Africain*, Dakar 1961, pages 300-1.

The bellows used by metal workers in West Africa many years ago. This one is worked by hand. Compare it with the Egyptian bellows on p. 14.

find the places where gold-bearing ore existed under the ground. They had to dig shafts into this ore, and get it out, by hand tools. They did not have any machines to do this for them. They had to crush the ore by hand, and then smelt it in furnaces so that the gold would come out of the ore.

Yet each year, in the sixteenth century, they got a total that was nearly half as much as the amount of gold produced by modern machinery in the colonial period. As late as in 1938, for example, the production of West African gold was only $21\frac{1}{2}$ tonnes.

The *export* of goods pays for the *import* of other goods. In exchange for their cotton-cloth and gold and other goods, West Africans were able to buy many foreign products that they wanted or needed.

They bought a lot of Saharan salt, something that everybody needed. They bought luxury goods, such as silks that came from Asia. They bought thoroughbred horses from Egypt and Tripoli. They bought swords and knives and kitchen things from the little workshops of early industrial Europe, or from the craftsmen of the Arab countries of the Middle East. They bought hand-written books of learning for their Muslim schools and libraries. And as trade grew with European sea-merchants, especially after 1600, they bought guns and gunpowder, bars of iron, rings of copper, jewellery, hats, and a host of other items.

Trade routes and traders

We have seen how trade routes across the Sahara were opened in the distant past. They were used by very many merchants trading between the Western Sudan and North Africa. Inside West Africa, other trade routes were opened. They were used especially by the Dyula traders of the Mali empire, the Hausa traders of northern Nigeria, and other

153

Kinds of West African currency. These copper 'manillas' were made in standard sizes and weights. They were used in the Guinea trade with sea-merchants.

trading peoples. By 1600 you could say that every region of West Africa was part of this internal trading network.

Transport was by camel in the Sahara. Camels and donkeys were used in the Sudan. South of the Sudan the transport was by men and women carrying things on their heads along the forest trails.

After 1500, with the coming of many ships from Europe, a new system of trade with sea-merchants began to expand along many parts of the coastland of Guinea.

This big expansion in trade was still important only for a minority of West Africans. But the minority steadily got bigger.

Where cities grew, the biggest merchants were often the rulers of the countries in which the cities stood: kings and their counsellors, chiefs and elders. These were men who needed wealth in order to pay for governments and soldiers, and maintain their courts, and make gifts to visitors, and live well themselves.

A caravan approaching Timbuktu.

King Tunka Manin of Ancient Ghana, as we have seen, monopolised the gold and salt trade[1]. Other kings did this, too.

This was why, when European ships sailed up the Benin River, for example, and dropped their anchors off Gwato, the river-port of Benin, they entered into trade not just with anyone they met but only with agents and merchants selected by the king of Benin. 'Nobody is allowed to buy anything from Europeans on this coast,' observed a Dutch report of the seventeenth century,[2] 'except the agents and merchants whom the king has named for this purpose. As soon as one of our ships drops anchor, the people inform the king, and the king appoints two or three agents and twenty or thirty merchants whom he empowers to deal with the Europeans.'

It was much the same in the Western Sudan. Passing through Bornu at the beginning of the sixteenth century, Leo Africanus reported that the king of that empire was especially interested in buying horses from North Africa and Egypt. He paid for these horses in various ways, but notably in war-captives who were used as slaves in North Africa and the Mediterranean countries. Yet the merchants who brought the horses, and took away the captives, were allowed to deal only with the agents of

[1] See Chapter 4, *Revenue and wealth of Ghana,* page 41.
[2] The same was true of earlier times.

155

Above *and* below: *Asante weights. These were used for weighing gold dust.*

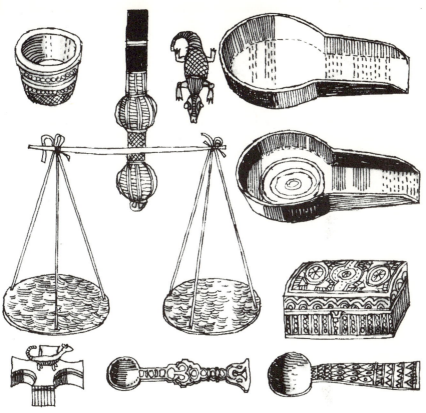

Asante equipment used for weighing gold dust. It includes the scales, the kuduo in which the gold dust was kept, the spoon for ladling it out, the shovels, the measure and the weights.

the king himself. If the king happened to be away when they arrived at his capital, they simply had to sit down and wait until he came back again.

What did the kings and merchants do with their wealth? Social conditions did not exist when rich men could think of *investing* their wealth; of handling it, that is, in such a way as to produce more wealth. They mostly used it for their expenses, for gifts with which to ensure the loyalty of allies and servants, and for displaying their power. The emperor of Kanem-Bornu, according to Leo Africanus, had the equipment of his cavalry made in gold, 'stirrups, spurs, bits and buckles'. Even his dogs had 'chains of the finest gold'. But the giving of gifts was perhaps the most important way of using wealth. Taking their

157

wealth with one hand, and giving it away with the other, the kings and chiefs helped to keep it circulating among people.

How they traded

Whether they worked for Dyula companies, or for kings or chiefs, or on their own account, West Africans were good traders. The European sea-merchants soon found this out. They thought it was going to be easy to get the better of African traders; they discovered they were wrong.

'These people,' an English sea-merchant called John Lok reported to his friends in England, after getting back from a voyage to the Guinea coast in 1553, 'are very clever in their bargaining. They will not overlook a single bit of the gold they offer for sale. They use their own weights and measures, and they are very careful how they use them. Anyone who wants to trade with them must do so honestly, for they will not trade if they are badly treated.'

This trade was mostly done by *barter*: that is, the exchange of one lot of goods for another lot of goods, without using money.

Barter trade called for great care. Prices often changed. Traders had to be on the lookout not to 'lose their bargains'.

European trading ships.

158

In certain trades, as John Lok observed, Africans used their own weights and measures. The gold-traders of Asante, for example, had long developed a very complicated set of weights for the sale of gold-dust. For a long while, these were made in the measures of weight used by the traders from the Western Sudan. After about 1600, they began to be made for measures of weight used by the European sea-merchants.

West African traders also used various measures of value: or of what we call money. These measures were seldom or never coins or paper-notes, such as those of today. They were cowrie shells, or pieces of brass, or lengths of iron bar, or cloths of cotton.

This West African 'money' of those days was useful, but it was clumsy. Here is a table that shows the value of cowries in the 1850s:

40 cowries	=	1 string	=	$\frac{1}{4}$d to 1d
5 strings	=	1 bunch	=	3d to 6d
10 bunches	=	1 head	=	1s 9$\frac{1}{2}$d to 2s
10 heads	=	1 bag	=	18s to £1

So you had to have 20,000 cowries in order to buy something worth 18s in the English money of that time.

Cities

In the year 1602, a Dutch visitor described the city of Benin. It seemed very big to him.

When you go into it you enter a great broad street, which is not paved, and seems to be seven or eight times broader than the Warmoes street in Amsterdam [the chief city of Holland]. This street is straight, and does not bend at any point. It is thought to be four miles (6$\frac{1}{2}$ kilometres) long.

At the gate where I went in on horseback, I saw a very big wall, very thick and made of earth, with a very deep and broad ditch outside it... And outside this gate there is also a big suburb. Inside the gate, and along the great street just mentioned, you see many other great streets on either side, and these also are straight and do not bend...

The houses in this town stand in good order, one close and evenly placed with its neighbour, just as the houses in Holland stand... They have square rooms, sheltered by a roof that is open in the middle, where the rain, wind and light come in. The people

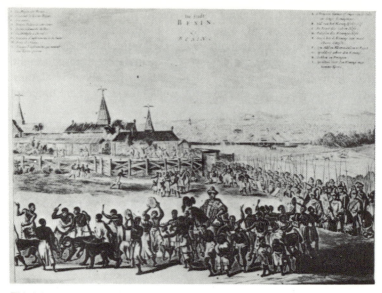

This is how a Dutch visitor drew Benin and the Oba's palace in the seventeenth century.

sleep and eat in these rooms, but they have other rooms for cooking and different purposes. . .

The king's court is very great. It is built around many square-shaped yards. These yards have surrounding galleries where sentries are always placed. I myself went into the court far enough to pass through four great yards like this, and yet wherever I looked I could still see gate after gate which opened into other yards. . .[1]

Little or no stone was used in building the cities of West Africa, for it was easier and cheaper to build in wood and clay. This is why West Africa has so few ancient ruins, even though, as in Yorubaland, it had many cities that were large and prosperous. The wealthy city of Jenne, for example, was built entirely of short-lived materials. Leo Africanus tells us that 'the king, the men of religion, the doctors of learning, the merchants and those of wealth and authority' lived in 'houses made like huts, of clay and thatched straw'.

Yet absence of stone was not a sign of absence of civilisation. This same traveller found that the people of Jenne were 'very well dressed'. That is not surprising. They enjoyed a big trade with the Akan peoples

---

[1] Recorded in O. Dapper's *Description of Africa*, first published in Amsterdam in 1668. Dapper was a geographer, who collected reports from travellers.

in the south and those of the Western Sudan in the north. 'It is because of this blessed city of Jenne,' wrote the author of the *Tarikh as-Sudan*, Abd al-Rahman as-Sadi, in 1665, 'that caravans come to Timbuktu from every side', for Jenne, standing where it did, had long become 'one of the great markets of the Muslim world'.

The architecture of Timbuktu was much the same, though it had some buildings in brick as well. Soon after 1500, Leo Africanus found 'many handicraft workers, merchants and cotton-weavers' there. European goods were much in use. There was also an abundance of grain and other foods. Milk and butter were in good supply. The king possessed a big treasure in gold. 'The royal court,' Leo wrote, 'is very well organised and splendid. When the king goes from one town to another with his

Part of the ancient city of Kano.

train of courtiers, he rides a camel; but horses are walked behind by his servants. Should there be any need for fighting, the servants take charge of the camels and all the soldiers mount horses.' The king had about 3,000 horsemen and a much larger number of infantry. The best of these horses were brought across the Sahara from North Africa.

Gao, capital of the rising Songhay empire, was described by the same traveller as 'a very large town without any defensive wall'. He thought that most of its houses were poor and ugly, but reported that there were 'several fine ones where the king and his courtiers live'. Gao's inhabitants included many rich traders who spent their time in travelling on business. 'Bread and meat are very abundant, but they have no wine or fruit. Yet their melons and cucumbers are excellent, and they have enormous quantities of rice. Fresh-water wells are numerous there.'

Leo considered that the revenues of Songhay were large, but so were its expenses. Luxury goods brought across the Sahara for the kings, nobles and rich merchants were very dear. Imported horses, woollens, swords, cavalry harness, medicines and jewellery all cost far more than they did in the countries where they were made.

Yet the cities grew, in the northern grasslands as well as in the forests of the south. They became a fruitful part of West African civilisation.

CHAPTER TWELVE
Religion, the arts, and learning

Even today, when times have greatly changed, the beliefs and customs of West Africa (like other parts of Africa) continue to reflect the social and spiritual development of the past. Out-of-date though many of these customs and beliefs may seem, they were a vital and necessary part of everyday life in historical times. They explain much of the success and power of West Africa's civilisation.

The value of religion

The origins of religion in Africa, as in other continents, lie far back at the beginning of human society. They took shape in remote times when mankind first multiplied and spread across the world.

This means that some of the origins of West African religion were formed in that very early but remarkable 'nursery' of early cultures which grew up in the green and fertile Sahara during Stone Age times. That is a reason why African religions often resemble each other, at least in some of their ideas of worship. The sacred ram, for example, was a symbol of the supreme god of the pharaohs of ancient Egypt; but so it was for the Berbers of the Sahara and old North Africa; and so it still remains for some West African peoples. The python was honoured in ancient Meroe, capital of the African empire of Kush on the Middle Nile more than two thousand years ago; and the python has been similarly honoured in other African lands.

But West African religions by the sixteenth century had long since grown into forms of their own. These were extremely varied, for they reflected the great variety of ways in which men and women lived and worked. We can think of them, briefly, as having served a double purpose. In the first place, they provided an *explanation* about how people came to be what they were and the world what it was. Secondly, going on from this religious explanation, they provided the *social power* by which people could make laws and customs, and ensure that these were respected.

How did they do this? The answer is complicated. It rests in the fact, already noted at various points in this book, that religion and politics went hand-in-hand in traditional civilisation. Like Europeans of the Middle Ages (AD 800-1350), Africans lived in an 'age of faith'. They believed, in short, that political authority came not from men but from God and the spirits. Those who exercised power on Earth could do so, in other words, only if they were accepted as speaking and acting with the good will of the departed ancestors, who, in turn, were men's protectors and helpers in the world of the spirits. Rulers could rule only if they were spiritually appointed to do so; and their subjects obeyed them not simply from respect for the king's power and law, but also for reasons of religion.

It would be possible to give many examples. Among the Asante, for example, the office or position of chiefship was referred to as *akonnua*. This may be interpreted as the 'stool', though it also had a spiritual meaning. Asante who were appointed to be chiefs went through various ceremonies, but the final ceremony or ritual was the 'en-stooling' of the chief with the supreme ancestral stool of his particular chiefdom. From that moment the appointed chief, duly en-stooled, could speak with religious as well as with political power. It was regarded as belonging to the whole people and no longer only to his own descent-line or 'big family'. Such attitudes were common to many peoples.

Governments without kings, such as those we have discussed for the Igbo, also relied on religion as the basis for political power, though they did so in different ways from the Edo, Yoruba, Asante or other centrally-organised peoples. The Tallensi of northern Ghana, for example, ruled themselves in a number of village governments without kings. Power was shared out among different descent-lines, but these were held together by religious rituals. Underpinning all these rituals, among the Tallensi, were those which affected the men who held senior offices in village government. These were the chiefs and the Earth-priests. Only if proper ceremonies were carried out, and religious duties observed between chiefs and Earth-priests as between 'men and their wives', could the Tallensi prosper. Otherwise, it was believed, disasters such as sickness or famine would strike at all the Tallensi.

And so these religions, like other religions, helped men to live together, expressed their higher hopes and aspirations, and linked the individual to the community. As we should expect, some of these religions have remained important. Like all other religions of the age before science, they included much magic and witchcraft. Yet they also worked out their own *body of thought* about the beginning and the growth of mankind, and about the workings of the universe into which

A Ghanaian chief (Omanhene of Akrokeri) celebrating the annual Yam Festival.

mankind was born. They thought out ways of explaining how and why the world was created and how and why the world developed.

These explanations were not scientific by modern standards. Yet they could and did reflect the deeper moral truths of life, the difference between right and wrong, between good and evil, between the obligations of the individual and the duties of society. Often they were expressed in proverbs and stories. Much moral and practical wisdom may be found in the traditional sayings or proverbs of West Africa, linked as these often are to religious beliefs. The traditional wisdom of the Akan, for example, is expressed in more proverbs than will be found in the Bible or the Koran.

Many such sayings took the form of sharp comments on people's behaviour. 'A lot of mice may dig a hole,' ran the Akan proverb, 'but it does not become deep.' Or 'when your guns are few, so are your words.' Readers will be able to add examples from their own people's proverbs.

There were innumerable stories, too, which told 'home-truths' about good or bad behaviour, folly or wisdom, arrogant pride or decent

165

humility. Of Ananse Kokrofu, the Great Spider, the Akan used to tell this tale:

> Ananse collected all the wisdom in the world and shut it up in a gourd. Then he began climbing a tree so as to keep this precious gourd safe at the top. But he got into difficulties only half-way up, because he had tied the gourd to his front, and it hampered him in climbing. His son Ntikuma, who was watching at the bottom, called up: 'Father, if you really had all the wisdom in the world up there with you, you would have had the sense to tie that gourd on your back.' His father saw the truth of this and threw down the gourd in a temper. It broke on the ground, and the wisdom in it was scattered about.
>
> Men came and picked up what each of them could get and carry away. Which explains why there is much wisdom in the world, but few men have more than a little of it, and some men have none at all.

Creative arts

The many arts of West Africa, dancing, singing, the playing of musical instruments, sculpture and the like, were also an important part of sixteenth-century civilisation. Sometimes they were only for amusement or for adding to the fun of daily life. But often they were inspired by moral and religious beliefs, and were placed at the service of social and spiritual customs. In being thus linked to religion, West African arts were no different in *content* — in what they meant and did for people — from the arts of all other peoples who lived in an age of faith. But they were very different in their *form* — in their shapes, fashions and styles.

By the sixteenth century, West Africans had long developed many *art forms* of their own, often of very great skill and beauty. Today these masks and dances and sculptured figures may seem strangely out of date. Yet they are worthy of much respect, quite apart from their artistic beauty, because they, like the religions and proverbial wisdom of West Africa, helped to express the beliefs and hopes by which men and women lived.

In any good museum you can find splendid carving in wood and ivory that illustrates the skill of those old artists who worked in clay and metal. Think of the energy and life that speak in traditional music and dancing. Consider the discipline that is needed for all that, the restraint and modesty but also the power and daring. Or listen to the drums that

An ivory gong made in Benin.

men had learned to make and play so well. With their drum language, skilled men could speak of many things. Here, for example, is the fragment of a drummer's song of praise to Tano, the river god of the Asante, as recorded many years ago:

> The stream crosses the path,
> And the path crosses the stream:
> Which of them is the elder?
> Did we not cut a path to go and meet the stream?
> The stream had its beginning long long ago,
> The stream had its beginning in the Creator:
> He created things,
> Pure, pure Tano. . .

Many of these old arts and songs have passed away, together with the beliefs, ideas and customs which gave them birth. A new life has

A ceremony of the Dogon who live in the central region of the Sudan (now in Mali).

opened. But the depth and value of the old life, so much a parent of the new, can be seen only when we give these arts of the past the honour they deserve.

Education and schooling

Outside the cities of the Western Sudan, teaching was restricted to popular instruction in the skills and customs that were used in everyday life; to training in traditional law; and to the preparation, also by example and by word of mouth, of priests, practitioners in herbal medicine, and other specialists.

All West African religions possessed a body of complex beliefs, which trainee priests had to learn and know how to use. They learned this either from the priests of shrines in their home and nearby villages,

A dance of the Bambara (Mali).

or sometimes in regular 'academies' established at a regional centre. In the same way, all who wished to practise as doctors, whether in the use of herbs or at shrines, had to be taught their art from men and women who possessed the necessary qualifications and reputation. Metal-workers, weavers, boat-makers, drummers, warriors and others had to be schooled not only in the material techniques of their respective crafts, but also in the spells and special customs which were believed to be essential to success in their work.

Apart from these requirements about rules of behaviour, of religion, and of craftsman skills, there were also the needs of government. Many peoples had organised themselves in communities which gave much power, for the taking of community decisions and the keeping of law and order, to special associations or groups of men and women. Entry into these groups or societies was generally by rites that were secret. These rites had to be taught to would-be members.

All the members of such associations also had to know about the history of their own people or branch of a people. They were expected to know about their law, their methods of enforcing the law, and their punishments for those who broke the law. Where peoples had organised themselves in states with central governments and kings, there had to be schooling in the skills and methods of administration by civil service. Many states had groups of elders whose job was to learn the traditions of their country, recite these on proper occasions, and teach them to younger men.

There was altogether a great deal of schooling in sixteenth-century civilisation. But with some exceptions, important though few, it was a matter of word-of-mouth teaching of skills, customs, laws, traditions and the like. It was done for the most part without the aid of writing and reading.

This was also a stage of society in which education was generally thought of as being a part of religion. It was not based on modern science, and so could do little to promote technical progress. Skilled craftsmen were trained in the methods of the past, and were content to follow the old methods. They felt no need to experiment with new methods. Having a religious attitude to their methods of production, they were even against experiment.

So we have to think of this civilisation as both moving forward and standing still. It was moving forward all the time because of its energy and growth and wealth. And yet it was also standing still because of its conservative attitude to methods and techniques.

This aspect of standing still should not lead us into underestimating the achievements of sixteenth-century civilisation. The farmers who

An Igbo dance mask.

170

farmed, the miners who found metals, the smiths who worked so skilfully in these metals, the weavers and woodcarvers, the artists and musicians, the chiefs and counsellors, the traders and tellers of tales: all these and their fellow-specialists were successful because they had discovered and learnt a great deal about their work. All this discovery and learning came from many years of steady development.

Important centres of Muslim learning

Here is the place to say something more about Islam.

Two universal religions were at work in the sixteenth century; Islam and Christianity. We call them universal religions, open to all, because they differed in this important respect from the religions created in West Africa, Muslims and Christians believed (as, of course, they still believe) that it was their duty to send out missionaries and convert everyone else to their faith. People who believed in West African religions generally did not think like this. They thought of their religion as belonging only to themselves and their own people.

Christianity had little influence. Apart from a handful of missionaries along the coast, it was absent from West Africa. Islam, on the other hand, was by now important in the Western Sudan and was already pushing missionaries into the forest lands and down to the coast of Guinea. Yet Islam in this period remained largely a religion of the cities, towns and big market-centres. Outside these there were very few Muslims.

In the towns and cities, where Islam was widely accepted, literacy and book-learning appeared in West Africa. There is no knowing when Islamic schools, founded for the teaching of the Koran and the *sharia*, the laws of Islam, first appeared. Muslim teaching of some kind certainly existed in the city of Gao as early as the beginning of the tenth century, and many Muslim missionaries were at work in the Western Sudan during the eleventh century.[1] We hear of the growth of Islamic schools in the empire of Mali during the fourteenth century, as well as in the Songhay cities of the fifteenth century. By the sixteenth century, West African Muslim scholars were writing on many historical, legal, moral and religious subjects.

The book by Leo Africanus, which refers to about 1500, has much to say on this. Of the old capital of Mali, Niani on the upper Niger, Leo wrote that 'they have many mosques, priests and professors who teach in

[1] See also pages 68 and 137 above.

the mosques', and, as we have already noted, he considered the people of Niani as 'the most civilised, intelligent and highly reputed' of all the peoples of the Western Sudan.

'In Timbuktu,' he tells us, 'there are many judges, professors and holy men, all being generously helped by the king, who holds scholars in much honour. Here, too, they sell many handwritten books from North Africa. More profit is made from selling books in Timbuktu than from any other branch of trade.' Gao, on the other hand, could boast of no such brilliance. 'The people here,' Leo considered, 'are absolutely

A teacher in Northern Nigeria reading from a text of the Koran.

ignorant. There is probably not one in a thousand who knows how to write. But the king of Gao,' he adds with a touch of humour, 'treats them as they deserve. For he taxes them so heavily that they are scarcely left with enough to live on.'

In these and other cities of the Western Sudan, learning drew not only on the talent and work of local people, but also on those of Muslim scholars from other lands. 'God has drawn to this fortunate city,' wrote a Timbuktu author about Jenne, 'a certain number of learned and of pious men, strangers to the land, who have come to live here.' This was another reason why the Islamic schools of Timbuktu and Jenne became famous in the whole Muslim world.

Three famous writers

Timbuktu and Jenne had many well-known writers. The most renowned of the sixteenth century was probably *Ahmad Baba.*

Born in Timbuktu in 1556, Ahmad Baba composed many works on Islamic law as well as a biographical dictionary of Muslim scholars. At least thirteen of his works are still in use by the '*ulama*[1] of West Africa. His library was so good that it was held in high esteem for many years after his death. His bravery and independence of mind were also much respected. It is easy to see why.

When the Moroccan invaders seized Timbuktu in 1591, Ahmad Baba refused to serve them. Fearing his influence and accusing him of organising a rebellion, the Moroccan invaders took him in chains across the Sahara to their capital of Marrakesh. There they held him for many years before allowing him to come home again. So it may be said that Ahmad Baba, who never ceased to protest against the invasion of his native land, was not only an outstanding scholar but was also in his daily life one of the forerunners of West African nationalism.

Two important histories of the Western Sudan were also written by scholars of Timbuktu. They are the *Tarikh al-Fattash*, the History of the Seeker for Knowledge, completed in about 1665; and the *Tarikh as-Sudan*, the History of the [Western] Sudan also completed in about 1665. Both were written in Arabic, for this was the literary language of these learned men, just as Latin was the literary language of the scholars of Europe. Both were the work of West Africans born in Timbuktu. The chief author of the first was *Mahmud Kati*, who was born in about 1468 and is said to have lived to the age of 125; while the

---

[1] This is an Arabic word meaning 'men of learning'. Its singular is *mu'allim*. In West Africa this word often appears in its Hausa form, *mallam*.

A page from the Tarikh as-Sudan.

second was *Abd al-Rahman as-Sadi,* who was born in 1596 and lived until about 1655.

Both scholars had good careers. Kati was only twenty-five when the Songhay ruler, *Askia* Muhammad the Great, took over power from *Sunni* Baru; Kati became a member of the *Askia's* personal staff. He went to Mecca with the emperor and was thus well placed to see and understand the events of his time. He began his great book in about 1519, but his sons and grandsons, who were also scholars, continued to work on it and brought the story of Songhay and Timbuktu down to about 1665.

Abd al-Rahman as-Sadi was born only five years after the Moroccan invasion, the results of which he saw when still a child. He tells us in the *Tarikh as-Sudan* that it was because of all the sad events he had witnessed in his youth that he decided to write his book. In a moving preface he recalls how he saw 'the ruin of learning and its utter collapse' under the hammerblows of Moroccan onslaught. He explains

And because learning is rich in beauty and fertile in its teaching,

174

since it instructs men about their fatherland, their ancestors, their history, the names of their heroes and what lives they lived, I asked God's help and decided to set down all that I myself could learn on the subject of the Songhay princes of the Sudan, their adventures, their story, their achievements and their wars. Then I added the history of Timbuktu from the time of its foundation, of the princes who ruled there and the scholars and saints who lived there, and of other things as well.

For some of these 'other things' we can be very thankful: they include, for example, many of the early stories of Ancient Ghana and Mali.

This long history of Muslim learning and writing has never ceased in West Africa. On the contrary, it has grown and spread with the passing

The dignity of kings was increasingly recognised; this is the funeral head-figure in an Asante royal burial. It is made of solid gold.

A shrine in the Palace of the Oba of Benin.

of years. Today the *'ulama* of West Africa, whether in the northern country of the plains or the southern country of the forests, have many libraries and pupils. Their libraries contain works by many West African and other Muslim authors, and range from books written centuries ago to books of the present time.

In later years, Christian scholarship began to make its contribution to West African education and schooling; but this, in the sixteenth century, was still to come.

CHAPTER THIRTEEN
The organisation of society

Past chapters have shown that ways of life had greatly changed by 1500-1600 when compared with those of earlier times. Bigger food supplies had become available because of better tools, improved farming methods, and wider markets. This had helped the growth of population. Already West Africa contained far more people than at the beginning of the Iron Age, and most of them were better fed.

These social changes had led to political changes. Many different ways of self-rule were now on the scene. There were many 'governments without kings', as described in Chapter 10. Often these were strengthened by dividing people into age-sets which gathered together persons belonging to different descent-lines, or 'big families'. Always they were strengthened by the worship of the gods through revered ancestors.[1] There were many systems of rule by chiefs through 'title societies', such as those of Awka and Nsukka, or special associations such as Ekpe among the Cross River peoples, Ogboni among the Yoruba, and Poro among the peoples of Sierra Leone.[2]

Big states and empires had been built by powerful kings. For a long time these rulers had continued to be appointed by councils of chiefs who were the heads of senior 'big families'. This produced what may be called an early form of 'constitutional monarchy'. The emperors of Ancient Ghana and Mali, for example, were obliged to rule according to the 'constitutional' laws and limits laid down by tradition, and safeguarded by councils, consisting of the heads of 'big families'.

As time went by, the kings and chiefs got more power over the mass of ordinary people. There arose new forms of government by groups or classes of nobles who tended to alter the traditional rules to their own advantage.[3] Throughout the Western Sudan the rise of Islam after the fourteenth century did much to change the customs of former times, in government as in trade and religion. We have noted important examples

---

[1] See Chapter 12, *The value of religion*, page 163.
[2] See Chapter 19, *Sierra Leone and the Poro Association*, page 254.
[3] As, for example, in the Wolof empire, Chapter 6: and the Yoruba kingdoms, Chapter 10.

of the way in which Muslim kings strengthened their positions against the descent-line chiefs: in Songhay under *Askia* the Great, or in the Hausa states under rulers such as Muhammad Rumfa of Kano.[1] This trend continued, and there came the rise of the 'king's men'. This means the rise of appointed officials who were not members of the 'big families', and who were loyal only to the king their master.[2]

This strengthening of the authority of kings at the expense of senior chiefs did not happen only in areas influenced by Islam. We shall see that the *alafins* of Oyo also strengthened their personal authority with the growth of their empire in the seventeenth century,[3] and that the same thing happened with the rise of 'king's men' in Dahomey, and in the Asante empire during the eighteenth and nineteenth centuries.[4] The old ways, in fact, were continually being modified into new ways. Nothing in any of these systems of government was ever 'standing still'. On the contrary, all these varied methods of self-rule, ranging from popular rule in village governments to rule by chiefs or kings, were constantly going through a *process of change.*

The dividing-up of society

As this *process of change* went on, and more peoples formed themselves into states under elders, chiefs or kings, something very important happened to society. Its old natural equality began to disappear. It became *stratified.* It became divided, that is, into different social *strata*: different 'layers' of power and wealth. Some men, usually because of their birth, had the right to become chiefs. Others could not become chiefs, but had the right to elect them. Others again could not elect chiefs, but only had the right to say how chiefs ought to behave. Still others were pushed down into a lowly position where they had to obey their masters without question.

These 'layers' may be thought of as *horizontal* divisions, with all the senior chiefs, for example, on one level of power, all the free farmers on a second, all the unfree servants or slaves on a third. Together with these different 'layers' there remained, however, older divisions of another kind. These were *vertical* divisions which separated all the people of one clan from the people of other clans, all the inhabitants of one village

[1] *Askia* the Great, Chapter 7; Muhammad Rumfa, Chapter 9. For a general discussion and more details, see the last three sections of this chapter.
[2] See especially Chapter 21, *Hausa developments: rise of the 'king's men'*, page 274.
[3] See Chapter 16, *The empire of Oyo*, page 217.
[4] See Chapter 18, *The Asante empire*, page 244.

from their neighbours, all the descendants of one set of ancestors from the descendants of other ancestors. These vertical or 'up-and-down' divisions were in some ways even more important to West African social development than the horizontal divisions or 'layers', and they were already very ancient by the sixteenth century.

There also took place a third kind of dividing-up of society, caused by the changing and better ways in which people worked together. Craftsmen formed themselves into different groups, according to their skills: metalworkers, boat-builders, fishermen, farmers, diviners, priests, singers of songs, and many others. Some of these groups of craftsmen and specialists possessed much social power; others possessed little. How much social power each group possessed varied from place to place. Among some peoples, for example, metalworkers were greatly honoured; among others, they were not.

This dividing-up of society had already gone very far in West Africa by the early years of the sixteenth century. There had appeared in West Africa, as elsewhere in the world, a form of social organisation in which some people were masters and other people were servants. People had built, in other words, a ladder of social power. Kings stood on the top rung, slaves on the bottom. In between there was everyone else, standing on rungs that were higher than the rungs below them, but lower than the ones above.

This dividing-up of society into different 'levels' or 'layers' was not, of course, a chance invention by clever kings and chiefs. It reflected the new ways in which people worked together, produced wealth, exchanged goods, and lived in society. It marked an important if often painful stage in history; and it happened in nearly every part of Africa as in nearly every part of the world. And, of course, we are still in this stage.

But men were seldom able or content to go on standing for long on the same rung of the ladder of social power. Slaves pushed upward into freedom. Kings were sometimes pulled downward. Poor men climbed to wealth. Rich men became poor. This movement up and down the social ladder greatly influenced the events of political history. It could not, for example, always be a peaceful one. Quite often it set one people or state against another, and promoted wars and conquests. The progress of one people had to be at the expense of some other people.

One further point. We have said that the dividing-up of society occurred nearly everywhere in the world. But it needs to be remembered that it went much further, and became much more painful, in many of the countries of Europe and Asia. There, because of much greater development in production and exchange of goods and wealth, society became rigidly divided into separate *classes* of masters and servants, with a few people having great wealth and power, and most people having little or none. There, too, movement up and down the ladder of social power became difficult or rare, at least until after the social upheavals which followed the French Revolution of 1789.

This stiff and harsh dividing into classes had not yet happened in West Africa. The horizontal divisions into 'layers' of power remained less influential than the vertical divisions into different clans, descent-lines, and communities. This is why most West African governments during the sixteenth century and onwards were much more democratic, much more respectful of the rights of individual persons, than were the governments of Europe.

By the sixteenth century, for example, most of the land of Europe was in the private possession of a landowning class. In West Africa, even today, most of the land is not so divided. Yet the horizontal 'layers' in West African society were of growing importance; and we shall now discuss them a little further.

Masters and servants

Old records and traditions tell us little of the way that ordinary folk lived, but much of the magnificence of kings. Travellers from North Africa were greatly impressed by the power and wealth of West African rulers. Here, for example, is a North African description of the court of the emperor of Mali. It is that of Ibn Batuta, who travelled through Mali in 1352 during the reign of *Mansa* Suleyman, but it remained true of later times as well:

> The lord of this kingdom has a great balcony in his palace. It is called the Bembe. There he has a great seat of ebony that is like a throne fit for a large and tall person. It is flanked by elephants' tusks. The king's arms stand near him. They are all of gold; sword and lance, quiver of bow and arrows. He wears wide trousers made of twenty pieces of stuff, and they are of a kind which only he may wear.
>
> Before him stand about twenty Turkish or other pages, who are brought from Cairo. One of these, standing on his left, holds a silk umbrella that is topped by a dome and bird of gold. The bird is like a hawk. The king's officers are seated in a circle near him, in two rows, one to the right and the other to the left. Beyond them sit the commanders of the cavalry.
>
> In front of him there is a person who never leaves him and who

is his executioner; and another who is his official spokesman, and who is named the herald. In front of him there are also drummers. Others dance before their king and make him merry. . .

There we have a glimpse of some of those groups of men who had the right to serve the king and the state in special jobs or offices according to their training and position in society: counsellors, military officers, spokesmen, drummers and others. But what about the mass of ordinary people?

They were generally divided into the 'free' and the 'unfree'. We have to treat these words with care, because the actual amount of freedom and unfreedom greatly varied with time and place; and it was always possible for free men to become unfree, mainly by being captured in war, or for unfree men to become free by hard work, loyal service, or good luck. All the same, these big divisions into 'free' and 'unfree' became more widespread and important during the sixteenth century.

They were clearly recognised. In Hausaland, for example, men understood very well the difference between the mass of ordinary folk who were free, the *talakawa*, and all those who were not free, the *cucenawa*. In Bornu, the nobles ruled over three big social groups known as the *kamba*, *kalia* and *zusanna*, whose amount of freedom got less from the first to the second, and less again from the second to the third. Writing of the people of the seaboard of modern Ghana in 1700, a Dutchman, called William Bosman, observed five main 'layers' among the peoples whom he knew there. The first were kings and rulers. The second were chiefs whom 'we should call civic fathers, their duty being to take care of their city or village, and to maintain law and order'. The third 'layer' were those who had 'acquired a great reputation by their riches, either got by inheritance or obtained by trade'. The fourth were farmers and fishermen. The fifth were slaves.

Free men seldom lived or worked just as they liked. Their freedom usually needed the protection of chiefs and lords. This protection was given in exchange for taxes or regular payments of one kind or another. In this way, free men often became vassals or subjects of sub-chiefs, or of big chiefs, or of kings and emperors. These vassals owed service to their lords; but their lords owed them protection in return. It was on this two-way system of service that many big political systems of the sixteenth century were founded.

Unfree men were in much the same general position as the majority of free men, except that they had fewer rights and were often pushed down into very humble positions in society. They seldom or never had any political say in deciding how chiefs should behave. They were usually 'tied' to a certain place and occupation, and were forbidden to move away or change their work. In the empire of Songhay, for example, unfree women were even forbidden to marry free men, a ban that was applied so as to ensure that the children of slaves should remain slaves, and not be free because the father was free. *Askia* Muhammad slightly changed this law about the marriage of the unfree (or slaves), but the result was much the same. He laid it down that a slave woman might marry a free man, but that her children would still be slaves. The point about laws of this kind was to ensure that the king and his chiefs should continue to have a large source of free or cheap labour.

Kinds of service

It is often difficult to draw a clear line between men who were counted as being free, and men who were considered as slaves. Since nobody worked for money, free men as well as slaves had duties they could not escape, and often these duties made them do very much the same kind of work. One helpful way of seeing how things were is to consult the *Tarikh al-Fattash*, which gives a detailed picture of everyday life in the Songhay empire of the sixteenth century.

The *Tarikh al-Fattash* tells us at one point that *Askia* Muhammad, who became emperor in 1493, acquired twenty-four special peoples as part of his estate. It describes who these peoples were, and what they did in return for the emperor's protection. We can regard them either as vassals or slaves.

They served in different ways. Some of them had to cut fodder for the Songhay ruler's cavalry. Others were riverfolk and fishermen. These owed the ruler of Songhay a certain amount of dried fish every year. 'It consisted,' says the *Tarikh al-Fattash*, 'of ten packets of dried fish to be paid by those who could afford as much. . . And every time the king was asked for river transport, he got it from the canoes of this people, and they also supplied the crews.'

Another of these vassal or slave peoples of the *Askia* were called Arbi. Their job was to be bodyguards and house-servants of the king. As many as five subject peoples (groups of people whose exact numbers we do not know) were metalworkers. 'They owed a duty to the king of one hundred spears and one hundred arrows every year for each family of them.'

And so it went on, each vassal or subject group having to provide this or that service to their chief or king, and each chief or king, in his turn, having to protect them from enemies and to help them in times of trouble. Good rulers were men who fully accepted this two-way system of service. Bad rulers were those who took what was due to them, but gave no help and protection in return.

There was, we should remember, a lot of movement up and down the ladder of power. Free men were taken prisoners in wartime, and were thrust down to the bottom rung; they could be used or sold as slaves. The Muslim rulers of the Western Sudan often raided their non-Muslim neighbours so as to secure supplies of free labour; and their non-Muslim neighbours now began to do the same in reverse. Lawbreakers were also reduced to slavery for serious offences. Regular slave markets were held. In the city of Gao, for example, Leo Africanus observed 'a market where many slaves, men and women, are sold every day. A girl of fifteen is worth about six ducats.[1] Little children are sold for about half the price of grown-ups.' Many such slaves were sent northward across the Sahara.

We should also note, at the same time, that slavery in West Africa was seldom the harsh and pitiless fate that was reserved for those who were later taken across the Atlantic to the mines and plantations of the Americas. There, across the Atlantic, slaves were treated worse than cattle. Their fate was a hopeless one. Few could ever become free men and women. Traditional slavery in West Africa was a much milder affair.[2] Often it scarcely deserved the name of slavery at all, being only a form of service which carried special duties and obligations. Slaves could easily work themselves into freedom. They could marry into their owners' families. They could become rich. Sometimes they even became chiefs and kings, like *Mansa* Sakuru of Mali.

Civil service developments

Government through a highly-trained and educated civil service is a modern development. But states and empires of this period had civil services of a less complicated sort. Their rulers governed through a system of governors and sub-governors; and each of these had his own *bureaucracy* (a word that comes from the French for office). These office-holders or officials operated an early form of civil service.

This started a long time ago, certainly in the days of Ancient Ghana. There are no detailed accounts of how the lords of Ghana organised their government. But they must certainly have had some kind of civil

[1] A ducat was a coin in use among North African traders.
[2] This was untrue of some countries, such as Mauretania, where Berber peoples continued to treat their slaves with cruelty and contempt.

service. For they were able to secure law and order over a very wide region of the Western Sudan, and to draw tribute from many peoples.

With the passing of the years, we learn more about the old methods of government. A writer of the early fourteenth century, Al-Omari of Cairo, has described how *Mansa* Kankan Musa of Mali (1312-37) carried on his rule. It was one of this emperor's customs, we are told by Al-Omari, 'that whenever someone who has been charged with a certain task or important affair reports to the king, the latter questions him on everything that has happened from the time of his departure to the time of his return, and in great detail. Legal cases and appeals also go up to the king who examines them himself. Generally, he writes nothing himself, but gives his orders by word of mouth. For this, he has secretaries and offices.' Already, in fourteenth-century Mali, there were the beginnings of a regular civil service.

Yet early forms of civil service such as these tended to be easy-going and unreliable. The officials might be prompt and obedient when the king or governor was present. When the king or governor was absent, they might stop bothering about his orders. Or they might simply go on doing things as they had always done them, no matter what the king or governor had ordered. The governments of these early states, in short, were very loosely organised.

The sixteenth century brought developments in government. Kings and governors began to need more reliable methods of giving their orders, and of having these orders carried out. Life had got more complicated, with growing wealth and power. So governments became more closely organised. The rulers of Benin, for example, introduced important reforms in methods of government. These were, it seems, especially the work of Oba Esigie, who came to power at the beginning of the century and ruled for nearly fifty years. Esigie emerged as victor in an old power-struggle, which had been fought by many Benin kings before him, against Benin's strongest group of nobles, the Uzama. These Uzama nobles had previously enjoyed the right to choose, by election among themselves, who was going to be the king of Benin. Now they lost this right, and from this time onwards, the eldest son of a dead king took the throne.

Kings, nobles, governors

In this particular change we can see not only how the power of the king of Benin had grown, but also how the traditions of the Edo people influenced those political ideas which had come from Yorubaland in earlier times. For the Uzama nobles of Benin had been in many ways like the Oyo Mesi nobles of Oyo, whose power continued to include the right to elect the *Alafin* of Oyo. But while the Oyo Mesi among the Yoruba continued to enjoy this right, the Uzama among the Edo did not.

At the same time as taking away some political power from the Uzama, the king of Benin created two new kinds of noblemen: palace chiefs and town chiefs. In this he was no doubt seeking to balance two important influences in the state. While the palace chiefs were usually connected with the court, the town chiefs were often self-made men who had done well in trade or warfare, or in some other specialised way of life which did not depend on having court connections.

With all this, the sixteenth-century kings of Benin became more powerful in their city. Yet they do not seem to have strengthened their hold over the Benin empire. Benin princes became rulers of different parts of the empire, even outside Edo-speaking areas, but they ran their own affairs very much as they pleased. Meanwhile, too, rebellious or defeated generals, exiled chiefs, and traders were setting up little Edo states of their own. They helped to spread Benin ideas and the Edo language, but not the power of the *Oba* of Benin.

Somewhat similar changes were taking place in Yorubaland. In Oyo itself the hereditary council of nobles, the Oyo Mesi, retained their former powers as the chiefs of senior descent-lines, but these powers were not increased when the empire grew larger in the seventeenth century. While the subject-kings of outlying parts of the Oyo empire continued to enjoy a fair measure of self-rule in local affairs, they were bound to the *alafin*, but not to the Oyo Mesi nobles, in a number of new ways:

1 The *alafin* appointed resident officials in the different provinces. Their duties were to look after the collection of taxes, settle political quarrels, and stop the development of plots against the *alafin's* rule. These officials were usually men who had been slaves; they were called the *Ilari*.
2 The *alafin's* authority was strengthened by the spread of worship of Shango, the god who was regarded as the special protector of the *alafin* and his power.
3 All chiefs had to supply troops for the *alafin's* wars, attend the *alafin's* yearly festival at Oyo, and serve him in other regular ways.[1]

Internally, whether subject to Oyo or not, the Yoruba states were organised for government in much the same way. All the Yoruba

[1] See also Chapter 16, *The empire of Oyo*, pages 217-220.

governing councils of the sixteenth century, for example, appear to have dealt with a wide range of everyday affairs — with questions of morals and religion, public health and security, justice and foreign relations. They controlled the public treasuries into which the taxes were paid. They were in charge of public building, trade, national defence.

In the Western Sudan, too, there was a steady improvement in methods of government. Here the customs of Islam helped towards the formation of regular civil services staffed by 'king's men': by officials, that is, who owed their appointments not to their birth but to individual skill and service to the king. *Sunni* Ali of Songhay (1464-92) had divided Songhay into provinces and had appointed governors and commanders with staffs of their own. *Askia* Muhammad (1493-1528) developed this system further still, improved it and increased the number of officials. Songhay was thus divided into the provinces of Kurmina, Dendi, Baro, Dirma and Bangu. Each had its own governor, called *fari* or *farma* or *koy*; the senior among them was the *kurminafari*.

At the seat of central government, the *askia* (like *Sunni* Ali before him) governed through a 'civil service' of officials. There was a large number of war chiefs, as we shall see in a moment; and a still larger number of civil chiefs. The latter, for instance, included the *barey-koy*, who was in charge of all court arrangements, and was assisted by the *kukura-koy*, whose job it was to provide food and other necessary supplies, and by the *garei-farma*, master of the camp. There was also the *katisi-farma*, head of the 'finance department', assisted by the *waney-farma*, responsible for questions of property, by the *bara-farma*, who was concerned with wages, and by the *dey-farma*, who looked after such buying and selling as had to be done on behalf of the government. Farming problems were likewise the business of the *fari-mundia*; forestry matters that of the *sao-farma*; while the *asari-mundia* was head of the 'department of justice'. Besides these, there were many other officials. Similar civil-service systems were used in the Kanem-Bornu empire under *Mai* Idris Alooma (about 1580-1617), in the Hausa states, and elsewhere.

Professional armies

Another way in which the means of government developed was in the methods of making war. These became more effective, more highly organised.

Chiefs and kings and emperors of earlier times had relied on simply 'calling up' their subjects, their vassals, or their allies. Some of them, like King Tunka Manin of Ghana in the eleventh century, could put very large armies into the field by this means of 'call-up'. But these were temporary armies. They were *amateur* armies. They served for a campaign or a war, and then everyone went home again until the next time.

The rulers of the sixteenth century found that this method of amateur war-making was not convenient to their needs. They began to create full-time armies, *professional* armies.

They did this for several reasons. With the growing development of central government, kings needed troops who were always available, who could move at once, and who could be relied on to obey orders. This last point, incidentally, explains why kings often employed their slaves as professional soldiers. Another reason was that the weapons of war were becoming more expensive and more difficult to handle. Firearms, for example, cost a lot to buy, while cavalry horses were expensive both to buy and to feed. They also called for special skills in using them; and only regular training could provide these skills. Kings saw that if they were going to lay out wealth on cavalry horses and firearms, they had better give these to men who were going to spend their life as soldiers, who would be properly trained, and who would stay closely under the king's own command.

Askia Muhammad of Songhay seems to have led the way in forming professional armies. His famous predecessor, *Sunni* Ali, had relied on the old-fashioned 'call-up' of earlier times. Muhammad, taking over a large empire and determined to make it larger, was not content with an amateur army: he wanted a full-time army, and he built one up.

How he did this may be seen in the *Tarikh al-Fattash*. Briefly, a full-time army was raised and placed under the command of a full-time general, the *dyini-koy* or *balama*. The *Askia* also formed a full-time navy on the Niger. *Sunni* Ali had included Niger boatmen in his amateur military system. The *Askia* turned these into professional sailors. This Songhay navy on the Niger he placed under the *hi-koy*, or admiral of the canoe-fleet. Another officer, the *tara-farma*, had command of a full-time force of cavalry.

Mai Idris Alooma of Kanem-Bornu was another sixteenth-century ruler who took advantage of all this development in the means of making war. He imported muskets and instructors from Tripoli, and built up a small group of musketeers. He found these useful for three reasons. First, they were professional soldiers, and so were always available for duty. Second, they trained regularly with their weapons, and so were good at using them. Third, they were war-prisoners who had become the king's slaves, and so were bound to obey him.

Soldiers also began to become professional in the Guinea states. Some of the Yoruba governments raised full-time military forces. Special groups of professional warriors emerged in Igboland. These were men who sold their war-making or defensive services to those countries or rulers who might need them. Such warrior-mercenaries, or professional soldiers, were also busy along the great trade routes, providing escorts for the caravans, defending markets, chasing off raiders. Sometimes, as we have seen in the case of Gonja, soldiers like these helped to form new states.[1]

It should be remembered that these long-service troops were only the core or nucleus of the army. Every state still depended on calling up amateur soldiers during time of war, for none of them had enough professionals. What sometimes happened now, in contrast with the past, was that the skill of the professionals was learned to some extent by the amateurs, especially in conquering states like Songhay where large armies fought many wars.

All this had mixed results. War became more frequent and more destructive. Ordinary folk suffered accordingly. But professional armies also strengthened the power of kings and governments, and, in doing so, made it easier to keep law and order over wide regions. Ordinary people could gain from this. The same contradictory process of loss and gain occurred in many parts of Asia and Europe.

These different influences, for good or for bad, worked together in West Africa during the sixteenth century. They led to political progress, but they also opened the way to many troubles.

Law and order

Some people had many laws, many social rules and regulations, and went to great trouble to enforce them. Other peoples got along with far fewer laws, and bothered far less about applying them. It depended on where people lived, and how they lived. The sixteenth century saw changes in this field, too.

There was a growth in the means of *enforcing* law, whether by specially appointed officials, by special associations elected or recognised for the purpose, or by the formation of soldier groups who took their orders from judges or kings (though judges and kings were often the same men). But there was also a growth in the means of *making* law. This development of African law, or what is sometimes called

[1] See pages 95-96.

customary law because it was not written down, was an important aspect of the civilisation of the sixteenth century.

It has been little studied; and it is not a subject we can follow here. But one unusual problem in this development of law does call for special comment. There came a clash between Muslim law and traditional African law. (Later on, a similar though more limited clash would occur between African law and European or Christian law.)

Muslim law rested on the *sharia*, a code of beliefs, observances, and rules laid down long ago and based on the teachings of the Koran. In its pure form, the *sharia* not only preaches that there is only one God, but does not approve of all forms of sorcery and witchcraft. From its first introduction, accordingly, Islam conflicted repeatedly with West African beliefs in many gods and in many forms of witchcraft.

It clashed, of course, for practical as well as religious reasons. We have mentioned in Chapter 7 how the rulers of Songhay tried to balance the interests of the Muslim people of the towns with those of the non-Muslim people of the country-side.[1] One reason for this opposition of interests lay in the very different rules which governed the inheritance of wealth among Muslims and non-Muslims. Another practical reason, especially important when it came to deciding on the choice of kings or chiefs, lay in the difference between the Muslim system of succession, which provided for power to descend from father to son, and many of West Africa's non-Muslim systems, which provided for power to descend, for example, from father to sister's son.

Clash of beliefs

These and similar differences in custom and belief had important political results. There was often an outright clash between those who continued to believe in their traditional religions, and those who accepted Islam. We have noticed some examples of this. When the non-Muslim followers of Sumanguru occupied the capital of Ancient Ghana, the Muslim merchants left the city and went to Walata, ruled by Muslims. Something of the same kind happened later on, when the non-Muslim Fulani drove out the Muslim rulers of Takrur.

The force of this clash varied with the times. Often there came a compromise, or settlement, between the two kinds of religion. Some peoples accepted Islam, but none the less kept many of their old beliefs and customs. As well as the *sharia*, in other words, they also had the

---

[1] See pages 73 and 75.

'*ada.* In the sixteenth century, however, the clash was often acute in the Western and Central Sudan, because the late fifteenth century had seen a big expansion of Islam in the towns and cities. Later on, as we shall note, the cause of Islam suffered many reverses, but asserted itself once more in the eighteenth century.

Before leaving this subject, we can usefully return for a moment to the case of Songhay discussed in Chapter 7. By the time *Sunni* Ali came to the throne in 1464, Islam was becoming strong among the merchants and leaders of the Songhay cities and market-centres. *Sunni* Ali accordingly made concessions to their beliefs and customs, and he went out of his way to declare his respect for Muslim scholarship. 'Without learned men,' he is said to have remarked, 'there would be no pleasure in life.' But *Sunni* Ali based his political and military power on the support of the non-Muslim farmers and fishermen of the countryside; and his tremendous record of success shows that in this he calculated wisely.

Yet Islam went on gaining converts and influence in the cities and market-centres, so that *Askia* Muhammad, coming to power at the end of the century, found himself in the opposite position to that of *Sunni* Ali. Although the *Askia* was careful not to offend non-Muslim feelings, at least on questions of court ceremonial, he ruled as a strict Muslim and introduced many legal reforms. In order to devise these laws, and make certain that they were properly in line with Muslim thought, he applied for advice to a famous scholar of North Africa, Al-Maghili (who died in 1504).

This pro-Muslim policy served *Askia* Muhammad well. He built a still greater empire than *Sunni* Ali had done. But the conflicts between Muslim and non-Muslims, in Songhay as elsewhere, continued. They had their full effect with the Moroccan invasion of 1591. For the *ulama* of the Songhay towns then tended to accept the Moroccans as their natural Muslim allies against the non-Muslim people of the Songhay countryside. When *Askia* Ishaq II faced the Moroccan army at the disastrous battle of Tondibi in 1591, his chief secretary and adviser, Alfa Askia Lanbar, actually persuaded him to abandon the field. Later on, this Muslim official even betrayed some of the Songhay chiefs to the leader of the Moroccan invaders. In behaving like this, of course, the *ulama* of cities like Timbuktu were really trying to recover their old independence. They backed the Moroccans against the Songhay rulers, although, once the Songhay were defeated, they turned round and became hostile to the Moroccans. But their attitude during the invasion tells us a lot about the political importance of the conflict between Islam and West African religion at that time, and in later times.

190

CHAPTER FOURTEEN

New pressures from outside

West Africa's many-sided civilisation of the sixteenth century was the work of West Africans. But this work was often influenced, and sometimes with deep effect, by pressures from outside. Important among these, now as in earlier times, were the opportunities and demands of long-distance trade.

For century after century, the gold and other products of West Africa were carried through the Sahara by the 'ships of the desert', the slow but persevering camel caravans which brought to West Africa, in exchange, salt and other things that were valued by West Africans because they did not produce these goods themselves, or did not produce them in sufficient quantity. This *interaction* of West and North Africa had first become a central part of history in the early days of Ghana and Kanem.

In the sixteenth century these old and valued trading links were much disturbed by political troubles both in North Africa and in the Western Sudan. This had important consequences in the seventeenth and eighteenth centuries. To understand how and why they came about, we must leave West Africa for a while, and look at what was happening elsewhere.

Changes in North Africa: the Turkish empire

The old trade routes through the Sahara were in three main 'groups': those in the west, those in the centre, and those in the east.

The first group of routes, the westerly routes, linked West Africa by way of Mauretania to the rich Muslim states in Morocco and al-Andalus (southern Spain), and, through these, to the cities of western Europe. The second group of routes, less used than the first, linked the great markets of the Middle Niger by way of Tuat with Algeria and other markets of the central Maghreb.[1] The third group of routes, the easterly routes, linked Hausaland and Kanem by way of Agadès and Ghat with

---

[1] Maghreb: Tunisia, Algeria, and Morocco.

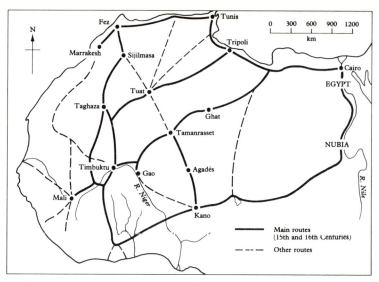

24   *Caravan routes across the Sahara in the fifteenth and sixteenth centuries.*

the Fezzan (in southern Tunisia today), Tripoli and Egypt. Another important route went eastward from Kanem-Bornu by way of Darfur to the Middle Nile, and so to Egypt.

There were cross-routes as well. Caravans from the Middle Niger, for instance, could and often did go westward so as to take the westerly routes to the north; or they went north-eastward to Aïr and then to Tripoli by way of the great oasis of Tuat.

Events now worked together to disturb the trade along nearly all these routes. So far as the westerly routes were concerned, this was largely the result of wars between Muslims and Christians in Spain and Morocco. Pushing the Muslims out of Spain, the Portuguese and Spanish came south across the Mediterranean. In 1471 the Portuguese captured some of Morocco's Atlantic ports, including Tangier; in 1505 they captured still more of these ports. The Spanish, meanwhile, seized some of Morocco's Mediterranean ports. At the same time new conflicts broke out inside Morocco itself.

Later, in the second half of the sixteenth century, the Moroccans recovered most of their ports and began a slow recovery. But much had been destroyed. Sijilmasa, the ancient market city which lay at the northern end of the westerly caravan routes, had been reduced to ruins and had never recovered. Even more serious for West African trade, there was now a frontier of warfare between Muslim Morocco and

Christian Spain. Trade continued between the two; but it lost much of its former freedom of movement. In losing this, it became smaller in value.

Made poor by these costly wars, the Moroccan kings looked about for means of filling their empty treasuries: as we have seen, they picked on Songhay. They strove to capture the wealth of the Western Sudan. Their venture, as we shall discover, had little success; but it meant another big interruption in the peaceful flow of trade between West and North Africa.

At the same time a new power was rising in the eastern Mediterranean. This affected the central and easterly caravan routes, though with varying impact.

The empire of the Ottoman rulers of Turkey now began to expand westwards into Africa. Egypt became its target. Ruled since 1250 by a line of powerful soldier-kings, the Mamluks, Egypt had known prosperity and freedom from invasion, especially under Sultan Baybars (1260-77) and Sultan Kala'un (1279-90). But since then, military rule had weakened Egypt. It was now attacked from two directions.

1 In 1509 a Portuguese fleet under Francisco de Almeida fought and defeated an Egyptian fleet in the Indian Ocean. This gave Portugal control of the narrow straits which lead from the Indian Ocean into the Red Sea. By controlling these straits, the Portuguese hoped to capture the ancient and valuable trade which had long passed between Egypt and the western states of India. In trying to capture this trade, the Portuguese largely ruined and put an end to it.

This Portuguese intervention might not have mattered very much since goods could still go overland between Egypt and the East, had it not been for another big development. This was the new westward expansion of the Ottoman empire. Here we may note the main dates, for these are important in the story.

2 In 1517 the Turkish armies conquered Egypt. In 1551 they occupied Tripoli. Irregular raiding companies[1] carried the power of their country still further westward through North Africa. They made themselves the masters of the coast of Tunisia and Algeria, founding new Turkish-dominated states along this seaboard.

A bitter Mediterranean rivalry now developed between the Christians of southern Europe and the Muslim Turks advancing through North Africa from Egypt. Much of the sixteenth century passed in small harsh battles between the two sides, each seeking to win control of sections of

---

[1] The Europeans of the Mediterranean, who often fought these companies, called them corsairs or pirates.

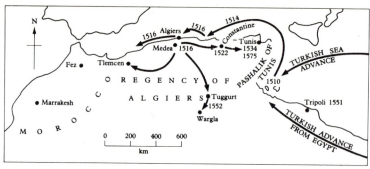

25 *The Turkish advance on North Africa.*

the North African coastline and so acquire mastery of the trade with West Africa. In 1571 a famous sea battle was fought between the Christians and the Muslims off Lepanto, a place on the western coast of Greece. The Christians won this battle, but were unable to follow it up. They failed to win control of the Turkish province of Tunisia or the Turkish-ruled state of Algeria.

All these wars and upheavals damaged the trans-Saharan trade, especially on the western routes. After the ruin of Songhay and the establishment of Turkish power along much of the North African coast, it took some time before trade could recover. The movement of goods between West Africa and southern Europe by way of Tunis and Algiers, and between West Africa and western Asia by way of Egypt, was repeatedly barred by new frontiers of war or hindered by new imperial rivalries.

And when, finally, trade could again flow easily between West Africa and North Africa, the world had greatly changed. The 'ships of the desert' were fast giving way to the ships of the ocean. Because of their progress in long-range sailing and ocean navigation, the sailors and merchants of Europe were firmly on the scene.

The coming of the Europeans to West Africa

Not many Europeans had sailed to West Africa before 1500. After that, their numbers rapidly and regularly increased. They also sailed increasingly to India and other Far Eastern lands, as well as to the Americas, having first reached those countries at the end of the fifteenth century.

This overseas enterprise was by no means an accident. It was the product of important developments in Europe. One of these was the *national growth* of western and southern Europeans, notably the Spanish, Portuguese, Dutch, English and French, together with their expanding financial and military power. Another was the *commercial interest* which led these peoples, firstly the Portuguese and Spanish, into trying to break the Muslim hold on international trade with Asia and West Africa. Faced with Muslim control of North Africa and Egypt, the Europeans now tried to 'get round the back of the Muslims' by sailing far to the south and east. A third and decisive development was Europe's new *technical ability* to build ocean-going ships and sail them out of sight of land.

Until the 1430s the seaboard nations of Europe possessed no ships that were good enough for long-range voyages.[1] Before that time, only the peoples of the East knew how to make long voyages by sail. Of these peoples the Chinese were the most advanced. It was the Chinese who made the great naval and navigational inventions which led to the building of large ships that could survive the storms of the ocean. It was they who designed sails which could enable these ships to sail against the wind, 'into the wind' as sailors say; and it was they who first used instruments, like the compass, which could tell seamen in what direction to steer, even when their ships were far from any coast.

These Chinese inventions were taken over by other peoples who sailed the empty waters of the Indian Ocean and the eastern seas. Foremost among these other maritime peoples were the Arabs. Through the Arabs, inventions of this kind became known to the Europeans of the Mediterranean. Now moving into the age of modern science, Europeans borrowed the new methods of sailing and navigating, improved on them, and began to build long-range ships of their own. In this the Italians, Spanish and Portuguese took a leading part.

So far as West Africa was concerned, and for reasons that we need not discuss here, it was the Portuguese who mattered. Under an enterprising nobleman called Prince Henry (1394-1450) they led the way. The Prince assembled a valuable library of charts and maps. He found money for the building of ships and the recruiting of crews, and ordered these to sail down the western shores of Africa.

Until the 1430s the sailors of Portugal had never managed to come beyond southern Morocco. They had feared to come any further, because, apart from superstitious beliefs about the climate and conditions at sea and on land beyond Cape Bojador, the winds along this

---

[1] Vikings of Scandinavia had sailed to North America several hundred years earlier. But these Viking voyages were not followed up.

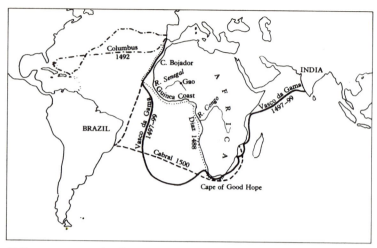

26 European voyages of exploration after 1433.

part of the coast blow nearly always from the north to the south.[1] The
Portuguese could sail southward with the wind behind their ships and
sails, but these ships and sails were not good enough for them to turn
round and go back northward against the wind. They had a saying which
tells the story:

> Who sails beyond the Cape Nun shore,
> Turns back then, or returns no more.

Now they built ships and sails which could master the winds, and in
1434 they came far south beyond Cape Nun. Year by year, they sailed
further. In 1446 their captains reached the mouth of the Senegal River.
In 1472 they entered the Bight of Benin, having reached Elmina the year
before. In 1482-83, they got as far as the mouth of the Congo. In 1488
Diaz rounded the Cape of Good Hope at the extreme southern point of
Africa. Ten years later Vasco da Gama led three ships right round the
Cape of Good Hope, up the eastern coast of Africa as far as Malindi (in
modern Kenya). There he found an Arab pilot, Ibn Majid, who took him
across the ocean to India. With this voyage, the Portuguese had passed
through the ocean gates of the 'Golden East'.

Seamen of other European countries followed, boldly risking long
months at sea in small slow sailing ships and suffering many deaths and
disasters, but drawn on always by the powerful hope of loot and profit.
The Spanish were among them, but the main Spanish effort lay in the

[1] For more information on the reasons for Portuguese enterprise, see Chapter 15, *The
sea-merchants*, page 209.

196

This map was made in 1375 for European merchants, and shows how Europeans then imagined the majesty and powers of the kingdoms of the Western Sudan. The figure at the bottom is the Emperor of Mali; who holds an orb and sceptre in his hands, and wears a noble crown. The wall represents the Atlas Mountains.

Caribbean, first reached by Christopher Columbus[1] in 1492, and afterwards on the mainland of the Americas. After the Portuguese and Spanish there came the French and English and then, towards the end of the sixteenth century and later, the Dutch and Danes, the Swedes and Germans of Brandenburg (as the state of Prussia in Germany was then called). All these Europeans fought and quarrelled with each other, disputed their 'rights' to this or that region of the sea and coast, and yet steadily added to European knowledge and experience.

Sometimes this work of exploration was violent and destructive, for early European captains often tried their hands at raiding and looting. For the most part, though, West African states were too strong to be attacked with much hope of success by soldiers from the sea. This being so, the raiding and looting soon gave way to peaceful trade and then, here and there, to friendship.

A new partnership

Coastal Africans now found that they could buy metal goods and other useful things from traders who came right to their beaches. This was highly convenient for these Africans of the coast, who had formerly had to buy such goods through middlemen from the Western Sudan. Europeans, for their part, found that they could sell their goods for gold and ivory and pepper, all items of great value when resold in Europe, but which they too had formerly had to buy, through many middlemen, from the traders of North Africa. The records show that Africans and Europeans alike welcomed this new coastal trade, and did their best to make it grow.

In the sixteenth century, these business dealings were useful only to peoples living along the Guinea coast itself. The main bulk of West African trade still went overland by the central and eastern routes across the Sahara. But the future of the coastal trade was to be of the highest possible importance.

Throughout the century, it should be emphasised, the trade was largely one of partnership between Africans and Europeans. Both sides had benefit. They bargained keenly with each other, but they also respected each other. If this partnership could have continued into the future, history would have had a very different tale to tell.

As the years slid by, the two-sided benefit from this coastal trade became increasingly a one-sided benefit, with Europeans gaining more

[1] Columbus was an Italian from Genoa, but he sailed in Spanish service.

and more, and Africans less and less. The trade developed *away* from a peaceful exchange of raw materials and manufactured goods, and *towards* a massive trade in captives and in slaves. The foundations of the oversea slave trade, a development of terrible meaning for several African peoples, were laid in the sixteenth century.

Here we shall examine only why this happened. For the main growth of the oversea slave trade occurred in later years.

Beginning of the Atlantic slave trade[1]

The slave trade grew big because of European activities in the distant lands beyond the Atlantic.

In 1492, having sailed westward across the Atlantic, Christopher Columbus and his men arrived at some islands of the Caribbean Sea, which lies between North and South America. Knowing nothing of the existence of the American continent (although northern Europeans had in fact reached it many centuries earlier), Columbus believed that he had come near to India. So he called these Caribbean islands the West Indies, a name they still bear. Others followed Columbus. They entered the vast land masses of North, Central and South America.

These others, who were Spanish soldiers and adventurers, ruined the American peoples whom they found. Their intention was not trade, but loot; not peace, but war; not partnership, but enslavement. They fell upon these lands with greed and the fury of destruction. And the American peoples, unlike the Africans, were unable to defend themselves. Being at an earlier stage of social and technical development than the Africans, they fell easy victims to Spanish violence. Along the coast of Guinea, the Portuguese and other Europeans had begun by trying their hands at violence. But they had given that up. The Africans they met were too strong for them. In the Americas it was different.

There was widespread destruction of the 'Indians', the name that was mistakenly given by these raiders to the native-born American peoples. A Spanish report of 1518, only twenty-six years after the first voyage of Columbus across the Atlantic, says that when the island of Cuba was discovered it was reckoned to contain more than a million 'Indians', but 'today their number does not exceed 11,000. And judging from what has happened, there will be none of them left in three or four years' time, unless some remedy is applied.'

---

[1] A summary of the results of the oversea slave trade will be found in Chapter 22, pages 284-286.

No remedy was applied, in Cuba or anywhere else; or none that made much difference. Whole populations of enslaved 'Indians', forced to work for Spanish masters in mines and on plantations, withered and died, rebelled and were killed.

Trying desperately to find new sources of free labour, the Spanish rulers began sending out Spanish people under conditions no better than slavery. But they could not find enough of them. Where else to look for slaves? The answer was West Africa. Already the Portuguese and Spanish had imported a few West African captives into their own countries. Now they began to carry West African captives to the West Indies and the mainland of the Americas.

In this they faced many problems. They had to seize or buy their African captives and bring them back to Spain and Portugal. They had then to get these men across the Atlantic without ruining their health

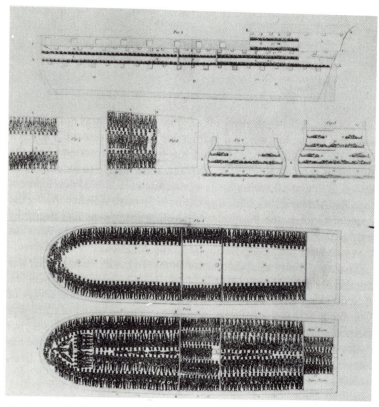

The 'storage plan' for the Liverpool slave-ship Brooker, active in the last quarter of the eighteenth century, shows how African captives were packed for the Atlantic passage.

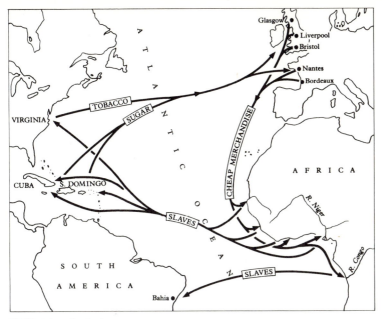

27 The triangular trade.

That was a big problem in the foul old sailing ships of those days. Lastly, they had to turn these captives, or those who were still alive after the crossing of the seas, into slaves. But this, too, proved very difficult. For the Africans resisted enslavement by every means they could. They broke out in revolt after revolt, led by heroes whose names we shall never know. They fought to the death. They spread fear and panic among the Spanish settlers. They went into the mountains or deep into the forests, and formed free republics of their own. They made history in their fight for freedom.

But Spanish arms and organisation, together with the golden profits of the slave trade, proved too strong. In 1515 the Spanish shipped back to Europe their first cargo of West Indian sugar, then an expensive luxury. And in 1518, a grim date in the history of the Atlantic slave trade, the Spanish carried their first cargo of captives *directly* from West Africa to the West Indies. After that, throughout the sixteenth century, the slave trade grew rapidly.

It continued to grow in later years. As the wealth and size of the American plantation-colonies became ever larger, so also did the demand for slave labour. There developed what was to become known as the *triangular trade*. This was a commercial system which greatly

201

helped to build the industrial and technical progress of western Europe in the eighteenth and nineteenth centuries, and especially the progress of Britain and France.

This new and profitable trading system, starting in the late sixteenth century, was called triangular because it had three distinct stages or 'sides'. Each of these 'sides' brought a profit to the merchants and manufacturers of western Europe.

In the first stage or 'side' of this trade, merchants in the big ports of western Europe bought, and shipped to West Africa, goods such as cottons, alcoholic spirits, metalware and firearms. These goods they sold to African chiefs and kings in exchange for slaves. The slaves were prisoners of war or condemned criminals. If they had stayed in West Africa, they would have been domestic or household slaves in the sense we have discussed on page 183. African chiefs and kings often exchanged such 'slaves' among themselves. They saw no reason for not selling them to Europeans. So it was fairly easy for the Europeans to buy captives.

The second 'side' of the triangular trade lay in taking these captives across the Atlantic, usually in chains, and in selling them to plantation-owners in exchange for sugar, tobacco, rum and other products. And the plantation-owners turned the captives into slaves.

The third 'side' consisted in taking the American products back to Europe and selling them at very high prices.

A Senufu religious mask.

202

On the Guinea coast the Europeans went on buying gold and other goods. Increasingly, though, they concentrated on buying captives, for the profits of the 'triangular trade' became ever greater. The profits became so great that in the eighteenth century the Europeans even brought gold from Brazil to the *Gold Coast* (modern Ghana) in order to buy captives they could not otherwise obtain there.

This slave trade greatly enriched Britain and France, as well as some other nations of Western Europe. But it made West Africa much poorer. Most of this still lay in the future; yet the beginnings of this evil trade were also part of the sixteenth-century scene. The cloud then was no bigger than a man's hand; but soon it grew into a tempest, and the tempest of the slave trade blew and raged for years, even for centuries.

SUMMARY

1500 to 1600: Development and change

If you could jump back four hundred years, and visit the West Africa of the sixteenth century, you would find it very different from West Africa today.

Of course the people would look like our own people of today, because they were the ancestors of our own people, except that none of them would be wearing European-style clothes. But there were far fewer people. Towns were quite small. Roads were just tracks. There were no machines of any kind.

Yet that West Africa was also very different from the West Africa of still earlier times. In fact, the years between 1500 and 1600 marked a big advance on earlier times. They form the central part of our picture of the past. Why is this? Let us summarise.

The sixteenth century was one of much *development*:

1 Men learned new political skills. Regular civil services began to appear. Laws were improved. The power of 'big family' chiefs began to be balanced by the power of ordinary people who rose by their work or good sense.

2 Trade, and making goods for trade, got bigger. There was more wealth to share around, even though the shares were very unfair to poor people. The trans-Saharan trade went on being important, but a new coast trade started with the European sea-merchants.

3 Reading and writing developed, sometimes with brilliant results, in the Muslim cities and big market-centres. The peoples of the forest

country and the coastland developed their arts of public speaking, their story-telling, their proverbial wisdom, the preservation of their history, as well as their fine sculpture in wood and ivory and metal, their skills in dancing and in drumming.

Those are some of the reasons why the sixteenth century forms the central part of our picture of the past. But we can also think of this exciting century in another way. We can think of it as the ending of one long period of West African history, and the beginning of another.

That century harvested the fruits of the work of past West Africans, in politics and war, in trade and in making goods for trade, in the arts of everyday life. But that century also sowed the seeds of a different future. It prepared the way for many *changes*.

For nearly five hundred years, ever since the Almoravid invasion of the eleventh century, the peoples of West Africa had stayed safe and free from outside interference. West Africans had paid for this safety by also staying outside the currents of science and the invention of machines that were flowing then in Europe. But they gained as well from this safety. They built a strong and useful civilisation of their own.

Now this safety from outside interference began to be swept away. Little by little, West Africans were drawn into the tide of world events. Europeans began arriving on the coasts of Guinea in ever-growing numbers. And in 1591, sounding trumpets of disaster, Sultan Mulay's soldiers came south across the Sahara and wrecked the Songhay empire.

So the sixteenth century had two big trends: one was towards *internal development*; the other was towards *changes by pressures from outside*.

After 1600, as we shall see, development continued. But so did outside interference. This interference spread across West Africa. Beginning in small ways, in the end it exploded into the colonial invasions of a hundred years ago.

These are the reasons why we can think of the sixteenth century as marking the end of old West African history, and the beginning of modern times.

PART THREE
The seventeenth and eighteenth centuries

CHAPTER FIFTEEN

A period of great change

The seventeenth and eighteenth centuries, AD 1600 to 1800, continued and in certain cases speeded up the process of political change in every main region of West Africa.

In the Western Sudan the time of the old empires was now at an end. By 1600 the imperial power of Mali had practically disappeared; and only its glorious and ancient reputation stayed in the minds of men. The Songhay empire lay in ruins, having been invaded and plundered by Sultan Mulay's troops. Even the new or 'second' empire of Kanem-Bornu had begun to decline in influence by 1700.

The end of the old empires brought upheaval and confusion. Many peoples faced the need to build new states of their own. This was especially the case in the western and central regions of the Western Sudan; and here the need was reinforced by what happened to the trans-Saharan trade.

Changes in the trans-Saharan trade

Partly because of these events in West Africa, and partly because of changes in North Africa noted in the last chapter, there were alterations in the caravan business across the desert. The western routes, which had for long been so important to West Africa, were used less and less. Now there were even years when they were not used at all. By the end of the eighteenth century, according to the survey of a Frenchman called Venture de Paradis, there was only one caravan along the main western route every two or three years, while many other routes were often out of action.

Such rare caravans as these travelled usually between Timbuktu and Wadan in the far west, thence passing northward by way of Wadi Nun to the cities of Morocco. One by one the market cities, which had relied on regular trade for their support, perished or declined. North of the desert, Sijilmasa, once so comfortable and prosperous, never recovered from its ruin during the many conflicts and invasions of Morocco in the sixteenth century. South of Sijilmasa the old Saharan oasis towns of the westerly routes fell into decay or vanished altogether. The market cities of the central and western region of the Western Sudan suffered in the same way. They lost wealth and power.

These were among the reasons why new states in the Senegambia, Middle Niger, and central regions of the Sudan took different forms from before. With the decline of the cities, the cause of Islam was weakened. Now it was the turn of the non-Muslim peoples of the countryside to take a lead. We shall see how this worked out, and also how, late in the eighteenth century, the cause of Islam once more grew strong with many important consequences.

Trade on the central Saharan routes was damaged much less, and later considerably recovered; while trade on the eastern routes, going north from Hausaland, Bornu, and Wadai east of Lake Chad, almost certainly got bigger during this period. What had really happened, in short, was that the bulk of the trans-Saharan trade had now shifted from the western to the eastern routes.

Changes in the Guinea region

Meanwhile in the forest and coastlands of the Guinea region, the new trade with sea-merchants had begun to be important for many peoples. After 1600, so far as West Africa as a whole is concerned, the slow camel caravans of the desert were rapidly out-rivalled by Atlantic sailing ships. These vessels were still very small by our standards of today. But they were very large when compared in carrying capacity with a train of camels. So these were years of steady expansion of Guinea trade with the sea-merchants. Through this, West Africa was carried ever more deeply into the affairs of the rest of the world, with large gains for some West African peoples and serious losses for others. Because of all these developments, it became necessary to build new kinds of states and find new ways of keeping law and order.

We shall therefore find the seventeenth and eighteenth centuries a period of great complexity and vivid interest. There is much upheaval and confusion, but there is also a continued growth of West African civilisation. Many bold and remarkable men appear on the scene, battling to overcome the problems of the times. Many new solutions to political and other problems are forged with skill and courage and success. There are many disasters, but also many successes.

In studying the record of this long and complicated period we shall find it helpful to change the geographical order used in earlier chapters.

So we shall begin with Guinea and work from east to west, taking Guinea to include the forest and part-forest country as well as the seaboard itself; and then go on to consider the Sudan.

The sea-merchants

We have noted the growing influence of sea-merchants from Europe. But for a long time this influence was felt only along the coast, and even here it was often of small importance. Later it became very important. Before going any further, and in order to get a balanced picture, we must pause to see just what this oversea influence was, and how it took shape.

By the early years of the seventeenth century, sea-merchants from several European nations were arriving on the coasts of Guinea. But they had no political or military importance in West Africa.

Their ships were weak and unreliable. Their sea-maps and sailing instruments were primitive. They knew little of Africa, while much of what they thought they knew was wrong.

To the perils of the ocean and the fevers of Guinea there were added other risks. These Europeans were not united. They fought each other fiercely and often. At first the Portuguese had the upper hand over the English and the French. Then the Dutch came into Guinea waters and took the lead, the Dutch being at that time the foremost trading nation of Europe. In 1637 the Dutch attacked and captured the Portuguese castle at Elmina with the help of local Africans. Five years later the Dutch threw the Portuguese out of the *Gold Coast* altogether.

European rivalries on the West African Coast

Having broken Portuguese control of Europe's trade with Guinea, the Dutch now tried to set up their own control. But other rivals at once came on the scene, notably the English.[1] There followed years of battle and ambush between these Europeans. These violent rivalries were watched with keen attention by coastal Africans. The Africans sided now with one European group and now with another, according to their judgement of where their best interests lay.

Yet the sea-merchants kept coming, and gradually worked their way to a peaceful partnership both with each other and with African

[1] England and Scotland became united in 1603, but the word 'British' came into general use only in later times.

merchants along the coast. Once again it is easy to see why. Behind these sea-merchants there were powerful political and commercial companies and interests in Europe. These were now getting themselves strongly established in the West Indies and on the mainland of the Americas. They needed the Guinea trade as part of their system of commerce; therefore they needed peace among themselves. So the coastal trade steadily became more extensive and less violent. Soon it was being carried on peacefully at dozens of regular markets along the seaboard. Of the forty-one trading castles that were eventually built by Europeans in modern Ghana, for example, no fewer than twenty-eight were constructed before 1700.

Dates of some important trade castles on the Guinea Coast

Gold Coast (Ghana)	*when built*	*by whom*
Elmina	1482	Portuguese
	after 1637	rebuilt by Dutch
Axim	1508	Portuguese
	after 1642	rebuilt by Dutch
Cape Coast	1655	Swedes
	after 1665	rebuilt by English
Cormantin	1638	English
	after 1665	rebuilt by Dutch
Christiansborg	1652	begun by Swedes
	after 1661	completed by Danes
Anomabu	1753	English
The Gambia		
James Fort	1651	Germans (Courlanders)
	after 1661	rebuilt by English

While the seventeenth century was thus the period of the *establishment* of the European-American trade with Guinea, the eighteenth was the period of its large *expansion*. By the year 1800 there was scarcely a single coastal people without a close interest in this trade. And by that time the influence of the trade had pushed inland to many peoples who lived quite a long way from the coast.

Yet the Africans, though deeply influenced by the coastal trade, for long held the upper hand. The Europeans were masters on the water, but Africans were masters on the land, and made sure that they remained so. Only late in the eighteenth century, with growing European control of trade along the coast, did this balance of power begin to come down on the European side.

Many people in far-away Europe, now beginning to feel strong

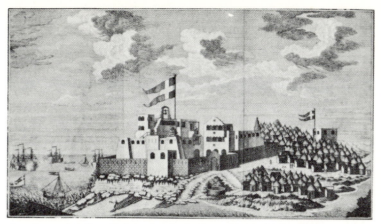

A trading castle built at Christiansborg by the Danes. The Danish flag is flying over it.

enough with their ships and their soldiers to go anywhere they wished and do anything they liked, fell into the mistake of thinking that the Guinea trade was all run by Europeans. But the truth, as the traders on the coast well knew, was quite different.

'There is no small number of men in Europe,' a Dutch official at Elmina Castle, William Bosman, wrote home to a friend in 1700, 'who believe that the gold mines are in our power, and that we, like the Spanish in the West Indies, have nothing more to do than to work the mines with our slaves. But you should understand that we have no means of getting to these treasures, nor do I believe that any of our people have ever seen a single one of these mines.'

Even on the *Gold Coast*, where so many European castles were built, the sea-merchants landed and settled only with permission from the people of the seaboard. The Europeans might sit strongly in their forts, but they still had to pay rent for the land on which the forts were built. Beyond their walls, they could dominate the country only for the range of their musket-shots. Often these Europeans were attacked in their castles, and sometimes these castles were taken by African armies. In 1693, for instance, the big Danish fort of Christiansborg in Accra was seized by the soldiers of Akwamu, held for a time under the flag of Akwamu,[1] and given back to the Danes only after the latter had paid a large amount of gold.

Throughout this period, in short, the Africans were generally in complete control of their side of the trade. Often they were strong

[1] The Akwamu flag showed an African waving a sword, as a sign of the power of Akwamu.

enough to punish European misbehaviour and insist on compensation for damages. They also made use of the Europeans for their own political plans and needs.

Growth of the Atlantic slave trade

Yet there was one thing that the Africans could not control, and this was to mean a lot. They could decide to some extent what the Europeans wished to *sell* them. But they could not control what the Europeans wished to *buy* from them. And what the Europeans wished to buy, more and more, and soon with a driving eagerness that overcame all opposition, were slaves.

We shall consider the *results* of the oversea slave trade later in this book.[1] Here we need notice only one or two important points about it.

It began, as a large and regular *system of trade*, only after about 1625. This was when the Portuguese were well established in Brazil; the Spanish on other parts of the mainland of South, Central and North America; the English, French, Dutch, Danes and Spanish on the islands of the Caribbean Sea. All these opened more and more mines and plantations. They wanted more and more slaves. They went to Africa to find them. They found many millions of them.

Why did they succeed in this? The key to understanding why the slave trade began, and why it grew, lies in the master-servant organisation which existed in many states and among many peoples. As in other countries of the world, then or at other times, chiefs and kings regularly turned war-captives and certain classes of law-breakers into slaves. These slaves, as we have seen, were not very different from most other men and women except that they had fewer rights. As often as not, they were just servants who had special duties and work they had to do.

And just as in other countries, then or at other times, these kings were easily persuaded to sell, barter, or simply give away their servants or slaves. So it was easy for European kings, when they found their own supplies of European or American-Indian slaves coming to an end, to get some from Africa. In 1562, for instance, the English captain Sir John Hawkins was presented with a lot of war-prisoners, whom he turned into slaves and sold across the Atlantic. He got these Africans in exchange for some military help that he gave to two kings of Sierra Leone. Slave-trading was a cruel aspect of the world of that time, but many rulers and rich merchants had their part in it.

[1] See Chapter 22, pages 284-286.

We have seen, too, that the slavery of Africa was a much less cruel servitude than the slavery which now developed in the Americas. Yet it seems unlikely that African kings, chiefs and merchants would have stopped selling their servants and war-captives even if they had known the fate to which they were sending these men and women. For these kings, chiefs and merchants were under two very powerful and growing pressures to continue selling men and women.

In the first place, the Europeans now began to ask for slaves more than anything else, even more than gold and ivory. If they could not buy captives at one market along the coast, they simply went on to the next market; if denied by one chief, they applied to his neighbour. Secondly, kings and chiefs now began to feel the need for guns. And only the Europeans, at that time, could provide guns.

Just as iron-pointed spears had proved better than clubs and stones a thousand years earlier, so now the musket became the most powerful weapon. A situation began to arise where chiefs and kings felt safe only when they were sure of a supply of firearms. But these chiefs and kings, living in a non-industrial society, were unable to make firearms for themselves. They had to buy them from abroad. Apart from a few that came south across the Sahara, all the firearms had to come by sea. Yet the Europeans insisted on selling their guns in part-exchange for captives. So the oversea slave trade, begun in a small way, soon became a big export to the Americas of captured men and women.

There were many cases where African kings, chiefs or elders, seeing how destructive this slave trade had become to peace and prosperity at home, tried hard to bring it to a halt. We shall look at some of these cases later on.[1] But the pressures were too strong for them. Little by little, the oversea slave trade spread to the lands behind the coast, profiting repeatedly from the disunity among African states.

Firearms

This spreading influence was also linked to changes in ways of government. The rise of professional armies came at about the same time as the arrival of the first firearms, and with the wars and troubles of the seventeenth century. Large quantities of muskets now began to be imported. From England alone, at the height of the eighteenth-century Guinea trade, the gunsmiths of Birmingham were providing more than 100,000 a year.

[1] Chapter 22, *Resistance to the slave trade,* pages 286-288.

Here also there were gains as well as losses. By selling these guns, Europeans helped to spread war among Africans, since the buying of guns called for the capture of war-prisoners who could be sold into slavery. But the guns also strengthened Africans against European invasion or attack. The Europeans saw this very clearly. Yet they on their side were as powerless to stop the sale of guns to Africans as the Africans were powerless to stop the sale of war-prisoners to Europeans, and for the same reason: they could never get agreement among themselves. The Dutchman, William Bosman, then living in Elmina Castle, explained this in a letter written home in 1700.

> The main military weapons [of the *Gold Coast* Africans] are muskets or carbines, in the use of which these Africans are wonderfully skilful. It is a real pleasure to watch them train their armies. They handle their weapons so cleverly, shooting them off in several ways, one man sitting, another creeping along the ground or lying down, that it is surprising they do not hurt each other.
>
> Perhaps you will wonder how the Africans come to be furnished with these firearms. But you should know that we sell them very great quantities, and in doing this we offer them a knife with which to cut our own throats. But we are forced to do this. For if we [the Dutch] did not do it, they would easily get enough muskets from the English, or from the Danes, or from the Prussians. And even if we governors [of the official European trading corporations] could all agree to stop selling firearms, the private traders of the English or the Dutch would still go on selling them.

A chain of cause and effect

Looking back today on all those confused events, one can see a clear chain of cause and effect running through much of the story of the coastal lands of Guinea, and even to some extent of the forest lands.

First, there is the small beginning of coastal trade. New markets and centres of African power appear along the coast. New states emerge. These build themselves into a controlling position, as middlemen, between the European sea-merchants on one side and the African inland merchants on the other.

In the second half of the seventeenth century there comes an enormous expansion in the demand for slaves for the mines and plantations of the Americas. Encouraged by the sea-merchants, the coastal rulers try to supply this demand. They have to make wars in order to get hold of enough captives.

These wars are increasingly made with guns brought from Europe. But the European demand for slaves sharpens the African need for guns; and this need for guns in turn makes greater the need for captives with whom to buy the guns. By the eighteenth century the politics of Guinea are deeply influenced by the exchange of African captives for European manufactured goods, with guns high on the list of these.

We have spent a little time on these matters because, although they were only a small part of the overall West African picture in the seventeenth and even in the eighteenth century, they were a part of growing importance. They set the scene for many big events and further changes. They show how it came about that large populations of African origin were settled in the Americas. They explain why the influence of the sea-merchants, so very small at first, was able to grow so big as the years went by. They help us to understand many of the political and military happenings of the period.

CHAPTER SIXTEEN
Benin, Oyo and the Delta states

The prosperity of Benin, and beginnings of decline

The power of the *obas* of Benin, at least outside their city and its neighbourhood, diminished slowly during the seventeenth century, but rapidly during the eighteenth. The reasons for this arose in general from the changing nature of politics and trade along the coastland of the eastern Guinea region.

The sea-merchants were now bringing many more openings for profitable trade. These, in turn, led to more attempts by local people to win their independence from the *oba's* rule. There were new wars. As the wars multiplied, so also did the number of firearms that were bought from the sea-merchants. Gone were the days when the *oba* could hope to keep the control of expensive weapons in his own hands. Now these weapons were also getting into the hands of rivals and rebels.

With the rising quantity of firearms in many different hands it became less and less easy for the *Oba* of Benin, or any other powerful ruler in this region, to make sure that his peoples remained obediently loyal. The traditions of Benin speak of bad or harsh *obas* in this period; behind such traditions we can glimpse the mounting problems of government, as warfare and rebellion spread across the land.

But these disturbing events did not necessarily mean a decline in general prosperity. At least until the middle of the eighteenth century, and perhaps later, Benin remained a city of wealth and comfort. Benin chiefs and their families continued to live very well. A Dutch visitor, David van Nyendael, wrote about them in the year 1700:

> The rich among them wear a white calico [cotton] cloth about one yard (1 metre) long and half as broad... Over that they wear a finer white cotton dress that is often as much as sixteen or twenty yards (15-19 metres) in length. This they pleat neatly in the middle, casting over it a scarf about a yard (1 metre) long... Wives of great chiefs wear calico cloths woven in this country. These cloths are very fine, and very beautifully patterned in several colours. The

women wear necklaces of coral that are very nice to look at. Their arms are decorated with bright copper or iron bangles. Some of them wear bangles on their legs, while their fingers are thickly crowded with copper rings. . .

This Dutchman's report shows that local industries still prospered in Benin, especially the crafts of weaving and metal-working, just as they had in the past. It also shows the self-respect and dignity of the people of this famous city. Van Nyendael wrote that the inhabitants of Benin were generally 'good-natured and very civil', as well as generous in their treatment of strangers.

But they certainly expect that their good manners shall be repaid in the same way, and not with arrogance or rudeness. And to think of forcing anything out of them is to think of arguing with the moon.

They are very prompt in business, and they will not allow any of their ancient customs to be set aside. But once we [foreign merchants] comply with these customs, then the people of Benin are very easy to deal with, and will leave out nothing needed for a good agreement. . .

History has many examples of great cities which continue to be comfortable while the states and empires around them totter and fall. So it was with the great and ancient city of Benin.

Its dignified way of life, the result of centuries of social and political growth, continued to surprise and please the strangers who came here from beyond the seas. They admired its government, it courtesy, its laws, its tolerance. They praised its hospitality and care of visitors. They respected its sense of independence.

Yet the seeds of political decay were sprouting many weeds by the end of the eighteenth century. Gradually, this old empire fell apart. And as it fell apart, the security and comfort of Benin itself began to fail. The rulers and their priests, threatened by many perils, became more dictatorial. Their wisdom shrank. Their civilisation narrowed. One may see this even in the changing styles of Benin's wonderful art of sculpture in brass. These styles became less sensitive and delicate, more warlike and crude, closer to the spreading insecurity and confusion of the times.

The empire of Oyo, a great power

West of the lower Niger, in Yorubaland, events again took a different course. Under its supreme leader, the *Alafin*, the empire of Oyo grew in strength and influence during the seventeenth century.[1] It reached the peak of its strength soon after 1650, and continued as a great power in this region for more than a hundred years, dominating most countries between the Volta River in the west to Benin and the Niger in the east. It maintained during this time, through Egbado, a firm hold on the coastal trade with Europeans at Ajase (Porto Novo); and it increased its authority over its subject peoples by a big and efficient army, consisting of a full-time cavalry force together with part-time levies of troops from all its tributary states. The Oyo cavalry became famous and much feared.

High among Oyo's successes in this main period of expansion was the domination of Dahomey. This was completed in two phases; first, in four successful expeditions between 1724 and 1730 and secondly, to reassert these successes, between 1739 and 1748.

After these years of military expansion, the problem for Oyo's leaders was to decide whether to go on with expansion or concentrate on building up the trading wealth of the empire. This problem was not resolved until the reign of *Alafin* Abiodun (1770-89). He won a bitter struggle against the militarist views of Bashorun Gaha. Then he turned vigourously to policies of economic development, especially of the trade in slaves with Europeans along the coast. There were now said to be 6,600 towns and villages under the *alafin's* direct or indirect rule.

But *Alafin* Abiodun, concentrating on trade, neglected his army. This weakened the real power of the central government. Under the next ruler, *Alafin* Awole, there came a period of decline. Local revolts broke out and proved difficult to put down. By this time the *alafin's* authority was supported in Oyo itself by a complicated public service under leading officials such as the Ona Efa, in charge of justice, and the Osi Efa, who controlled the financial affairs of the empire. Elsewhere the *alafin* ruled through representatives, the *ilari* and *ajele* chiefs, who lived at the court of each of the subject-states, enjoyed religious power as priests of the shrines of Shango, and acted as the *alafin's* political spokesmen.[2]

So long as the army was strong, the *ilari* had much power. Now, they began to lose it. Besides this, the empire had grown so large that it was very difficult to govern through officials who made no use of writing. Orders and reports had to be sent back and forth by word of mouth, because Oyo had no-one who could read and write.

---

[1] For the background, see Chapter 10, *Later Yoruba history: the growth of Oyo*, pages 124-127.
[2] See Chapter 13, *Kings, nobles, governors*, pages 184-186.

Yoruba religious carvings.

The *alafin* was still by no means a dictator. His personal power was limited even in the eighteenth century when the empire stood at the height of its power. As a constant check on his actions and decisions, there was his council of senior 'big family' nobles, the Oyo Mesi, under their leader the *bashorun*. As with other Yoruba states, the whole system was based on a balance between the *alafin* and his 'king's men' or appointed officials, on one side, and the Oyo Mesi and other nobles on the other side. And the power of the latter could be decisive because they kept the right to say that an *alafin* had lost the confidence of the ancestors, and must therefore commit suicide,[1] whereupon they could choose another *alafin*. Yet here again the system developed another 'built-in' balance. This took the form of chiefs who controlled the Ogboni association. If necessary these chiefs were able to countermand the Oyo Mesi's decision that an *alafin* should be deposed. Rivalries between these various holders of political and religious power now added to Oyo's difficulties.

In the last years of the eighteenth century, many disputes broke out between the ruling *alafin* and the powerful Oyo Mesi nobles. The chiefs of other Yoruba states now took a hand in these disputes, siding with either the *alafin* or the nobles according to local interest or calculation. So the careful balance of political power within the empire became increasingly upset. Here we see another aspect of the long conflict between the traditional *Ebi* system — of family relations between the Yoruba rulers — and the Oyo drive for a single great Yoruba state.

The troubles of the *alafin*, like those of the *Oba* of Benin, were also increased by the growth of the coastal trade in slaves and firearms. This helped to spread warfare and raiding. These in turn tended to promote revolt among the less loyal subject states of Oyo. There were increasing calls on the military and financial power of the *alafin*. These led to greater demands on the subject states for soldiers and taxes. Such demands were not popular.

The challenge to Oyo came in fact from three directions:

1 There was first of all a growing difficulty in keeping control of the trade routes to the coast. These ran through forest lands where Oyo had never enjoyed much power, mainly because its cavalry could not operate in the forest. Growing strong in their middleman position between the sea-merchants and Oyo, and taking advantage of the troubles between the *alafin* and his nobles, the little states along and near the coast grew increasingly rebellious. They took advantage of the disputes at court between the Oyo Mesi and the *alafin*.

2 At about the same time the power of Oyo began to be challenged from a new direction. For a long time the Fon people of Dahomey had paid tribute to Oyo.[2] Now they too entered the coastal trade in firearms, and, gathering their strength, made a bid for their independence. Oyo's armies were able to master the situation for many years but in

---

[1] The method of announcing this decision to an *alafin* was to send him parrot's eggs.
[2] See Chapter 17.

the end, largely because of the disputes in Oyo, they failed. During the nineteenth century, when the power of Oyo had very greatly declined, the Fon were to turn the tables and themselves invade Yorubaland.

3 Thirdly, soon after 1800, there came a threat from the north. The rising strength of the Fulani rulers of Hausaland began to press down on the northern states which were subject to Oyo. The *alafin* of that time lost Ilorin in this way. Nupe threw off its loyalty. By the early years of the nineteenth century the empire of Oyo, for all these reasons, had really ceased to exist outside the northern region of Yorubaland; even there its power was declining.

As elsewhere in West Africa, the old systems in eastern Guinea were in crisis or collapse; and new forms of government, shaped more closely to the needs of the new times, began to rise and take their place.

The Delta states

The many small states of the Niger Delta and Cross River, formed as we have noted in Chapter 10 from many different peoples, took full advantage of the quickly growing trade with European sea-merchants.

As the ships from Europe and the Americas entered creek after creek along this maze of ocean-fronting waterways, market after market sprang into being.

Professor Onwuka Dike[1] has described this energetic process. He explains that the places where these markets grew were widely separated from each other. After all, there was plenty of room in the Delta: going along the coast, it is more than four hundred and fifty kilometres from the Cross River in the east to the River of Benin in the west, and there are many useful creeks and river outlets in between. Usually, the points of settlement were 'islands like Bonny dominating the mouth of a river which linked the hinterland to the sea. In time, each community developed the independence and individualism so typical of island dwellers. Every river mouth, every centre of trade, and, in some areas, every town had its overlord'.

Government in the Delta

By now, too, new methods of government had taken shape in the Delta.

---

[1] In his book, *Trade and Politics in the Niger Delta, 1830-85*, Oxford 1956.

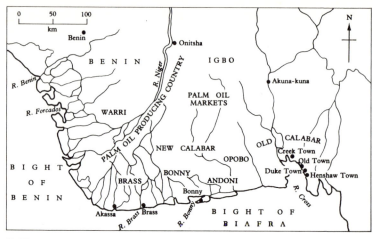

28 *The city-states of the Niger Delta.*

They combined to form what is called a 'city-state'. This means just what it says: a state composed of a city or big central settlement, founded for reasons of trade or other interests, but governing only itself, its surrounding villages, and nearby land or waterways. History has many examples of city-states, the most famous in Europe being those of the ancient Greeks: Athens and Sparta and their like.

There were many such states in the Delta after about the middle of the seventeenth century. And, as Professor Dike explains, 'each city-state had all the apparatus of rule which enabled it to maintain law and order, administer justice, make war and peace, organise and prosecute peaceful commerce'.

But the city-states of West Africa, like those of ancient Greece, also had several different forms of government. Some, like Athens, were republics. Others, like Sparta, were monarchies: that is, they were ruled by kings. Among the second were Bonny (a word corrupted by sea-merchants from Ibani), New Calabar (Kalabari), and Warri: these were ruled by kings elected from members of their wealthiest and most prominent families. Among the republics were Brass and the market-towns of Old Calabar in the Cross River (Creek Town, Henshaw Town, Duke Town and Obutong); these were ruled as republics by members of special political associations.

The Old Calabar towns, for example, were governed by Ekpe, an Efik word for leopard. The Ekpe or Leopard association was a shrewd and effective means of government by a minority of powerful men, but all

222

local men could find a place on one or other level of seniority.[1] Its main job was to protect the interests of the merchants of these towns. Everyone who could afford to pay its entrance fees could join Ekpe. But the merchants made sure that fees for entry to the top or ruling grades were high enough to keep power in the hands of the wealthiest among them. This 'merchants' government' supervised all dealings with the Europeans, punished the latter when they misbehaved, and at the same time made and enforced the laws for lesser men slaves. This was a mixture between a limited democracy and rule by wealth.

Whether their government was monarchic or republican, the day-to-day life of the people was organised through the *House System*. This was another new development. It took the place of traditional ways of rule through clans of big families. The House was a kind of co-operative trading company based not so much on kinship as on commercial association between the head of the House, his family, his trading assistants, and his servants.

There were many such Houses in the Delta, although their full development came only after 1800. Some of them, like those of the Pepples of Bonny, became known throughout the western world. Often they were very large. They included not only the members of the House family itself, but also a big number of workers and servants or slaves. All these were employed not only in trading with the sea-merchants and with other Africans, but also in clearing and planting land, in founding new settlements, and in manning the trade-canoes and war-canoes of each House. The House system was a good example of the way in which new solutions were invented for the new problems of the times.

The trade of the Delta

All these city-states of the Delta grew prosperous on the Atlantic trade in slaves. One reason for this lay in their *middleman* position of monopoly. Because they occupied every river-mouth, and were skilful in politics, they obliged the ships from Europe and the Americas to deal with them, and only with them. Another reason for their prosperity lay in the fact that the lands behind the Delta were rich in population.

This density of population helped to feed the trade in captives. As time went by, the trade became highly organised, being carried on by

---

[1] See also Chapter 19, *Sierra Leone and the Poro Association*, pages 254-256.

well-established rules and regulations for more than two centuries. Many of the black people of the Americas descend from parents who were bought from the traders of the Niger Delta.

We may compare this long-standing export of people, this forced emigration to the Americas, with the similar export of people that was going on from Europe at the same time. Just as millions of people were taken out of West Africa, so also were millions of people taken out of Europe in these centuries: Italians, Germans, Irish, Scots, Poles and many others. Few of the latter, it is true, were sent abroad by being captured and sold as slaves; they were none the less forced by hunger and unemployment to leave their homes and seek a new life across the seas. The real difference lay in the actual conditions of life for the Africans and the Europeans who were thus removed from their homelands. These conditions were far worse for the Africans, just as they would remain far worse for most black Americans in later times.

How flourishing this Delta trade was may be seen in many records of the time. An English captain[1] who wrote about Bonny, for long the biggest of the Delta states, described it as 'the wholesale market for slaves, since not fewer than 20,000 are sold here every year. Of these, 16,000 come from one nation, called the Ibos, so that this single nation has exported over the past twenty years, not fewer than 320,000 of its people; while members of the same nation sold at New and Old Calabar, in the same period, probably amounted to 50,000 more.'

Like the slave-dealing merchants of the English ports of Bristol, Liverpool and London, or of the French ports of Nantes and La Rochelle, the chiefs and merchants of the Delta states prospered by all this trade.

The trade was well organised. Regular markets were held, governed by strict rules. This same English captain wrote:

> The preparation for these markets generally occupy the Bonny people for some days. Large canoes, capable of carrying 120 persons, are launched and stored for the voyage. The traders add to their trade-goods by obtaining from their friends, the captains of the slave-ships, a considerable quantity of goods on credit. . . Evening is the period chosen for the time of their departure, when they proceed in a body, accompanied by the noise of drums, horns and gongs. They generally come back at the end of the sixth day after their departure, bringing with them 1,500 to 2,000 slaves,

[1] Captain John Adams, who knew West Africa between 1786 and 1800, and whose book was published in 1822.

224

who are sold to Europeans the evening after their arrival, and taken on board the ships.

Buying and selling with the European and American captains was a tricky business. There was much bargaining. The money used was generally composed of trade goods like iron bars, rolls of cotton or quantities of yams (needed by the slave-ships to feed their captives as well as their crews during the voyage across the Atlantic); cowrie-shells were also an important form of money. Any attempt by the European traders to bully or cheat their African partners was likely to be answered by a boycott. The Africans, operating through associations like Ekpe, simply closed the river to European trade until the Europeans made good the damage they had caused. Here in the Delta the Europeans had no castles and few shore stations. Instead, they lived in old ships, called hulks. These hulks were permanently anchored near the shore of the trading towns.

The complications of this trading system may be seen from the deals that were made. In 1676, for instance, the captain of the English ship *Bonaventure* bought a hundred men, women and children, and had them duly branded by his crew with the special mark of the British Royal African Company: *DY* for Duke of York. For these carefully selected captives he paid five muskets, twenty-one iron bars, seventy-two knives, half a barrel of gunpowder and various lengths of cotton stuff.[1]

Time and patience were needed for such bargains. Here is an extract from the records of another English ship, the *Albion-Frigate*, which arrived at New Calabar in 1699. First of all, as the customs prescribed, the captain sent messengers ashore to greet the king of New Calabar and ask him to start a deal.

The king agreed but not with the prices that the English offered. 'He gave us to understand that he expected one bar of iron for each slave more than Edwards [the captain of another English ship] had paid him. He also objected to our metal basis, mugs, beads and other goods, and said they were of little value at the time.' Bargaining continued. The next day 'we had a conference with the king and principal natives of the country, about trade, and this lasted from three o'clock until night. But it had no result. They continued to insist on having thirteen bars of iron for a male, and ten for a female.' The Europeans of the *Albion-Frigate* thought this too expensive. They had supper with the king and went

---

[1] This trade was now done in special 'units of exchange' called 'trade ounces'. Each 'ounce' consisted of a certain number of goods of various kinds, according to their cost in Europe. See footnote on page 258.

In the Niger Delta: British traders (under the umbrella) are going upriver to bargain. This picture was drawn in 1832.

back to their ship. Agreement was reached only after another four days of argument.

This well organised trade was usually conducted with very little violence or confusion. The merchants on both sides gained from this. But poor men still suffered very badly.

Like their fellow-sufferers who were forced to leave Europe by hunger and unemployment, the Africans who were sent abroad faced terrible weeks at sea in foul old ships, got bad food and met shipwreck and frequent death. But unlike the European emigrants, they were often chained during the dreaded 'Middle Passage' from fear that they would revolt against their oppressors. This fear was well justified, for brave or desperate revolts at sea were many. Once the captives were landed across the Atlantic, they were condemned to lifelong slavery under the most cruel conditions.

The story of these Africans does not belong to this book. Yet the story is also part of the history of Africa. In one way it was a very sorrowful part, in another way a triumphant one. For these Africans, shipped like cattle across the seas, none the less wrote a great epic in the history of mankind.[1] Without them, the civilisation of the Americas could never have flourished as it has.

[1] See Chapter 22, *Africans beyond the seas*, pages 288-290.

CHAPTER SEVENTEEN

Dahomey in the seventeenth and eighteenth centuries

General notes

The thinly-wooded land of Dahomey (now renamed the Republic of Benin) is part of the open country which divides the forests of Nigeria from those of modern Ghana (see also the vegetation map on p. 5). This is one of the reasons why its history shows many differences from that of its neighbours.

Modern Dahomey, as a glance at the map will show, includes the coastland between the frontiers of Nigeria and Togo as well as the inland country for some six hundred and fifty kilometres to the north. These frontiers were established by French colonial invaders at the end of the nineteenth century.

In the seventeenth century the position here was very different. There were then two different sets of states. One of these was along the coast itself, the length of seaboard which European traders then called the *Slave Coast*. It consisted of a string of small city-states. The other lay in the inland country not far from the coast, and was composed of a number of more loosely organised states. The most important of these was formed by the Fon people based at Abomey.

Most of these peoples, whether along the coast or in the interior, have traditions which point to a common origin in a region called Tado in what is central Dahomey today. By 1600, however, they were long since divided into different groups. Those along the coast now discovered the same chances of trade with sea-merchants as their neighbours in the Niger Delta or along the *Gold Coast* (modern Ghana). The empty ocean became for them, too, a 'frontier of opportunity'. They took this opportunity with energy and courage. They prospered with the new trade.

Close to the ocean surf, the best-known of these seaside states were Jakin, Whydah (also called Ouidah or Fida), and Grand Popo. Immediately behind them lay Great Ardrah or Allada, the principal power along this coast for most of the seventeenth century and the one that generally controlled its weaker neighbours. All of these took shape

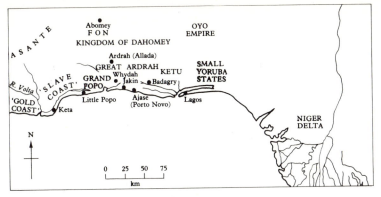

29 Dahomey and region in the eighteenth century.

around 1650: at about the time, in other words, that increasing sugar production in the West Indies began to make increasing demands for African labour. Later, other seaside states were formed. These included Badagry and Ajase (Porto Novo).

Ardrah and Whydah

These little states used the sea-merchants to their own advantage in the same way as in the Niger Delta. Their kings fixed prices for the sale of goods, including captives, and sent their agents to bargain with the ship's captains. They made the Europeans pay taxes. In order to trade with Great Ardrah, a European merchant called John Barbot reported towards the end of the eighteenth century, 'Europeans usually give the king the value of fifty slaves in goods, for his permission to carry on trade, as well as paying customs duties in respect of each ship. They also give the king's son the value of two slaves for the privilege of obtaining water for their crews, and the value of four slaves for permission to cut timber.'

At first these kings found that the Europeans quarrelled so violently among themselves that they spoiled the trade. They took steps to stop this. They shared out the trading facilities among the various Europeans, and reduced the amount of violent competition. The results were impressive. 'Whydah', wrote an English visitor, John Atkins, early in the eighteenth century, 'is now the greatest trading place on the coast of Guinea, selling off as many slaves, I believe, as all the rest together. Forty or fifty ships [French, English, Portuguese and Dutch] load their cargoes there every year.'

229

Then came a new challenge from the inland country. This same visitor explained why. The king of Whydah, Atkins reported, was in the habit of buying captives from his neighbours. 'But if he cannot obtain sufficient numbers of slaves in that way, he marches out with an army, and depopulates the country. He and the neighbouring king of Ardrah commit great depredations inland.'

Now the Fon people of the inland country, who were raided in this way, already had problems of their own. Like Ardrah and its neighbours, they were officially subject to the Yoruba of Oyo. In the fairly open country where they lived, they found themselves at the mercy of cavalry raids by the armies of Oyo who made them pay tribute. So the Fon of Dahomey came together in self-defence. They built a strong state of their own.

The Fon expansion

They did this on new lines. Until now, like other West African peoples, they had thought of their king or ruler as being a father to them. This was what is called the patriarchal[1] principle of government. The king's power is like a strong pot, and the people are the water in the pot: so long as the pot is not damaged or upset, the water is safe. But the Fon invented a different principle of government. They likened the king's power to the water in the pot: the life-giving water that was scarce and precious to them. The life of the nation was full of dangers and they likened it to a pot with many holes. Only if every citizen placed his finger on a hole would the water — the king's power — be kept from wasting.

This meant that the whole Fon people became directly involved in support of their king. Everyone served the king, because everyone's safety and happiness was believed to depend on the king. Government in this new kind of state became organised on army lines. Chiefs got power not by membership of this or that family, but by courage and success in warfare; and they could be promoted, down-graded, or transferred to other duties as the king thought fit. Even women were called into this work of supporting the king by direct service. Regular companies of women soldiers fought for the king, often with success.

By the eighteenth century the king, as 'guardian of all the Fon', had direct power through his own orders, or indirectly through the orders of

[1] From the word *patriarch*, which means, in this connection, the powerful head of a 'big family'.

230

The Amazons of Dahomey: a scene in the 1790s.

the ministers whom he appointed, over a large 'State sector' of economic and political life. Every year there was a census or public counting of the people, and also of the principal goods they produced by farming and handicraft industry. Through his *tokpo*, or minister of agriculture, the king controlled the amounts of land that were sown with millet, yams, maize and other crops. By doing this he made it possible, at least in theory, to avoid having too much or too little of any of Dahomey's crops. All honey was reserved for the use of the army, and no private sale of it was allowed. This was also the case with ginger, which the Fon regarded as a valuable medicine. A central part of the king's responsibilities was to make sure that every section of the Fon had a fair share of the country's wealth. This he did by holding 'annual customs' or special ceremonies, at which he gave away large amounts of the cowries which the Fon, like many other peoples of West Africa, now used as money. The king's job, in short, was not only to collect wealth. He also had to divide this wealth among all sections of his people.

Based on the town of Abomey, this remarkable state may be said to have begun its history with King Wegbaja in about 1650. Wegbaja was followed by Akaba in about 1685, and Akaba by Agaja in 1708. Agaja was an outstanding general and a statesman, who reigned for 32 years. Under his rule the state of Abomey or Dahomey became strong enough to capture the coastal states, though still forced to pay tribute to Oyo; and its people formed themselves into a nation.

King Agaja seems to have had two motives in attacking the coast. In the first place, there is evidence that he wanted to call a halt to the slave raids of the coastal states, and even to stop the export of Africans. It is certainly true that the number of Africans sent away from here became much smaller after Agaja's conquest.

Secondly, Agaja wanted to assure himself and his government and traders of better access to the sea-merchants: they were tired of having to pay for their guns and gun-powder at the very high prices demanded by the 'middlemen' traders of the coastal states. These prices the Fon found unusually high after 1712, for in that year the annual tribute exacted by Oyo, then the imperialist overlord of the Fon, had to include 41 cases of guns, each case having to contain 41 weapons. This meant that the king had to provide his overloard of Oyo with a total of 1,681 guns every year, as well as supplying weapons to his own army.

Agaja's warriors marched on Great Ardrah in 1725, and conquered and sacked it. Three years later they pushed south again to the smaller states of Savi and Whydah. In 1732 they took Jakin. After that, and for more than a hundred and fifty years, this coast was dominated by the kings of Dahomey.

But the Fon hold on the coast was not kept easily. Whydah and its neighbours tried to regain their freedom of action; in this they were sometimes helped and encouraged by European captains and agents. Not until the 1740s did Dahomey win complete control. Then Whydah became a Fon colony under the power of officials sent from Abomey, the capital of Dahomey. Of these officials, the most important was the *yevogan*. It was with him that the Europeans had to deal.

European influence was limited to the beach itself, and even there the Europeans were closely supervised by the *yevogan* and his staff. Only by special permission could Europeans visit Abomey. But as time went on, official European agents were generally allowed to go to Abomey and pay their respects at court. By 1793 the English agent[1] at Whydah could report that 'from Whydah to Abomey is perhaps the most beaten track by Europeans of any part of Africa'. Most of these visitors to Abomey thought that the king was an outright dictator. In this they were wrong. Though the king's power was undoubtedly very great, he still needed

---

[1] Archibald Dalzel (pronounced *Dee'ul*).

the assent of his counsellors. Even then he could not act without obeying many traditional customs which also limited his power.

Dahomey and Oyo

Formed in self-defence against raids from Oyo and raids from the coast, the Fon rulers had developed a considerable military strength. But dangers from outside their kingdom did not stop when Agaja seized control of Ardrah and Whydah. Agaja still had to face his overlord, the *Alafin* of Oyo, who did not welcome Dahomey's increase of strength and who was asked by the coastal states for help against Agaja.

As a result the *Alafin* of Oyo sent his famous cavalry into Dahomey in 1726, two years after Agaja's march to the coast. They completely defeated Agaja's army, and repeated their invasions in 1728, 1729 and 1730. But Dahomey still kept a hold on its coastal positions, though its rulers had to sell captives to Europeans so as to get guns and gunpowder.

All these conditions, but especially the imperialist pressure of Oyo, played a part in reinforcing the military and political growth and power of the Fon state. They likewise strengthened all those customs which were thought of as protecting or helping the king, since the king was the symbol of Fon safety. Royal customs which were believed necessary to the king's welfare had to be maintained at all costs, even when, as for a long time, these customs required the yearly killing at Abomey of a large number of human victims.

Built by Agaja, this strong state was further strengthened by King Tegbesu (1740-74). He concentrated on increasing the power and efficiency of his government. This made him unpopular with European merchants who began to prefer to trade elsewhere. Tegbesu was followed by Kpengla (1774-89) and Agonglo (1789-97). Rivalries for power now appeared. They broke out into a civil war between rival groups. Only with King Gezo (1818-58) did the power of Dahomey recover.

Though controlled by the Fon, some of the old coastal states continued to flourish. By about 1780, Whydah was the main market for the whole lagoon traffic along the shore. Badagry also became active in business.

Westward, other lagoon markets did well at Grand and Little Popo. These had good defensive positions in their creeks and lagoons. They managed for the most part to escape from Dahomey's control. They

First day of the Yam Festival in Asante: see Chapter 18. (From a drawing made in 1819).

dealt largely in ivory. Here is an English description[1] of one of them at the end of the eighteenth century:

> The houses are well constructed, and generally two storeys high with stone steps. There is a good market with the most abundant supplies of stock of every kind, and many delicious fruits. The [people] and chiefs are respectful, honest, and desirous for trade. Ivory abounds here in endless quantities, being constantly sent from the inland towns.

By this time, in fact, the *Slave Coast*, as the seaboard of Dahomey was called by Europeans, had ceased to be a major centre for the export of slaves.

---

[1] That of Lieut. Edward Bold.

CHAPTER EIGHTEEN

The Akwamu, Asante and their neighbours

The Akwamu and their rivals

While the Fon kings of Dahomey were building their power and making ready to push their armies to the coast, other strong leaders were at work in the forest lands to the west, in the southern part of modern Ghana. Here there occurred a long struggle for power, trade and security among a number of enterprising peoples. Important among these were the Akwamu and the Denkyira, and afterwards the Asante.

The state of Akwamu took shape in the modern region of Akim Abuakwa, on both sides of the Birim River, during the late sixteenth or early seventeenth century. Traditions say that the Akwamu had previously lived at Twifu Heman north-west of Cape Coast. Their new state prospered by trade in the gold of the Birim River district, and in other goods. Towards 1650 it became strong enough to look round for allies and for lands to conquer. In this, again, we may see the effort of the men of those days to combine small states into big states.

For the king of Akwamu and his advisers the problem was no easy one. To west and north-west they faced the power of Akim and other

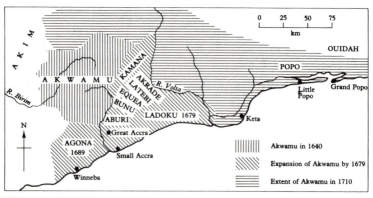

30 Stages in Akwamu expansion.

states that were allied with, or subject to, the state of Denkyira. There was danger from that direction. But to the south and south-west the position looked better for them. Here Akwamu was in contact with a group of little states — Aburi, Buni and others — which lay between Akwamu and the Ga and Fante towns and markets of the coast itself.

Now it was from these markets that Akwamu had to buy its guns, ammunition, and other foreign goods. To ensure the future of the state, the first need was to break through to the coast, subdue the Ga towns, especially Great Accra, and establish a direct trading partnership with the English, Dutch, and Danes. The Akwamu armies achieved this in 1677 under a strong leader whose name was Ansa Sasraku. In this the Akwamu set an example which the Fon of Dahomey would soon repeat to the east; and the Asante would soon repeat to the north-west.

Ansa Sasraku brought the Ga coast under his control between 1677 and 1681. He and his successors continued to expand their power and their trade. Helped by their trade with the Europeans, they enlarged their armies and sent them further afield. In 1679 they subdued the state of Ladoku east of Accra, and in 1689 the Fante state of Agona west of Accra.

These were big successes. The Ga towns of Great and Small Accra, for example, could raise an army of 9,000 men in 1646, and their power was not much smaller when Ansa Sasraku defeated them thirty years later. The Ga, however, were weakened by internal disputes. They split up after Akwamu's victory. Led by Ashangmo, successor to the more famous Okai Koi, some of them left their homes and went eastward to Little Popo on the Dahomey coast. But the majority remained where they were, opposing Akwamu when they got the chance and taking what aid they could from the commanders of the European forts.

There were now two big powers in the forest and coastland of modern Ghana: Denkyira in the south-west, and Akwamu in the south-east. Each sought allies. In this way Akim was generally the ally of Denkyira, while Asante, still small and weak, looked rather to Akwamu. Blocked by Denkyira and its allies on the west, Akwamu expanded eastward. In 1702 its armies crossed the Volta River and occupied some of the little states of the Dahomey coast, notably Whydah. In 1710 they went over the Volta again, and brought the Ewe of the Ho region under their general control. The Akwamu empire had now reached its greatest point of expansion. Its authority reached for more than 350 kilometres along the coast, and for some way into the inland country.

But this widespread power did not last. By 1710 Asante had become a strong state. Though friendly with Akwamu, Asante was hostile to Akim. Pushed and raided by Asante, groups of the three sections of the

Akim people, Kotoku, Bosome, and Abuakwa, pressed across the borders of Akwamu in search of a safer home. Every Akwamu king in the past had been worried by the threat from Akim. Now, with Akwamu's strength extended over so wide a territory, the threat became a very great danger. In 1730 there were many battles with the incoming Akim, who were mostly victorious. In a long war the Akwamuhene[1] was finally forced to flee. He led some of his people north-west across the Volta and settled there, while the remainder of Akwamu was divided among the Akim and their neighbours. Out of this war came the new Akan state of Akwapim.

After this defeat of Akwamu, the little city-states of the Dahomey coast became almost at once subject to the kings of the Fon. Westward from them, along the coast, the Ewe and the Ga regained much of their earlier freedom of action. Westward again, between Accra and Elmina, the peoples of the Fante group of states escaped from the overlordship of Akwamu only to fall, though not at once, under that of Asante. Elsewhere, Asante subdued Denkyira and won more victories.

Origins of the Asante empire

Of all the Akan peoples, the Asante were the most successful in bringing a large region of central Guinea under the control of a single government. They built an empire, much larger than that of the Akwamu or the Denkyira, and one that lasted much longer. This empire commanded the politics and trade of central Guinea for nearly two centuries.

Their capital at Kumasi grew into a large and bustling centre of political, commercial, intellectual and religious life. Here gathered men of action and men of thought: learned Muslims; chiefs and soldiers from the forest lands; envoys from many states; Dyula merchants from Bobo, Kong, and Jenne to the west and north; Hausa merchants from Kano, Katsina, and other eastern cities, together with Kanuri from Bornu.

Let us look ahead, for a moment, and see what Kumasi was like at the height of Asante power. A good description was written for the year 1817, when some English officials went there. They were greeted by nearly 5,000 people, most of whom were warriors, and by a great deal of military music. William Bowdich, who was one of the visitors, wrote:

> There was so much smoke from the firing of muskets shot off in welcome that we could see only what was near to us. . . We were

[1] Akwamuhene = king (*hene*) of Akwamu.

halted in the midst of a circle of warriors, where English, Dutch and Danish flags waved and flourished all around. . . The dress of the captains was a war cap, with gilded rams' horns projecting in front, the sides extended beyond all proportion by immense plumes of eagles' feathers. . .[and] they wore a vest of red cloth that was covered with charms in gold and silver, and loose cotton trousers with long boots of a dull red leather that came half-way up their thighs. . .

What we had seen on our way [coming from the coast to Kumasi] had made us expect something unusual. But we were still surprised by the extent and display of the scene which burst upon us here. An area of nearly a mile in circumference was crowded with magnificence and novelty. The king, his chiefs and captains, were splendidly dressed, and were surrounded by attendants of every kind. More than a hundred bands broke into music on our arrival. At least a hundred large umbrellas, each of which could shelter thirty persons, were sprung up and down by their bearers with a brilliant effect, being made in scarlet, yellow and the brightest cloths and silks, and crowned on top with [models of] crescents, pelicans, elephants, barrels, arms and swords of gold.

These English visitors of 1817 found the city of Kumasi much better than they had expected. 'Four of the principal streets,' one of them wrote afterwards, 'are half a mile long, and from fifty to a hundred yards wide. The streets are all named. There is a senior captain in charge of each of them. Every household burns its rubbish every morning at the back of the street, and the people are as clean and careful about the appearance of their houses as they are about their own appearance.'

What is the story of the state that could found and support so imposing a city?

At some time not long before and after 1600, groups of farmers began leaving the Adansi region, where they were then living, and moved some eighty or one hundred kilometres to the north. Scholars have suggested two main reasons for this movement or migration. Firstly, these farming groups wanted to find more land in which to cultivate their crops. Secondly, they wanted to win a share in the prosperous gold and kola trade which flourished to the north of them. Of these groups the most enterprising were the Oyoko clan; and they appear to have moved north soon after 1600.

They settled not far from a small lake called Bosomtwi in the country known as Amansie. There they cleared farms, gradually took the lead among their neighbours (who spoke Twi as they did), and built a town

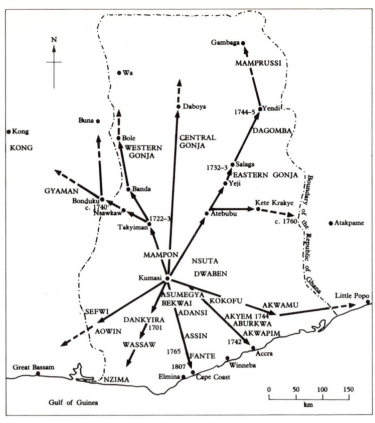

31 The expansion of the Asante empire.

called Asantemanso. They became active in the business of producing and selling gold and kola to merchants from the north as well as to merchants who came from the coast, and were joined by other groups from Adansi. They steadily grew stronger, and called themselves the Asante.

But they still had two big problems. They were subject to the powerful state of Denkyira, to whose ruler, the Denkyirahene, they had to pay tax and tribute in goods and slaves. They had serious rivals for land and trade in the Domaa, another Akan people who lived north-west of them. So long as these problems existed, the Asante could be neither very safe nor prosperous. And it was to solve these problems that they began to find ways of acting together. This happened soon after 1650.

At first their acting together was no more than a loose alliance of

240

The late Sir Osei Agyenan Prempeh II, the Asantehene.

different groups, Juaben, Kumawa, Nsuta, Bekwai, Mampong, and others, each of which had a little state of its own. They stood together when it suited them against their common overlord, the Denkyirahene, or against their rival, Domaa. They generally recognised a common leader, the best known of whom was Obiri Yeboa. But this loose alliance could not solve their problems. They needed to come still closer together so as to have the strength to become independent. This need led them, in about 1695, to an important *act of union.*

A kuduo from Asante, used as a container for gold dust.

This act of union was the work of two famous leaders, Osei Tutu and his friend and adviser, *Okomfo* Anokye (*okomfo* means priest). These two statesmen worked together to combine several neighbouring but separate Akan groups into a single strong union. They are said to have done this in about 1695 after Osei Tutu had been enstooled as ruler of the Asante. *Okomfo* Anokye declared that he had a mission from Nyame, supreme god of the Akan. Nyame, he declared, had ordered him to make the Asante into a great people. To spread this message the new Asante ruler, Osei Tutu, who was working closely with Anokye, called a vast assembly of people. At this gathering *Okomfo* Anokye 'brought down from the sky' a wooden stool that was partly covered in gold, causing this stool to come to rest on Osei Tutu's knees.

Having done this, *Okomfo* Anokye announced that the Golden Stool

Part of a gold necklace made by Asante craftsmen.

contained the soul or spirit of the whole Asante people. He told the chiefs and people that their power and health, bravery and welfare, were all symbolised in this Stool; and the chiefs and people accepted this. Osei Tutu then began to make laws for the Asante groups, who were thus welded into a union. Among the first of these laws was one of common citizenship, which forbade anyone to speak about any of the old *separate* histories of the now united groups. In this way the Asante acquired a *single* history about their past, and this single history was to act as a powerful means of keeping them united.[1]

The origins of the Asante, in short, are firmly linked in popular memory to a deliberate and highly successful act of statesmanship. This act achieved unity among Akan groups who were living side-by-side but governing themselves separately. When the Golden Stool 'came down

[1] The old separate histories were often remembered, but in secret.

243

from heaven', these groups gave up their separate governments and united under the single rule of Osei Tutu and his counsellors.

The Asante empire

Osei Tutu was enstooled as Asantehene, or king of Asante, in about 1695 after Obiri Yeboa had perished in battle against Domaa. He ruled until his death in about 1717 and was the first great builder of the Asante empire.

He began, as Professor Adu Boahen tells us, by reorganising the Asante army. He brought in

> the Akwamu military formation consisting of the Van (*Adonten*), the Rear (*Kyidom*), the Left (*Benkum*) and the Right (*Nifa*) wings. Each member state [in the Asante Union] was assigned a place in one of the wings, and each wing was placed under a commander who was at the same time the king of a state. Thus the Mamponghene was made the Krontihene or Commander-in-Chief of the Asante national army, the Esumengyahene and the Ejisuhene became the commanders of the Left and Right wings respectively, while Bekwai and Nsuta [two other states in the Union] were made members of the right and left wings. All the other *Aman* or states adopted this square military formation while they retained their places in one of the wings of the Asante army. If Osei Tutu borrowed this military organisation from the Akwamu, he and his successors certainly were able to develop it to an unprecedented peak of perfection and efficiency.[1]

Having built up his new forces, Osei Tutu turned first upon Domaa, avenged the earlier Asante defeat under Obiri Yeboa, and then got ready for the big struggle with Denkyira, ruled at that time by a king named Bosianti.

Denkyira was still the biggest power of all the country that lies in the south-western part of modern Ghana. This meant that Denkyira controlled the trade with Elmina castle; and Elmina at that time was the wealthiest market on the *Gold Coast*, the main source of European goods including guns, and the possession of the Dutch (who had taken it from the Portuguese in 1637). Needing guns and ammunition and other European goods, the Denkyirahene made much use of the Dutch at Elmina.

But in order to buy these guns and other goods the Denkyirahene, like

[1] A. Adu Boahen, *Topics in West African History*, London 1966, page 75.

244

other kings trading with the sea-merchants, had to pay for them in gold and slaves. He accordingly imposed heavy taxes, in gold and in captives, on his subject peoples. Among these subject peoples, as we have seen, were the Asante.

The Asante therefore had another strong reason for wanting to get the better of Denkyira. So long as they were separated from Elmina and other coastal markets by the power of Denkyira, they could never be sure of obtaining regular supplies of guns and other foreign goods. Yet war between Asante and Denkyira did not come at once. To begin with, Denkyirahene Bosianti tried to win Osei Tutu's friendship. Wisely preferring to negotiate rather than to embark on the risks and losses of war, he offered Osei Tutu compensation for past wrongs. He or his sub-chiefs even allowed Osei Tutu to buy guns from the Dutch at Elmina.

But Osei Tutu was not won over. Very strong in his own country, he was set on becoming independent of Denkyira. War broke out in 1699 when a new Denkyirahene, Ntim Gyakari, demanded from the Asante a larger tax than usual. By about 1701 the power of Denkyira was smashed, though at the outset of the war Asante was badly defeated. United as never before, the Asante then carried their war into the dominions of Denkyira. They brought most of these under their overlordship.

They captured much booty. But among the things they captured and brought home to Kumasi there was a piece of paper; and this piece of paper was important. For this was the rent agreement for Elmina castle. Signed originally by the Dutch with the coastal chiefs of Komenda, this Note, as it was called, had passed into the hands of the Denkyirahene when the chiefs of Komenda had fallen under his control.[1] From this time onwards, the Dutch at Elmina were in direct touch with Asante. The power of Asante, in other words, had reached the coast. This meant that it had also reached the Europeans in their seaside castles. Asante and these Europeans now faced each other directly, as friends or as enemies. Many important developments were to result from this.

Having defeated Denkyira and made most of its chiefs into his subjects, Osei Tutu turned his armies against the main ally of Denkyira. This was Akim, which had fought on Denkyira's side against Asante, and was even said to have lost as many as 30,000 soldiers in doing so. Osei Tutu marched against the Akim Kotoku, and made them pay tax to

---

[1] But the Ghana historian, K. Y. Daaku, has lately argued that Denkyira had never possessed the Elmina Note. He believes that the defeat of Denkyira simply caused the Dutch to go all out for good relations with Asante.

him. But the Akim armies did not give in easily. There had to be a second war against them.

This second war against Akim is said by the traditions to have been led by Osei Tutu, who was then killed by an Akim marksman while crossing the Pra River in 1731. But modern research in Ghana suggests that Osei Tutu really died in 1717; that the second war against Akim occurred in 1719; and that the name of the Asantehene who was killed on the Pra River was deliberately left out of the traditional records. These state, in any case, that the next Asantehene was Opoku Ware. He was probably enstooled in about 1720. He reigned for thirty years. Under this strong and very successful leader, the achievements of Osei Tutu and *Okomfo* Anokye were made firm and carried further.

Expansion and Reform

Opoku Ware's first big problem was a hostile alliance of the warriors of Denkyira, Sefwi and Akwapim, who all joined Akim in trying to crush the rising power of Asante. The allies failed in two harsh wars, during one of which an Akim army even took Kumasi and searched for gold in the royal graves.

But the union of the Golden Stool did not break down. Opoku Ware defeated the allies, and also brought the neighbouring states of Tekyiman, Banda, Gyaaman and Gonja on the Black Volta River under Asante rule. In 1744-45 he sent his armies into Dagomba, far to the north, and established Asante authority there as well, thus reinforcing his control of the trade routes to the Middle Niger. By the end of his reign, 'Asante was occupying an area much larger than modern Ghana'.[1]

Opoku Ware was followed by Kwasi Obodom, who reigned from about 1750 until 1764, when the royal stool was occupied by another outstanding ruler, Osei Kwadwo. King Osei Kwadwo strengthened the empire by military victories. More important, he introduced a number of political reforms designed to bring Asante government into line with the tasks and responsibilities of imperial conquest. These reforms consisted mainly of changes in the king's bureaucracy or civil service. They are important in the history of Asante. They are also a clear example of the way in which the growth of strong kingdoms led to an extension in the personal power of kings.

Up to Osei Kwadwo's time, men were appointed to positions of

---

[1] Boahen, page 76.

political power on the basis of *ascription*: that is, by inheriting this or that position of authority because they were members of leading descent-lines (descent, in this case, through mothers and not fathers). Now the empire had grown so large that new positions of authority were needed if the central government was going to be able to control its many distant provinces, as well as its many trading and military activities.

As in other strong kingdoms, Osei Kwadwo began to appoint chiefs on a new basis, that of *achievement*. He made it possible for men to become leaders not only because of their birth but also because of their devotion to the Asantehene, their courage in battle, or their skill in diplomacy and trade. In this way a new group of governors or commissioners came into existence, owing their promotion to merit and not to birth.

These political reforms, designed to strengthen the king's own power by increasing the number of officials who owed their appointment to royal favour and not to family inheritance, were carried further under Kings Osei Kwame (1777-1801) and Osei Bonsu (1801-24). Humble men could now win great positions in the state service. One such was Agyei, a salt-carrier in his youth, who rose under Osei Bonsu to be minister for foreign affairs. Another was Opoku Ferefere, who became the same king's representative in the empire's financial affairs.

These changes were accompanied by the adoption of new methods of ensuring peace inside the empire and the security of the king's power. This was done by raising a special force of police-troops, the Ankobia. They were always commanded by appointed officials and kept available in Kumasi, the capital, so as to be ready to deal with any revolt. Once again we may see how the growth in the personal power of kings led to the establishment of long-service troops who could defend the king and the 'king's men' (the new group of officials appointed by merit) from rebellion by hereditary chiefs (those who owed their positions to their birth).

These reforms were successful. They did not prevent many revolts by conquered provinces such as Gyaaman and Banda, whose peoples continued to desire their former independence.[1] But they gave the Asantehene a large number of fully reliable officials in every part of the empire. With these officials the king kept in touch, week by week and sometimes day by day, through a system of foot-messengers linking Kumasi to the outlying centres. Knowing what was going on, even in

---

[1] Gyaaman, for example, rebelled against Asante in 1752, 1764, 1799 and 1818, while Banda did the same in 1764 and 1818.

distant places, the Asante king could take preventive action in good time, and for this preventive action he had plenty of military strength. What weakened the Asante, later on, and brought the eventual downfall of this big empire, was the repeated clash with British invaders from the coast.

Yet for more than a hundred years the Asante dominated most of the country of modern Ghana, some of the inland country of the Ivory Coast, and parts of modern Togo. Here in central Guinea they succeeded in building another large and unified system of government and trade such as had existed earlier in the Western Sudan — under Ancient Ghana, Mali, Songhay, Kanem-Bornu — or in eastern Guinea under Benin and Oyo.

All the important rulers of West Africa recognised the strength and dignity of the Asantehene. Ambassadors went back and forth between them. Muslim clerks and teachers accompanied the Dyula and Hausa traders down the routes from Kano, Kong, Jenne and other states and cities of the Sudan. They were welcomed in Kumasi and other centres of the empire, and were invited into the service of the Asantehene and his government. In the nineteenth century, if not earlier, Muslim clerks were regularly employed to keep the records of the central government, and to conduct its official correspondence with foreign governments. Trade continually expanded. There were constant exchanges of ideas and information between Asante and other African states.

Asante, Fante and Britain

Southward along the coast of modern Ghana, the power of the Asantehene was well known to Europeans in their castles, and, through them, to the courts of European kings and the boardrooms of European and American banks and trading companies. But here in the south there were special developments which it will be useful to notice.

The Dutch and British in Ghana now became an important factor in African plans and policies. Denkyira, and then Asante, had made a trading partnership with the Dutch at Elmina and at one or two other forts. But the Asante and the Dutch were not the only partners in this business. There were also the Fante and the British.

Like the early chiefs of the Asante, those of the Fante, whose territory lay along the coast between Elmina and Accra, now came together in an alliance for their common good. Living near the sea, the Fante chiefs made a similar trading partnership with the British at Cape Coast and other castles. So there arose a second 'set of partners': the Fante made use of the British, just as the Asante made use of the Dutch. This soon brought Asante and the Fante chiefs into conflict. In 1806, after years of growing hostility, war started between them. It led to defeat of the Fante army at Abora.

Abora was not far from the shore. Pressing on after their victory, the Asante armies came right down to the water's edge. Their advanced guard occupied Kormantin and demanded the surrender of Fort Amsterdam, then held by their friends the Dutch, who at once gave in. The Asante generals next turned their attention to Anomabu, where the remnants of their Fante opponents had taken refuge under the walls of a British fort garrisoned by five officers and twenty men. These decided to help their Fante allies. The result was a battle for the fort itself.

In this way Asante and Britain came into conflict for the first time.

A gold pendant cast by the lost-wax method.

Later on, as British imperialism steadily took shape, hostilities like these were to break out time after time. But in 1806 peace was quickly made.

The fort held out against determined Asante efforts to storm its gun-defended walls, and both sides were glad to leave it at that. The British were far too weak to consider war against Asante, while the Asantehene, for his part, wanted only that the British, like other Europeans, should recognise his authority over this part of the *Gold Coast* shore. He was perfectly successful in obtaining this recognition. His armies again entered the coastal country in 1811 and 1814, destroyed the military alliance of the Fante, placed the Fante chiefs under Asante governors, and subdued Akim and Akwapim further to the east. As for the Europeans on the coast, by now consisting only of the British and the Dutch, they hastened to make their peace with the Asantehene. Not long afterwards, the Dutch left the coast altogether. By about 1820 the power of Asante was supreme.

Gonja, Kong, Bonduku

The story of the northern part of the modern Republic of the Ivory Coast is in many ways like that of the northern part of modern Ghana. Each had become linked with the expansion of inland trade since the expansion of the empire of Mali after about AD 1325.

We have seen how Dyula and other traders pushed their activities south towards the forest country, and how, after 1550, warrior groups from the north founded Gonja in northern Ghana. Much the same thing happened in the open country of the Ivory Coast. There is no doubt that strong trading centres existed in this country long before the founding of Gonja, notably at Kong and Bonduku. These trading centres gradually developed into self-governing towns which built themselves up into small states. They were mainly loyal to Islam, following the lead of their trading rulers; but of course they were also the product of inter-marriage and combination between Dyula traders and soldiers and the Senufu and other peoples who were already living in the land.

In the seventeenth century these little states became more highly organised. Gonja, established before 1600 in the northern part of modern Ghana, later expanded under a strong chief called Jakpa. Commander of a force of armoured cavalry, Jakpa came south from the region of Jenne, where he and his warriors had long been active in one way or another, and reached Gonja in about 1629. Not long afterwards, later in the seventeenth century, another warrior leader called Seku

Wattara likewise came south from the Masina region, along the Middle Niger, and invaded the little state of Kong, where he established himself as ruler. Strong in their cavalry, Seku and his successors brought the neighbouring countryside under their rule. Eager for a larger share in the gold and kola trade, they raided their neighbours. In 1725 they even marched as far north as the Niger at Segu, and attacked the Bambara ruler Mamari Kulibali.[1]

Kong remained an important state until the French colonial invasion of the last years of the nineteenth century. Bonduku, another key point on the trade route with the forest lands, had a somewhat different history. It was much influenced by its powerful neighbour, the Asante empire, and was placed under an Asante governor in the middle of the eighteenth century.

The Baulé and Anyi

The Baulé and Anyi of the southern Ivory Coast also belong to the history of the Akan. After the death of Opoku Ware in about 1750, there rose a dispute as to who should have the power. Sections of the Asante decided to leave home and seek fresh lands to the west. Some were commanded by a courageous woman called Awura Poku. She and her followers went away and settled in the country to the east of the Bandama River, which flows from the forestland of the modern republic of the Ivory Coast down to the ocean at Grand Lahou. The people whom they found in possession of the land they gradually pushed out, the Senufu to the north and the Guru to the west, although we may be sure that they also took wives and husbands from among these and other Ivory Coast peoples. These successive migrations from the Akan homeland formed the Baulé and Anyi during the eighteenth century.

Queen Poku died in about 1760 and was buried in her capital town of Warebo, which is near Bouaké. Her niece, Akwa Boni, followed her as queen of this Akan group, who now called themselves the Baulé. Under Akwa Boni, the Baulé took over the gold-bearing lands to the west of the Bandama region. Queen Akwa Boni died in about 1790. After that the unity of the Baulé was lost, because of quarrels between the heads of important families, and they never succeeded in creating the same close unity as their Akan relatives in the empire of Asante. Yet they continued to rule much of the southern Ivory Coast country until French colonial invasion at the end of the nineteenth century.

[1] See Chapter 20, page 265.

CHAPTER NINETEEN

Western Guinea in the seventeenth and eighteenth centuries

Most of the peoples of Western Guinea — that is, from the Ivory Coast to Senegambia — were variously influenced by new European trading opportunities after 1600. But the impact of expanding trade with Europeans was generally less important along the eastern (Liberian and Ivory Coast) sections of the coast than it was elsewhere.

The Kru and the Vai

There were several reasons why the sea-merchants came to this eastern part of the seaboard less frequently than elsewhere. They went to the Ghana coast rather than the Ivory Coast because they were attracted by the gold trade. They tended to avoid the coast of Liberia, and part of that of Sierra Leone, because the anchoring of sailing ships there could be difficult and dangerous.[1] To this simple picture, however, one must add two other points. The first is that neighbouring Sierra Leone had good harbours whether on the mainland or on islands near the shore; and these were used from the earliest time of European trade on the coast.

But there is a second important point in helping to explain why the Liberian coast in these two centuries remained unpopular with European sea-merchants. Here the principal people were the Kru. They were divided into two main groups, the Bete in the country of the Ivory Coast west of the Bandama River, and the Gueré who inhabited the seaside country of what afterwards became Liberia. Skilled with boats, the Kru

---

[1] The old sailing-ship captains had their own names for the Guinea coastline. These included:

The *windward Coast*, from about the Gambia River to Cape Palmas (eastern end of modern Liberia); and *The Leeward Coast*, east of Cape Palmas.

The main reason for these names was that the prevailing winds in this part of the Atlantic blow from the west or south-west, so that when sailors were on the western sections of the coast they thought of themselves as being to 'windward' (towards the wind), and when they were on the central and eastern sections of the coast they thought of themselves as being to 'leeward' (away from the wind).

Some of the *Windward Coast*, chiefly that of modern Liberia, was unfavourable to the safe anchoring of ships, and was little visited until the nineteenth century.

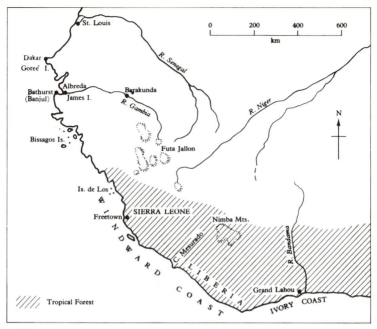

32 The coastline of the Ivory Coast, Liberia, Sierra Leone and Senegambia in the seventeenth century.

became valued as loaders and pilots and seamen for European captains, and they were also successful in the ivory trade. But they refused to deal in slaves, the commodity that the European sea-merchants wanted most of all. More than that, the Kru bought guns with the money they earned, and used these to defend themselves against slave-raiders. In this they were more fortunate than their western neighbours, the Vai, another enterprising people who tried the same tactics of self-defence for a long time, but were eventually driven into the slave trade as a means of getting the guns they needed.[1]

Interested in encouraging the ivory and gold trade, the Kru allowed the French to make a base at Grand Lahou, just outside their own country, in 1787. From here the French could tap the gold resources of the Akan country, and buy ivory from the Kru and other local peoples. As in Dahomey with other Europeans, and at some of the *Gold Coast* trading posts, the French were unable to extend their influence from Grand Lahou beyond the little fort they were permitted to build there.

[1] The Vai should also be mentioned as having invented their own local form of writing early in the nineteenth century.

253

Important changes came at the end of the eighteenth century, with the formation of ex-slave settlements in Sierra Leone and Liberia. Before that happened, however, there were many small states in this region. They had been formed in much earlier times and had built up political methods of their own. In the Sierra Leone region, for example, the real rulers of the country were the leading members of the special political and religious societies. The most important of these was called the Poro.

Sierra Leone and the Poro Association

Chapter 6 (*Senegambia before 1600*) has shown how strong little states of the Mende, Temne and others took shape in Sierra Leone as long ago as the expansion of the empire of Mali. These states had developed further by 1600, helped by the new ocean trade as well as their inland commerce. Some of them were monarchies, others were ruled by councils of chiefs. All of them shared with many other states, whether monarchies or not, a 'built-in' capacity to control the power of their rulers. We have seen how this worked, in segmentary societies, by balancing separate loyalties to individual family descent-lines with united loyalty to groups of families; and we have noted that this arrangement of 'checks and balances' on the use or abuse of power was always closely linked to religious beliefs.

Another method of 'checking and balancing' was the use of political associations. Sometimes these have been called 'secret societies'. But they were not secret. Only their ceremonies, meetings, and special equipment (such as masks) were secret: otherwise everyone knew about these associations, and, indeed, had to know about them. This method was much used by the peoples of Sierra Leone. They had many political associations for regulating the affairs of everyday life. Of these the most important was the Poro, an association which took shape several centuries ago. It was mainly through the Poro that these peoples ruled themselves. They used it to settle a wide variety of daily problems, and to control the power of their chiefs and kings.

The Poro had many branches and, as a method of self-rule, was especially useful to small communities of a few thousand people. Yet it would be a mistake to think that this method of government by political association was only fit for small communities. In many ways the Poro was like the much larger Ogboni association of the Yoruba, and there were times when several million Yoruba paid respect to Ogboni rules.

An essential point about the Poro, as about the Ogboni of the Yoruba or the Ekpe of the Cross River Efik, was that it linked religion with political controls. Every man had to join it if he was going to enjoy the respect of his neighbours. But he was permitted to join it only after going through a period of schooling. This usually took place when a boy was old enough to become a man, and was completed by the ceremony of circumcision. Poro schooling ensured that every man would understand the rules of good behaviour and would be able, in the measure of his talents or ability, to shoulder the responsibilities of grown-up life.[1] This did not mean that all members of the Poro had equal rights and duties. Though democratic in its membership, the Poro did not allow everyone to have a share of power. It gave power into the hands of chiefs and rich men who won it by seniority, or because they could pay the high fees which were needed to enter the senior grades of the Poro.

We have said, however, that the Poro was also an instrument by which 'checks and balances' were placed on the exercise of power. How could this be so if all effective power lay in the hands of chiefs and rich men? The answer lay in the religious side of the Poro. Its great authority rested on religious customs and beliefs. All men of power, in that age of faith, had to obey the moral and religious laws and regulations which were believed to have come from the ancestors and the gods.[2] The 'inner councils' of the Poro could not do as they liked. They had to obey the rules.

They acted in two main ways. At one level the 'inner councils' of senior elders looked after many everyday affairs such as traditional schooling, the control of local trade and market prices, political and military decisions, the administration of justice, and the providing of popular entertainments of dance and music. But they also operated at a higher and religious level. They were expected to look after the shrines of the ancestors, to make sure these shrines were properly used for prayer and ceremony, and generally to give ordinary people the assurance that all was well between them and the world of the spirits.

Did the various peoples who used the Poro work together? Historians are not agreed about this. Each people had its own Poro and its own 'inner council' of senior members. Sometimes there were states which grouped several Sierra Leone peoples together, and in these cases the 'inner councils' obviously did work together. Otherwise it seems that each 'inner council' had little contact with those of neighbouring peoples. What should in any case be noted here is that the Poro, like

---

[1] Women had a separate and parallel association, the Sande, with social powers but no political authority.
[2] See, for a further explanation, Chapter 12. *The value of religion*, page 163.

other such associations elsewhere, provided a skilful method, strong and yet flexible, of uniting communities behind common laws and rules; of confronting the problems of everyday life as well as answering the deeper questions of spiritual need; and, as the years passed, of adapting old ways of behaviour to new situations.

This was the complex political scene into which tens of thousands of Africans from other lands, released by the British navy from slave ships in the nineteenth century, were required to fit and build a new life for themselves. Out of this mixture of local inhabitants and of newcomers from other parts of Guinea and Congo there came the settlement of Freetown,[1] and afterwards the colony of Sierra Leone. This colony was the work of settlement during the nineteenth century; but, as its vivid history shows, it was also the work of the peoples already living in Sierra Leone, such as the Mende, Temne, and their neighbours.

Senegambia after 1600

Continuing westward from Sierra Leone, we find the same picture of local African enterprise and varying contact with the sea-merchants. But in Senegambia the contact was more frequent, and the trade more valuable, than along the seaboard of Liberia, of the Ivory Coast, or even of Sierra Leone; and the influence of the sea-merchants was therefore greater.

The British were especially interested in the Gambia River, rightly believing that this could prove a good channel for trade with the inland country. Along the banks of the Gambia they found hard-working people who were in touch with the inland peoples of the old kingdoms of Mali and the empire of the Wolof, and who also had little towns of their own.

An English captain[2] early in the seventeenth century described one of these Gambia towns, which he visited on a trading mission, as being strongly defended by a three metre fence. 'Inside the fence,' he wrote, 'they have built various rooms which are like little towers. From these they can shoot arrows and throw spears whenever they are attacked. Outside the fence, too, they have a deep trench which is very broad, and outside that again the whole town is encircled by posts and tree-trunks which are set fast in the ground and joined together, so as to make another fence about five-foot ($1\frac{1}{2}$ metres) high. Beyond that again they

---

[1] Where the first black settlers arrived from England in 1787.
[2] Richard Jobson in 1623.

256

have another fence like this. And the reason, they explained to me, is that they need these in order to defend themselves from the attack of cavalry' — from the raiding horsemen, that is, of the inland country.

This captain was impressed by the skills of the Gambians. He has left us a lively description that is useful not only for the Gambians, but also for many other folk along the coast, since it is quite certain that these same skills were practised elsewhere as well. Writing in 1623, he says that he found three main kinds of craftsmen among the Gambians: smiths who made weapons and metal tools; leather workers who made shoes, sandals and harness for horses; and clay workers who made many sorts of pots and also built clay-walled houses. But everyone, he adds, also worked at farming.

These Gambian trading states, ruled mainly by Mandinka kings, should be seen against a wider background. There were similar states along the neighbouring Casamance, Nunez and Geba Rivers, as well as in the Bissagos Islands. All these small states, ruling themselves by governments without kings or by governments with kings of little power, were similarly interested in trade, whether with the inland country or the sea-merchants. Notable among them, for example, were the Diola producers of wax and rice. Linking them were Mandinka-Dyula traders who were afterwards joined by a number of Portuguese mulattoes. Though in some ways less developed than the city-states of the Niger Delta, these 'western rivers' states were of much the same type. They were called into existence by a mixture of local political need and of response to the long-distance trade.

The Gambia

The estuary and lower reaches of the Gambia River have a special history of their own, because it was here that Europeans found particularly favourable trading opportunities, and safe anchoring ground for their ships. The first of them to make a regular base in the Gambia after 1600 were agents of the Duke of Courland, the ruler of a small German state on the southern shore of the Baltic Sea in north-eastern Europe. The Germans built a small fort in 1651 on what was later named James Island. After many disputes, in which the French and the Dutch also took a hand, the British Royal African Company seized this fort in 1661 from a Courland garrison reduced to seven men and two women. Twenty years later the French African Company acquired a foothold on the north bank of the Gambia, opposite James Island, at Albreda; and

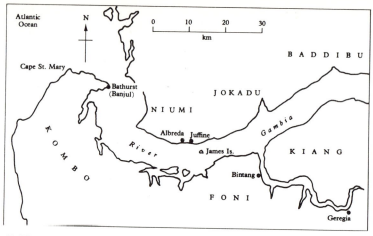

33 The estuary and lower reaches of the Gambia River.

for many years an uneasy peace then reigned between the agents of these rival companies.[1]

The eighteenth century was filled with wars between the British and the French, fighting each other for supremacy at sea; and most of these forts and trading states of Western Guinea changed hands several times. After the middle of the century the British became the stronger, and were able to base themselves at St Louis in the Senegal River as well as on James Island in the Gambia River. This introduced an early experiment in Crown Colony government on the lines of the British colonies in North America. In 1765 this coast between the Senegal and the Gambia was declared the British *Province of Senegambia*. Its governor lived at St Louis, with a second-in-command on James Island.

Yet this early and foreign attempt at uniting Senegal and The Gambia proved far from stable. In 1778 the French hit back. They seized James

---

[1] These companies were the outcome of new mercantile methods in Britain, Holland and France during the seventeenth century. They were corporations of merchants founded with government backing. Most of them went bankrupt in their early years, mainly because they had to deal in barter on the African coast: they had to exchange, that is, so and so many European goods for so and so many African goods.

Without a common money between the two sides, the companies found it hard to calculate how to make a profit. Later on, they invented a 'unit of exchange' called the 'trade ounce'. The value of this 'ounce', in terms of goods bought in Europe for the African trade, was usually fixed at double the cost of these goods in gold. This hundred per cent 'mark up' enabled the companies, as well as private merchants operating on their own, to make good profits in spite of losses by shipwreck and other causes.

The most important companies for Senegambia were the British Royal African Company, launched in 1661, and the French Compagnie du Sénégal founded in 1673.

258

Island and pulled down its fort. A year later the British retook James Island, but not St Louis. A peace settlement in 1783 confirmed this division of power, and the Province of Senegambia was abolished. After that there came a period of peace with The Gambia left to its own devices, until the British campaign to end the slave trade became important after 1807.

Renewed British interest in The Gambia, as a centre for the repression of the slave trade and a starting point for exploration of the Western Sudan, finally led to a lasting British establishment in 1816. This time the British made no attempt to restore their old base of James Island. They secured a new base on St Mary's Island, near the mouth of the river on the south bank, and renamed it Bathurst, the settlement which was later to become Banjul, the capital city of The Gambia.

Results of European presence

These European quarrels and changes did not have much importance for the Africans of Senegambia. They continued to trade with the European forts and warehouses, and it did not matter to the Africans if these were French, British, Dutch or Portuguese. Only much later, during the rise of European colonialism in the second half of the nineteenth century, did these coastal bases offer a serious threat to African independence. Then they became the bases for European colonial invasions.

Yet European trading presence along the seaboard had, as a whole, two important results for Senegambians. One was that it enlarged the power of the states near the coast at the expense of the inland states. This, as we have noted in the case of Cayor,[1] changed the balance of power and helped to undermine the old authority of the *Burba* Jolof. Thus in 1786 the *Damel* of Cayor was able to bring neighbouring Baol under his control, and to defeat the ruler of Futa Toro, the *Almamy* Abdelkader.[2] At the same time the people of the Cape Verde peninsular began their effort to throw off the overlordship of Cayor. In this they succeeded in 1810, when they formed a federation under the presidency of the chief of Dakar, a man whom they elected from the Diop family. In 1857 the French took possession of the peninsular as part of their drive for the conquest of Senegal. So that while the years of coastal trading

---

[1] See Chapter 6, *Rivals to Jolof, the rise of Cayor*, pages 58-59.
[2] See Chapter 20, *The western imamates*, pages 269-271. The Futa Toro had come under Muslim rulers after defeat of the last Denianke king in 1776.

benefited the coastal states, they also helped to open the gates to European invasion.

A second important result of European presence was in local expansion of the slave trade. It developed here in the same way as elsewhere. Local kings and rich merchants went into partnership with Europeans at the expense of the mass of ordinary folk. If they refused to sell captives from their own peoples, they proved very willing to go to war for captives from neighbouring peoples, or to buy captives from the traders of the Western Sudan. Some kings regretted this when they saw the damage to village life. But once the slave trade had begun, it proved very difficult to stop. If one king refused to make captives and sell them, another could always be found who would agree.[1] Kings found it more and more difficult to draw back, because they feared to deprive themselves of guns and gun powder. These could be bought only from Europeans, but Europeans would sell them only in exchange for captives.

By the end of the eighteenth century the kings of the Gambia River region were exporting more than 3,000 captives every year. Only the Europeans, it was found, could end the evil which they themselves had first created. This was to be among the tasks of the nineteenth century.

[1] For a Senegalese example, see Chapter 22, *Resistance to the slave trade*, page 287.

CHAPTER TWENTY
New states in the Western Sudan: Bambara, Fulani

Disorder and revival

As in the coastal regions of West Africa, great changes occurred in the Western Sudan during the seventeenth and eighteenth centuries.

Firstly, there came a decline of the big market cities such as Gao and Timbuktu.

This was partly the result of the Moroccan invasion of Songhay (1591). Law and order broke down across wide regions. Trade suffered. Some of the old market cities became quite unimportant, and today are almost forgotten.

Timbuktu was hard hit; Gao even worse. Such was the danger from the invaders that Gao is said to have been emptied of its inhabitants. Some were killed, many fled. And as Gao fell into ruin, there was nobody to look after the farms around it. Much careful irrigation, of water-supply by canals and ditches, became useless.

Secondly, as the power of the people of the towns or cities got smaller, the power of the peoples of the countryside and villages got larger. New states were built by the peoples of the countryside. Mostly, these states were not Muslim. Sometimes they were anti-Muslim, because they were built by people who felt that the people of the Muslim cities were their enemies.

Thirdly, the seventeenth century was also a time when professional armies became bigger, and got many more guns. The new states tended to be ruled, more and more, by men whose power rested on their armies. These armies became more destructive.

Fourthly, the eighteenth century, about 1700 to 1800, was generally a time of revival. Trade improved again: trade inside West Africa, but also trade across the Sahara. The disorders of the previous century began to be tackled, and at least partly ended, by new ways of government.

These new ways were part of a revival of Islam. They were invented, especially, by some Fulani groups. They led to what historians have called the Fulani Reforming Movement.

We look at these changes one by one.

Destruction of Songhay

Judar Pasha and his Moroccan army of musket-carrying soldiers seized the central area of the Songhay empire in 1591 when they captured the cities of Timbuktu, Gao and Jenne.

But the Songhay leaders did not give in. Defeated whenever they tried a big battle against the Moroccans, they fell back on guerrilla tactics. From their stronghold in Dendi, the southerly part of the old empire, they fought back in this way for more than half a century. In 1608, for example, the Dendi *hi koy*, or admiral of the Songhay fleet of war-canoes on the Niger, attacked Moroccan garrisons along the whole middle course of the river. A year later the Dendi *fari bar*, a leading Songhay general, carried out a very tough raiding march across the wide belt of land enclosed by the bend of the Middle Niger, and attacked the Moroccans who were then in occupation of Jenne. Other Songhay units followed this surprise assault by a series of guerrilla operations against Moroccan garrisons west of Timbuktu.

Hostilities of this kind continued until about 1660. They did nothing to restore Songhay: on the contrary, they only added to the ruin of this once prosperous country. By about 1650, Songhay was reduced to a weak group of little states in the south-eastern part of the old empire.

It was not so much the strength of the Moroccans that prevented the restoring of Songhay, as the total collapse of the empire once its central power was weakened. That system, as we have noted, had rested largely on the strength and prosperity of the cities; and this strength and prosperity of the cities had relied, in turn, largely on the subjection or enslavement of many peoples of the countryside. For them the Moroccan invasion was a chance of freedom. They seized it eagerly.

Many subject or 'slave' peoples or groups of peoples, of whom the largest were called the Doghorani, rose in revolt against their masters. They fought for their own interests, and these interests were in direct opposition to the restoring of Songhay.

With their central government destroyed and their armies smashed, the Songhay chiefs and generals faced not only the Moroccans, but many of their own subjects as well. Only a widely popular war against the invaders could have restored Songhay; but no such war was possible.

Middle Niger cities: the Tuareg

Early in the seventeenth century the rulers of Morocco began to tire of

Nomads of Mauretania.

their Songhay adventure. It had brought them much wealth in gold and other goods, but not as much as they had expected; and it had cost them dear. The Moroccan ruler, Sultan Mulay Zidan, successor of Sultan Mulay the Victorious, complained that as many as 23,000 Moroccan soldiers had died in this effort at conquest. Although he had taken the title of King of Gao, Timbuktu and Jenne, the Moroccan king decided to stop reinforcing his garrisons in those cities. These had conquered the Songhay suppliers of gold, but failed to reach the Akan sources of supply. The Akan, now trading with Europeans along the coast, began reducing their deliveries to the north.

After 1621 these cities along the Middle Niger were left to the rule of locally-recruited governors, called *pashas*, who offered no more than a feeble defence of the cities and nearby lands they were supposed to protect. These *pashas* and their soldiers intermarried with the local population. They gave birth to a group of Timbuktu people who were partly Moroccan in origin, and were called the *arma*. By 1700 the *arma* had little power left to them.

Timbuktu and Jenne became the target for attacks from the Bambara in the west.[1] But they and Gao also became targets for an old enemy, the

---

[1] See next section.

raiding warriors of the Saharan Tuareg. In about 1680 a section of the Tuareg, called the Wulliminden, seized Gao and made a camp there. From this base they turned westward up the Niger, warring continually with the defenders of Timbuktu. By 1720 the Wulliminden and Tadmekkei Tuareg had won control of much of the Middle Niger country, and in 1737 the Wulliminden actually captured Timbuktu for a time and made the local pashas pay them tribute. In about 1770 they made a permanent settlement at Gao.

These Tuareg were not, of course, only raiders. They were also interested in the trans-Saharan trade. They set about trying to restore it. They were not very successful in this, partly because they were so often at war with the peoples of the Niger country, and partly because these people were so often at war with each other. But it would be wrong to think that the trans-Saharan trade disappeared. On the contrary, in spite of all the dangers and obstacles, traders found ways of carrying on their business. In 1635, for example, some English merchants in Morocco were able to tell their partners in London that they were sending many English goods by camel-caravan to Timbuktu, Gao and other parts of West Africa, and were buying in exchange a lot of West African gold. Yet the great days of the gold trade across the desert were over.[1]

Bambara states: Segu and Kaarta

Among the country people who now began to raise their heads in the country of the Middle and Upper Niger were members of many different West African peoples who had lived here under various empires in the past. Some, like the Soninke or Sarakolle, were descendants of people who had lived in Ancient Ghana. Others, who belonged to the large and various Mande or Mandinka language-family, had been loyal to Ancient Mali. Others again, like the Dogon, had lived on the edge of these old empires. Spread among them in groups of varying size were the Fulani.

In the troubles that followed the destruction of Songhay, some of these peoples began to seek new fortunes of their own. Foremost among them were the Bambara. Under energetic leaders, the Bambara now built a small but strong state that was based on the Niger market-town of Segu and its surrounding lands. Somewhat later they built a second state that was based on the countryside of Kaarta to the north-west of Segu.

The traditions say that the Bambara state of Segu was founded by two

---

[1] See also pages 207-208.

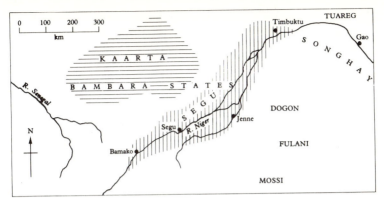

34 *The Bambara states.*

brothers, called Barama Ngolo and Nia Ngolo, soon after 1600. These two men were possibly at first little more than leaders of a well-organised band of raiders from the countryside. They took advantage of the confusion of the times in order to enrich themselves at the expense of their neighbours, building what the merchants of the cities no doubt regarded as a robber gang. But success brought them bigger and better ideas. Under their Ngolo chiefs, these hard-riding Bambara farmers settled down and formed their own system of law and order.

We do not know exactly how they did this. Towards 1650, however, they were established in the Segu region, mainly on the south bank of the Niger. They were led by an energetic chief called Kaladian. He seems to have ruled them until about 1680, and to have extended Bambara authority over a wide region of this central country of the Western Sudan. This empire included for a while the city of Timbuktu.

Mamari Kulibali and Ngolo Diara

Kaladian's empire fell apart with his death. The next big figure in this region, the famous Mamari Kulibali — Mamari the *Tiguiton* or *Biton*, Mamari the Commander — began his career with no more than a handful of followers. He reigned from about 1712 to 1755, and was the true founder of Segu. He defeated his Bambara rivals soon after 1712, fought off an attack by the king of Kong in about 1730, drove out another set of Bambara rivals a few years later, and left his successors with a fair-sized state.

The Bambara rivals whom Mamari drove out of the Segu region, in

265

about 1753, moved some three hundred kilometres to the north-west. There they founded a second Bambara state in Kaarta. This was the region where Kumbi, the capital of Ancient Ghana, had once flourished.

These two states dominated the country of the middle Niger until late in the nineteenth century.

Segu was always the stronger of the two. Under Mamari Kulibali it included the river country from the neighbourhood of modern Bamako all the way downstream to Timbuktu, together with the trading city of Jenne and markets along the river itself.

Mamari built his power according to the methods of the Songhay emperors after *Sunni* Ali. He relied on long-service soldiers and sailors. He formed a professional army many thousands strong, and also a professional navy on the Niger, from war-prisoners. These prisoners, reduced to a type of slavery, became regular soldiers and canoe-men. With these troops Mamari defeated all his rivals and neighbours — Soninke, Fulani, Malinke, Mossi and others.

Yet in building this military power, Mamari also created rivals for power. After his death in about 1755, events took a new turn. His son Dekoro became king of Segu, but had ruled for less than two years when the commanders of the soldiers took over. According to the traditions, King Dekoro was killed by the professional soldiers, bound together as they were in their condition of being a caste or group of 'slaves'. Then the king's power was taken by the *Ton-Mansa*, or 'commander of the slaves', who was the senior army general.

But this *Ton-Mansa*, like other ambitious generals then and since, fell victim to his own methods. He set an example which others could repeat. Three years later the soldiers killed him too, and elected in his place another general called Kaniuba Niuma, Kaniuba the Handsome, who was commander of the cavalry at Segu.

Kaniuba's reign was likewise no more than three years. Then the soldiers overthrew him in his turn and elected yet another king, Kafa Diugu, from among their number. Only in about 1766 did this disorderly soldier's rule come to an end. Then an outstanding leader called Ngolo Diara seized the throne. Ngolo Diara reigned for more than thirty years, put an end to the soldiers' political plots and plans, and restored the state of Segu to its former position of power.

Segu under King Ngolo became a large and busy city. In 1796, two years after Ngolo's death, the Scottish traveller, Mungo Park, the first European to come this way, estimated that Segu contained as many as 30,000 people. He found them living in four closely adjoining towns which consisted of clay-built houses with flat roofs, sometimes of two storeys. Segu's prosperity and size greatly impressed Park. 'The view of this extensive city,' he wrote, 'the numerous canoes upon the river, the crowded population, and the cultivated state of the surrounding countryside, formed altogether a prospect of civilization and magnificence, which I little expected to find in the centre of Africa.'

Under King Ngolo, the skilful Bambara farmers of the middle Niger countryside once again enjoyed the security and safe markets they had known in the days of Mamari the Commander.

The Fulani reforming movement

The Bambara states of Segu and Kaarta were a part of the political recovery in the Western Sudan after the collapse of Songhay and the final decline of Mali. But they were not the only part. Another of great importance was the rise of a new set of states under Fulani leaders, and, combined with this, a renewed effort to strengthen the powers and the ideas of Islam.

Most of the Fulani, as we have seen in earlier pages, were cattle-breeders who followed a wandering way of life. Now and then, linked with other peoples, some of them had settled down and grown used to living in towns. Mixed with Mandinka allies, the Fulani of Takrur had done this in the middle of the sixteenth century.[1]

Other groups of Fulani had also done the same, and, in doing so, had likewise changed their methods of government. Living in one place for long periods, they had accepted the authority of some of their ruling families; and these families regularly elected men to rule them as chiefs. In this, of course, they behaved like many other wandering peoples who had settled down and found that they needed chosen men to rule over them. Many Fulani ruling families now took part in a movement for Muslim revival. Unlike the Bambara leaders and their people, these Fulani became devoted Muslims.

Historians differ on the exact reasons for this. Broadly, however, we can see in this Fulani acceptance of Islam the same kind of motives as had inspired earlier kings and peoples in the Western Sudan. Islam's unified system of ideas about religion, law and order, and trading customs, could be valuable to men who suffered from the confusion of the times, for it promised a way of overcoming conflicts and rivalries. And many men undoubtedly remembered how the empires of Mali and

---

[1] See Chapter 6, *Tenguella Koli and the Denianke*, pages 60-62.

Songhay had become strong under Muslim rule, or at least under Muslim influence.

Among the Fulani their new faith had a revolutionary effect. First, it gave them a new unity among themselves. Secondly, it brought them into touch with the whole current of Muslim thought, whether from West Africa, from Egypt, or within the Western Sudan itself, and made them think about international questions as well as local questions. In this way they acquired new ambitions. There emerged what we may call the Fulani Reforming Movement. At its best, this held out a common vision and idea of how men should behave and live together, and of what men should strive to do for the betterment of life.

This new vision and idea wanted to revive the power and law of Islam throughout the Western Sudan. Of course, this ambition did not take shape quickly or all at once. Little by little, Fulani leaders gathered warrior bands. They began to set up new states in the countries where they lived, in those same countries which had suffered so many troubles since the decline of Mali and the ruin of Songhay.

We should note two important points. One point is that although this Muslim revival was often the work of Fulani people (or their close relations, the Tucolor), these were by no means alone. Others also took part. Among these the most important were the Mandinka, whose ancestors had built the empire of Mali, and whose traders, the Dyula, had done so much for the trade of West Africa. The Mandinka will generally have understood, far better than the Fulani, how to revive trade and why it was necessary to build up the strength of the market-cities once again. They had more trading experience.

Another point to remember is that this reforming movement was a complicated process. Much good came out of it; but also much misery. In the minds of the best of the reformers, the intention was to open a new period of social justice, security for all men who accepted Islam, and prosperity by trade. The whole of the Western Sudan should come within the *Dar al-Islam*, the home of Islam, the place where men obeyed the rules of Allah and lived at peace together. But it did not work out like this.

A great deal of progress was made in several ways; in trade and education, and in the spread of law and order. The Western Sudan regained its international connections. Muslim scholars once more travelled from capital to capital, including some who came from distant lands outside West Africa. Yet this progress was purchased at a bitter cost to many non-Muslim peoples who were raided, plundered, or turned into slaves. Later, in the nineteenth century, there were increasing wars; and not a few of these wars were the work of kings and warriors

The top of a state umbrella from Akwapim.

who used their devotion to Islam simply as a cover for seeking loot and privilege.

In the eighteenth century, however, the changes were impressive in a number of new states.

The western imamates

The first of these reforming states, of these Fulani-led states of Muslim revival, was the imamate of Futa Jallon. We call it an imamate because it was ruled by an *almamy* or *imam* of Islam. It lay in the hillside country that is now in the central part of the modern Republic of Guinea. Muslim reformers of the Fulani — *Mujaddadin*, 'revivers of Islam'[1] — together with allied groups of Mandinka and other local peoples, founded this state in about 1725. They subdued the non-Muslim farmers who were living in the neighbourhood, members of a branch of the Mandinka language-family called Dialonke.

This was a state of a new kind. It was organised in nine provinces (*diwal*) and many sub-districts (*miside*), and its political power was wielded by a religious leader, the *almamy*, while its military power,

---

[1] *Mujaddadin,* revivers of Islam, must be distinguished from *Mujahiddin,* warriors of Islam.

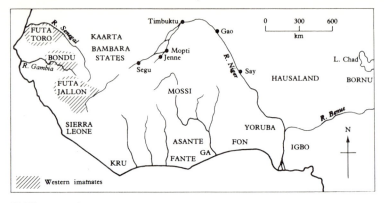

35 The western imamates.

commanded by the *almamy*, was based on a strict system of compulsory service. But the imamate of Futa Jallon was not simply a dictatorship of religious leaders. It retained many traditional features of West African political life. These included a measure of democracy. The *almamy* was very powerful, and claimed to rule in the name of God. But he still had to listen to the opinions of his counsellors; and these counsellors, at least when they were good men, spoke up for the complaints and needs of ordinary people.

Yet the part of democracy grew less with time. A new *almamy* was chosen every two years, at least after 1800; but the election was always from one of two ruling families, the Alfa or the Sori. With this narrow method of choosing their ruler, the leading families won more and more privilege and wealth. In the nineteenth century this was to lead to many revolts and changes. Here we need only note that the imamate of Futa Jallon, strong in its defensive hills, survived more or less intact until French colonial invasion.

A second imamate was formed in Futa Toro, in the land of old Takrur far to the west, among the northern neighbours of the Wolof. Here along the south bank of the Senegal River the Denianke kings had ruled since the Fulani-Mandinka invasion of 1559. Yet here too the influence of Islam had remained alive, though the Denianke kings were not Muslims; and Islam now acquired new power. In the 1770s there arrived in Futa Toro a group of Muslim reformers. They belonged to the clan of the Torodbe, and were led by a famous marabout, or religious leader, called Suleiman Ba. This *almamy* or *imam* defeated the ruling *silatigui* (a Mande word which means 'commander', and was the title of the Denianke rulers) at a decisive battle in 1776. The Torodbe then formed the imamate of Futa Toro. They ruled it severely and owned or

270

controlled all the fertile land. But they also gave peace to the people of Futa Toro, and introduced Muslim schools for children. Later, when these Torodbe grew more numerous and so became short of land, they began to take themselves and their ideas about government and religion to other parts of the Sudan.

The Torodbe belonged to the Tucolor, a West African people closely related to the Fulani. Once established in Futa Toro, they began to expand the trade with French merchants who came up the Senegal River, as well as with other Muslim centres of trade in the western region of the Western Sudan. They gave attention to Muslim learning and founded many schools for teaching the laws of Islam although, like their Fulani neighbours, their belief in Islam was combined with many ideas drawn from traditional customs. This included a great reverence for 'holy men' or marabouts who were supposed to possess magical powers, an aspect of life in that part of West Africa (as in some other parts) which may still be observed today.

A third new Muslim state, or *imamate*, was founded by another Fulani group soon after 1770 in the region of Bondu, lying between Futa Toro and Futa Jallon. The Scottish traveller Mungo Park, who passed through Bondu in 1795, has left us a good description of the country. He found it prosperous and at peace, though threatened by many dangers. The king, who lived in a set of clay-built houses surrounded by a high wall, received him hospitably and introduced him to his wives, who found their first sight of a European very surprising.[1] Park also found Bondu well provided with village schools, and visited many of them. He thought the children very well behaved and attentive. The cattle-breeders of the countryside, he observed, were quite wealthy, 'and enjoy the necessaries of life in a high degree'.

Importance of the imamate states

Summing up, what must be remembered about these states?
1 They were the first new states to appear after the times of trouble and confusion in the Western Sudan that had occurred during the seventeenth century.
2 They were a new kind of Muslim state. Inside them, many people of the countryside also accepted Islam, as well as the townspeople.

[1] They teased him good-humouredly about the whiteness of his skin and the size of his nose, saying that both were artificial. 'The first, they jokingly said, was produced when I was an infant, by dipping me in milk; and they insisted that my nose had been pinched every day till it had acquired its present unsightly and unnatural conformation.'

3 Their leaders gave an example to other Muslim leaders on the way to build new states. This teaching led, after 1800, to the formation of more Muslim states of a new kind.

4 They were ruled by leaders who had power for religious reasons, as well as political and military reasons. That was like the old states and empires of the Western Sudan or of the Guinea region. The difference was that these new states were ruled by strict Muslim customs.

They were also ruled by men who believed, much more strongly than Muslim leaders in the past, that their duty was to spread Islam, if necessary by war. They taught the duty of *jihad*, or holy war against non-Muslims. After 1800, the Western Sudan was to be the scene of many such wars.

A traveller's story

What was it like to travel in those days? Mungo Park met with difficulties through the actions of some of the kings through whose lands he travelled — not surprisingly, for he reached them through the territories of rival kings, and was easily suspected of being a spy. But he met with much kindness from ordinary people, and one of his stories about this deserves telling here.

Arriving at Segu for the first time, he had to wait on the bank of the Niger opposite that large and prosperous city, while the king of Segu decided whether or not to let him go across. He was hungry and alone. At sunset, while he was sitting under a tree and wondering whether he would ever see his own homeland again, a woman who had been working in the fields came up and spoke to him. She asked him why he looked so sad and tired. When he explained, 'she took up my saddle and bridle, and with looks of great pity, asked me to follow her'. Leading him to her hut, she lit a lamp and spread a mat upon the floor, and told him that he should rest there until the next day. Meanwhile she would find him some food.

In a little while, Park wrote afterwards, this kindly and hospitable woman returned with well prepared fish, which she baked on the embers of her fire and gave him to eat. After this she told the other women members of her family to go on with their spinning, and they worked through most of the night. While they were spinning, they made a song about their hungry visitor. This song 'was sung by one of the young women, the rest joining in a sort of chorus'. The words, Park tells us, went something like this: 'The winds roared and the rains fell, the poor white man, faint and weary, came and sat under our tree. He has no mother to bring him milk, no wife to grind his corn. Let us pity the poor white man: no mother has he. . .'

This moving little story shows once again how false an impression may be given by the bare record of events. Wars and quarrels between leaders, the rise and fall of states and kings and generals: all this can suggest that life was one long tale of violence. But in times of peace it was not like that; and times of peace were more frequent than times of war.

The eastward spread of Muslim reform

While these three new Muslim states were taking shape in the west, others of a similar kind began to appear further eastward. Here, too, formerly subject peoples made new states of their own; and here, too, the Fulani and their allies played a leading part.

Some of these Fulani lived in the Masina plains which lie in the neighbourhood of the Niger market-town of Mopti. Like their Bambara neighbours, with whom they were sometimes on good terms and sometimes on bad terms, they made a bid for independence. In about 1629 their chiefs, the Ardo, who were not yet converted to Islam, broke away from the overlordship of the Moroccan *pasha* or governor of Timbuktu, allied themselves with the Songhay of Dendi, southernmost province of the old Songhay empire, and waged war on every Moroccan or part-Moroccan garrison they could reach. Afterwards, they became subject to the overlordship of the rising power of Segu. Much later, in the nineteenth century, Muslim Fulani in these Masina plains built an empire of their own.

Further eastward again, beyond the Masina plains, other Fulani groups established themselves on the plains to the south-west of Gao. There, too, they were able to set up a little state of their own.

Other groups went on down the banks of the Niger. Not long before 1800 the religious leader of some of these, a marabout called Alfa Muhammad Diobo, founded the town of Say, not far from modern Niamey, which is the capital of the Niger Republic today. Alfa Muhammad's idea was to make Say into a centre for Muslim revival.

With the foundation of Say, as a glance at the map on page 270 will show, by 1800 the Muslim revival movement had moved right across the Western Sudan as far as the borders of Hausaland.

CHAPTER TWENTY-ONE

Hausaland and Bornu in the seventeenth and eighteenth centuries

Hausa developments: rise of the 'king's men'

We have seen in Chapter 9 how the sixteenth century brought wealth to Hausaland, but also wars and raids by envious neighbours. This contradictory situation went on in later times.

The collapse of Songhay was not a disaster here. On the contrary, it relieved the western Hausa states of the danger of invasion by Songhay armies, for these were now fully occupied against the Moroccans, and in any case were far weaker than the conquering Songhay forces of the days of *Askia* Muhammad the Great (1493-1528).

Many Hausa communities prospered increasingly from their farming, handicraft industry (especially cotton weaving), and enterprise in trade. But this prosperity was also reduced by the failure of the Hausa kings and ruling groups to unite among themselves. They had never been able to unite in the past. They were not able to do so now. This failure to unite was an obstacle to progress, for it meant that a great deal of effort went into wars and raids between Hausa communities.

These Hausa states continued the political development of earlier times.[1] Power began to be shared between people of noble families and people of ordinary families. The kings gave some of their power to people of ordinary families, to 'commoners' or 'king's men', so as to lessen the power of the nobles. This helped the Hausa kings to strengthen their own positions, which were often threatened by powerful nobles. So there developed here, as we shall see, another kind of 'constitutional monarchy': of rule, that is, by kings whose power is limited by political rules.

In all the principal Hausa states — Daura, Gobir, Kano, Katsina, Zaria (Zazzau) and some others — the power of the kings was kept secure by this appointment of 'king's men', and by the increased dividing of society into different groups or classes. In the eighteenth century there were four main divisions in Hausa society. *Firstly*, at the

---

[1] See Chapter 9, *Origins of the Hausa states* and *The Hausa achievement*, pages 105-108.

top of the ladder of power and wealth, there were members of the king's own descent-line, 'big families', and of other leading descent-lines. *Secondly*, there were freemen who had the right to cultivate land. *Thirdly*, there were the special group of 'king's men', many of them eunuchs, who were recruited from certain villages and who served in the king's government, often in posts of much power. *Fourthly*, there were unfree men who had no political rights. As well as all these, there were the educated freemen, the *mallams*, who acted as religious leaders but were debarred from holding political jobs or from owning big farms.

Out of this structure of different groups, of 'layers', there arose this constitutional monarchy of the Hausa kings. The king himself had a great deal of personal power. But he was able to act in important matters only with the agreement of his senior chiefs and officials. In securing this agreement, however, the king had one great advantage. The senior chiefs and officials were seldom or never united against him. On the contrary, they were carefully balanced against each other in two groups. In one group were the chiefs of leading 'big families' who held their positions by right of birth, while the other group consisted of the 'king's men'. Members of the first group might plot to overturn the king and win power for themselves. But in this they were opposed by members of the second group, who could not hold power outside their appointed jobs because they were of slave origin or were eunuchs. A clever Hausa king could play off one group against the other.

Consider an example from Zaria in those times. Here there were two leading officials, one from each group. The *madawaki* was the minister of war, commander of the cavalry and leader of the whole army; he was drawn from one or other leading descent-lines of hereditary chiefs.[1] Being a powerful nobleman, the *madawaki* might well be tempted to rebel against the king and seize the throne for himself. But this was where the constitutional 'checks and balances' came into action. For alongside the *madawaki* was the *galadima*, who not only looked after many civilian matters such as police, prisons and markets, but also controlled supplies to the army. So the *madawaki* could not do very much without the good will of the *galadima*. But the *galadima* was always drawn from the ranks of the 'king's men'. He was debarred by his origin from holding any political power except by the decision of the king, and was in any case the king's personal servant. This being so, he had no interest in helping a rebellious *madawaki*.

[1] In this title, *madawaki*, we see the influence in Hausaland of the methods of government of the Kanem-Bornu empire. The word comes from the Kanuri term, *mai dawaki*, or commander of the horses (cavalry). After the Fulani conquest of Zaria, in the nineteenth century, the word was modified to *madaki*.

The king used this opposition between leading officials in order to safeguard his power. Yet he too was confined by the same system of 'checks and balances'. If he wanted to go to war, it was not sufficient to persuade the *galadima* and other appointed officials of the wisdom of what he intended to do; he also had to have the support of the *madawaki* and other hereditary chiefs. Hausa government was therefore a complex and often delicate process of persuasion and rivalry between competing groups.

Internal wars

This useful type of government by kings of great but limited authority was offset, as we have noted, by a failure to unite the different Hausa states for their common good. Each state continued to serve its own interests at the cost of the others. Katsina was generally the most powerful of them between 1600 and 1700, but was often on bad terms with its neighbour, Gobir. These two states were great rivals for the caravan trade of western Hausaland. Katsina also waged war against Kano. In 1649 its king won a big battle against the king of Kano, and followed this by making an alliance with raiders from Jukun in the south. This alliance made little difference to Jukun activities: they continued to raid Katsina territory as well as that of Kano and other Hausa states.

Zaria's strength declined. After about 1750, adding to these troubles, the western Hausa states, especially Katsina and Gobir, had to face bold raids from Tuareg who were now established near Gao on the Middle Niger. The eastern Hausa states continued, as before, to feel the pressure of Bornu. After 1804, the position was much altered by the religious and social movement of the great Fulani leader, Uthman dan Fodio, and the foundation of the Fulani empire under his son, Muhammad Bello.

Bornu after Idris Alooma

It remains in this brief survey of political events to complete the story of Kanem-Bornu down to about 1800.

The great *Mai* Idris Alooma had come to power in about 1580. By about 1600 his rebuilding of the Kanemi empire was complete. He died in 1617, having brought its peoples many peaceful years.[1]

[1] See pages 101-103.

Bornu traditions then speak of three reigns, those of *Mai* Muhammad (1617-32), *Mai* Ibrahim (1632-39) and *Mai* Omar (1639-57), during all of which the empire remained at peace within itself, and often with its neighbours. These rulers carried on the work of Idris Alooma, and on the whole they did it well.

This long period of security and peace, more than half a century disturbed only by occasional frontier battles or minor quarrels at home, was the ripe and smiling 'harvest time' of Kanem-Bornu civilisation. While confusion and upheaval affected many other peoples of the Western Sudan, those of Kanem-Bornu had few such troubles. And although we know little of the detailed way of life of ordinary folk, we may well imagine that they made the best of these peaceful years. Farmers could work their fields in safety. Travellers and pilgrims could follow the roads without fear. Those who lived in towns and market-villages could prosper with the spread of trade that came both from everyday security and from unified rule over a wide country. There was growth of learning in the towns, and of schools in the villages. There was regular traffic between Kanem-Bornu and the Egyptian and Tunisian provinces of the Turkish empire in North Africa. *Mai* Ali, who succeeded *Mai* Omar in 1657, even made three religious journeys to Arabia.

Decline of Bornu empire

But *Mai* Ali, who reigned until 1694, had to face a different situation. It was while returning from his third pilgrimage in 1667, that the first grim warnings reached him of harsher times ahead.

The danger this time was not from the peoples to the east of Lake Chad, the Bulala nobles and their warriors who had rebelled so often against Kanemi rule. It came from the Tuareg of the Aïr oases in the north, and, at the same time, from the Jukun in the south. Both came raiding into Bornu, just as they came raiding into Kano and other Hausa states, their common motive being to seize some of the wealth of flourishing towns. Both gave *Mai* Ali and his armies some hard defeats. Twice he was besieged by these two enemies in his capital at Ngazar-gamu. In the end he managed to deal with each of them separately, and drove them back. The traditions say that a great famine struck Bornu in the later years of *Mai* Ali's reign, a disaster no doubt caused by these destructive raiding and defensive wars.

The great days of the Kanem-Bornu empire were almost over. After *Mai* Ali the traditions list seven rulers (or perhaps six, for one of them is in doubt) down to *Mai* Ahmad, who came to power in the last part of the eighteenth century, and later faced the first of Uthman dan Fodio's attacks. All these rulers saw the strength of their empire gradually decline. There occurred here the same general process as further to the west: central government found itself repeatedly weakened by revolt or independent action on the part of this or that subject people. Yet Bornu remained a powerful state whose traders continued to dominate the southern oasis trade across the routes to the Fezzan and Tripoli, playing a big part, too, along the 'gold and kola' route to Salaga in country under Asante rule.

Wadai, Darfur

Throughout the eighteenth century there were also many political changes to the east of Lake Chad. The rulers of Bagirmi and Wadai, backed partly by Fulani warrior groups settled there in earlier times, fought each other for control of Kanem, while the ancient authority of the Bulala kings and nobles vanished from the scene.

In this vast region, too, there now arose a movement for Muslim conversion and Muslim rules of government based on earlier Muslim

The ruins in Darfur of the great brick palace of Sultan Teirab (reigned 1752-87).

278

kingdoms of the seventeenth century in Wadai and Bagirmi. In Darfur, east of Wadai, a line of kings known as the Tunjur had built a non-Muslim kingdom in the distant past. This kingdom now fell to a new line of Muslim rulers. The tall ruins of their red-brick palaces and mosques, especially those of Sultan Muhammad Teirab (reigned 1752-1787), may still be seen among the foothills of Jebel Marra.

SUMMARY

1600-1800

We have seen how the sixteenth century, the years between 1500 and 1600, really marked the end of old West African history and the beginning of modern times.

The years around 1600 were in fact a turning-point for many peoples. They introduced a long period of transition, of far-reaching political, social and commercial change, during which more and more West Africans were drawn into the affairs of the wide world.

In the Western Sudan

The seventeenth century opened with the collapse of the Songhay empire in the central region, and the final decline of the Mali empire in the western region. These events were accompanied by a gradual but important shift of trade from the western routes across the Sahara to the central routes, and from the central routes to the eastern routes.

Gradually, out of much confusion, new states emerged. In the central region these included the Bambara states of Segu and Kaarta, ruled by non-Muslims. In the western region there began an important revival of Islam, mainly among Fulani and Mandinka groups: the Muslim states of Futa Toro, Futa Jallon, and Bondu were formed. This Muslim revival spread during the eighteenth century into the central region and afterwards into the eastern region.

Meanwhile, in the eastern region, the Hausa states had continued to flourish, and the Kanem-Bornu empire had entered a long period of peace and prosperity. East of Lake Chad, the further spread of the Muslim revival movement led to important political changes there as well.

In spite of all this change and upheaval, many peoples were able to protect their independence and continue with their traditional way of life. Notable among these were the Mossi and their non-Muslim neighbours in the central region.

Generally, the seventeenth century was a time of confusion, and the eighteenth a time of renewed political advance and recovery.

In Guinea

There were correspondingly large changes in all the regions of Guinea, but in very different circumstances.

Oyo rose to power in the eastern region, and built a strong empire. Benin city continued to be prosperous, but the power of its kings grew less, especially after about 1700.

New trading opportunities with the sea-merchants, and especially a great expansion of the Atlantic slave trade, deeply influenced the peoples along the coast. Prosperous city-states were founded in the Niger Delta, at Old Calabar, Brass, Bonny and elsewhere. Others emerged on the coast of Dahomey. The peoples of the *Gold Coast*, of Sierra Leone and of *Senegambia* were likewise deeply affected by the new coastal trade.

By the end of the seventeenth century these changes along the coast were of much influence on many peoples who lived in the lands behind the coast. The weak peoples suffered from the slave trade. The strong ones fought successfully in their own defence. Several of the latter determined to break the trading monopoly of the coastal peoples, and to come into direct contact with European merchants. Akwamu achieved this; and so did Dahomey; most powerful of all, so did Asante. And the Asante empire was to dominate the history of central Guinea from soon after 1700 until 1900, or for nearly two hundred years.

Towards a new challenge

The pressures of change did not end with 1800. On the contrary, they grew in some ways stronger still. The times of transition continued, and merged, as the nineteenth century went by, with an entirely new challenge to West Africa. This was the challenge of European colonial penetration and invasion. Later in the colonial period the pressures of change took new forms; just as now, in our own days of regained independence, they are doing so again. The modern reshaping of traditional West African civilisation is today in full development.

But this development of today springs from the developments we have read about here: from the history of West Africa before 1800. So we shall find it useful to round off our history by a summary of several matters of large importance.

CHAPTER TWENTY-TWO

1800: *West Africa and the world*

The Atlantic trade and the rise of colonialism

Within all these changes the way of life of most West Africans stayed true to their traditions of the past. Most people went on living by the rules and laws worked out and modified in previous times. These laws and rules came from the steady growth of their civilisation, and they offered what could often be a calm way of life, prosperous and easy-going, peaceful and self-confident. They pointed repeatedly to the interests of the whole community of the dead, the living, and the yet unborn; and they bade men and women serve the interests of their community. These laws and rules knew little of the god of the modern world, the god of individual competition. On the contrary, they tended to discourage any individual who might try to get more than his or her due share of wealth.

These laws and rules, the ideals of traditional African civilisation, were strong and valuable. They were the creation of many centuries of steady growth. They had a long and interesting history. They had helped to build the civilisation of West Africa.

But this civilisation also had its side of weakness. This was of two kinds.

Strength and weakness

One kind of weakness lay in West Africa's lack of unity. Against the threat of foreign invasion and conquest, West Africans seldom or never stood together. Although we may think of West Africans as belonging to the same great civilisation, it is also true that this civilisation was divided into many smaller ones. Each of these tended to think of itself as more or less entirely separate and different from its neighbours. Religious beliefs and customs often pushed one people against another. There was no 'common front' against invasion, and this greatly weakened African resistance.

Another and still more important weakness, and one we have already

For many centuries the kingdoms of Europe were able to make coins in gold, only by getting the gold from Africans. Here are some examples of European gold coins made from African gold.

283

noted, lay in the methods by which people produced wealth. These methods were not good for big increases in production or for using new ways of production.[1] Most people grew or made only what they needed for their own families, together with a little extra for trading at local markets. Having enough, they saw no need to change their ways of producing goods. They went on producing goods by the same simple methods as before, and with little or no aid from the mechanical inventions of Europe. So that by 1800, when compared with the strong countries of Europe, West Africa had become very backward in technology: in the use of machines, that is, and in the methods of industrial production.

This does not mean, however, that most Europeans were therefore happier or better off than most West Africans. On the contrary, the majority of the peoples of Britain and France, the most powerful nations of the nineteenth century, paid a terribly high price for their material progress. Country folk in England and France were forced into the hunger and disease of overcrowded and comfortless towns. Women and children were thrust without mercy into mines and factories. Countless numbers of industrial workers were starved or worked to death. Their lives were turned into a kind of slavery that was little different, in practice, from the slavery of the Africans across the Atlantic. This very suffering in Europe, however, put into the hands of rich and powerful men in Europe a strength and wealth which enabled them to conquer half the world.

Much of this new strength and wealth came from mines and plantations in the Americas, where Africans and their descendants toiled and suffered as slaves. Between 1600 and 1800 (and even after 1800), Europe drew many great benefits from the Atlantic slave trade.

We have studied the origins and growth of the Atlantic slave trade (Chapter 15). What were its consequences by 1800?

The slave trade: consequences for West Africa

It is well to remind ourselves, at this point, that West Africa traded with the sea-merchants in many goods besides slaves. Gold and ivory were important in the early times of trade, and continued to be in high demand throughout the long period we have studied. There was always some trade in other exports, too, notably in pepper, ostrich feathers, gum and several other products of West Africa. After 1600, however, it was

[1] See Chapter 11, *How the people lived*, page 147.

increasingly the European demand for slave labour that dominated the coastal markets and sent its influence far inland. In summing up the consequences of the Atlantic trade, we must direct our attention to this side of the business.

The slave trade was generally very bad for the peoples of Africa. But it was bad in different ways at different places. It was worst of all for the victims themselves. Once delivered to the captains of European and American ships, they were stripped, branded, and pushed into airless under-decks, crushed together, often chained by hand and foot. Like this they crossed the Atlantic in harsh weeks of sailing. Perhaps as many as one in every six captives died on the voyage across the ocean. Often the captives rose in brave revolt against their masters.

Back in Africa, the slave trade had other consequences. Many millions of strong young men (and a smaller proportion of women) were forced out of Africa by the slave trade. How many? We do not know. Probably the total number landed alive in the Americas was somewhere between ten and fifteen million people. Many others, of course, were lost to Africa in raids and wars for captives, as well as in the death of those who perished on the journey across the Atlantic.

Some African peoples were seriously weakened by their losses. But most were not. Most of the peoples affected by the slave trade could fill the loss by their natural growth. This is what happened in Europe, too. Between 1812 and 1914, for example, about twenty million people emigrated from Great Britain, so as to escape from hunger or unemployment; and yet the natural growth of the British population was such that the total population of Britain was bigger in 1917 than in 1814.

The main consequences of the slave trade, for West Africa, lay in two fields. The field of *production*. And the field of *politics*.

In the field of production, the slave trade obliged West Africa (like some other parts of Africa) to export its most valuable source of wealth, which was human labour.

Year after year, tens of thousands of African farmers and craftsmen were shipped away to work in American plantations, mines and cities. By their labour they created great wealth and profits: but for America and Europe, not for Africa. All that Africa received in exchange was the manufactured goods of Europe.

This exchange of raw material (as we may call human labour in this case) for manufactured goods was an early kind of *colonial exchange*. By it, the slave trade helped to make West Africa into a subject part of the economic system of Europe and America. In other words, the slave trade opened the way for the colonial system that was to follow in the second half of the nineteenth century. The slave trade helped to pull West Africa *back*, and to push Europe and America *forward*.

A few Africans did well out of the slave trade. But these were kings, chiefs, rich merchants. They gained at the expense of ordinary people.

In the field of politics:

1 The slave trade helped to spread wars and disorders, and the use of guns.
2 The slave trade weakened West Africa, made West Africa less able to defend itself, and more divided by internal conflicts.
3 When the Europeans wanted to invade West Africa, after 1800 and the end of the slave trade, they were able to take advantage of these conflicts between West Africans. In this way, too, we see that the slave trade was the father of the colonial invasions.

Resistance to the slave trade

On the African side, the slave trade grew out of the old customs of chiefs and kings. These were accustomed to regard all war-prisoners as property that could be sold or exchanged or simply given away. Certain groups of people were turned into permanent servants or house-slaves of rulers and rich men. We have seen how the lords of old West Africa took part in the buying and selling of men and women, sending many across the Sahara both before and during the ocean slave trade, in the same way as the lords of Europe and Asia did. We have discussed how the export of millions of Africans to the Americas was founded on customs such as these.

There were several African efforts to cut down the ocean slave trade, or to stop it altogether, when the damaging effects of this trade became clear. But such efforts largely failed, because the pressure of European and American demand was too great for them. Here are three examples.

The first occurred as early as the sixteenth century. In 1526 a famous king of the Bakongo state of Kongo, near the mouth of the river of that name, wrote an angry letter of protest to the king of Portugal. King Nzinga Mbemba, whose Christian name was Affonso, complained to the Portuguese king, his ally and partner in trade, that the slave trade was doing great hurt to his country. Together with certain Bakongo 'thieves and men of evil conscience', he wrote, Portuguese traders were 'grabbing and selling' his people, even including members of his own family. He wanted nothing from Portugal, he went on, except 'priests and people to teach in our schools, and no other goods but wine and flour for the holy sacrament'. Above all, he demanded that the Portuguese king, who was himself deep in the business of the slave trade, should recall his traders from Kongo, 'because it is our will that in these kingdoms of Kongo there should not be any trade in slaves nor any market for slaves'.

But the advantages and temptations offered by European-made goods, for which the sea-merchants increasingly demanded slaves, were too much for many of King Affonso's chiefs and sub-chiefs. They went on with the trade.

Another example occurred on the Dahomey coast of West Africa, the stretch of seaboard which the Europeans had named the *Slave Coast.* When King Agaja sent his armies to capture the city-states of Ardrah and its slave-dealing neighbours, in 1724, he wanted to bring the slave trade to a halt. He sent a message to the British government, by the hand of an Englishman whom his generals had found in one of the coastal towns, telling them that he wanted to stop the export of people from his country. The Fon of Dahomey, after all, had every reason to know the damage that was done by the trade, for they had suffered a lot from it. King Agaja was no more successful in ending the trade than King Affonso two centuries earlier, though he greatly reduced it. But he and later kings of Dahomey still had to sell captives into slavery, so as to buy the guns and ammunition which they needed.

A third example was noted in 1789 by a Swedish traveller who visited the imamate of Futa Toro in northern Senegal. A year before his visit, wrote this traveller, the *almamy* of Futa Toro had passed a law, 'very much to his honour', which declared that no slaves were to be taken through Futa Toro for sale abroad. But the *almamy* was up against a powerful trading system which yielded great profits; and this system defeated his good intentions.

Waiting in the Senegal River, as usual, were several French slave ships. Their captains, seeing they could not now hope to buy any slaves in Futa Toro, complained to the *almamy* against his law. They asked him to change his mind and do away with the law. He refused to agree. He followed this refusal by sending back to the agents of the French slave-trading company a number of presents they had given him, adding that 'all the riches of that company would not make him change his mind'. Faced with this refusal, the French captains discussed among themselves what they should do next. Then they found that the inland slave-dealers, also angry at the *almamy's* new law, had worked out another route for taking captives to the coast. So the French captains weighed anchor and sailed down the coast to this new market; and there they supplied themselves with the captives whom the *almamy* had prevented them from buying in the Senegal River.

There were other such acts of resistance, or attempted resistance. They all failed. And they failed because the slave trade, until soon after 1800, was a central part of the commercial system of the western world, the system to which large regions of Africa now increasingly belonged. Only a change in this system could stop the trade in slaves.

The beginnings of this change occurred in the closing years of the eighteenth century and led, among other things, to the foundation of Sierra Leone and Liberia. But we should also look at another main consequence of the Atlantic trade. This happened outside Africa, and yet it is, in many ways, a large and very remarkable part of African history. Large populations of African origin were taken to the lands beyond the Atlantic. Their toil, skills and achievements played a big role in building the civilisations of the Americas. Without Africa's contribution, those civilisations could never have become strong or rich.

Africans beyond the seas

By 1800 about half the population of Brazil were Africans, or the descendants of Africans. So were about half the population of Venezuela. So were a smaller but still large part of all the populations of the trans-Atlantic republics, whether in North, Central or South America, or in the Caribbean islands.

It was these men and women of African descent who conquered the wilderness of the Americas, clearing and working countless farms and plantations, founding and opening innumerable mines of iron or precious metals. Harsh and painful as it was, the oversea slave trade (like the not much less harsh and painful movement of millions of hungry or jobless men and women from Europe) laid the foundations of the American republics.

These Africans beyond the seas have their place in the story of Africa, the story of West Africa, for what they attempted and achieved was also a reflection of the strong and independent civilisation from which they came. Whenever they could, and from the earliest years of their enslavement across the Atlantic, they broke from their bondage and fought for their freedom. Unable to return home across the seas, they marched away into the South American wilderness and formed new states of their own. Many such islands of liberty were formed. None was more famous or successful than the African kingdom of Palmares, established in north-eastern Brazil in about 1605, which beat off many assaults by Dutch and Portuguese settlers or soldiers, and was overthrown by the Portuguese only in 1694, nearly a hundred years after its formation. Here in Palmares, thousands of Africans who had escaped from slavery joined together in a new life of their own, elected their own rulers, and governed themselves by the methods remembered from Africa.

Another famous example of African struggles for freedom across the seas was the heroic and successful campaign for liberty and independence that was conducted by the ex-slaves of the French Caribbean colony of St Domingue. In 1789, at the moment of the French Revolution, this French colony in the Caribbean was probably the wealthiest colony in the world. Its tens of thousands of African slave-workers produced enormous quantities of sugar; whole European communities lived off the profits.

When news of the French Revolution of 1789 reached St Domingue, these slaves claimed their share in its ideals and benefits. They demanded their freedom. Denied this, they rose in revolt against their masters. In years of hard fighting against large armies sent by France, and afterwards against large armies sent by Britain, these men of St Domingue won their freedom and founded the Republic of Haiti. Yet *more than half* these soldiers of freedom had made the 'middle passage' across the Atlantic. More than half, in other words, had been born in Africa, had spent their childhood in Africa, had learned in Africa their respect for freedom; while nearly all the rest were the children of parents or grandparents born in Africa. And they were led by Africans; by men of genius and courage such as Boukman, the unforgettable Toussaint Louverture, and Dessalines.

Raised by Toussaint and his Africans, the banner of freedom across the Atlantic was carried from people to people. Many threw off their bondage. Large numbers of men of African origin fought in the armies that made the United States what they are today. It was a general of African descent, Antonio Maceo, who became a leader in the military struggle for Cuban independence against Spain which began in 1868.

Like other men of vision, Maceo had no time for racism, for the false idea that one race of men is better or worse than any other. Some of the whites of Cuba disagreed with him. They were Spanish settlers who thought that white was going to be better than black even in an independent Cuba.

One day Maceo was approached by a Spanish Cuban who suggested that the regiments of the independence army should be divided into whites and non-whites. Maceo made him a reply which became famous in Cuba. 'If you were not white,' Maceo said to this man, 'I would have you shot on the spot. But I do not wish to be accused of being a racist as you are, and so I let you go, but with the warning that I shall not be so patient another time. The revolution has no colour.'

In Europe, too, West Africans who had won their freedom had begun to win honours and respect as well. One of them, whose name was Ibrahim, became personal secretary to the Russian emperor Peter the Great. Another, a young Nzima from Axim in modern Ghana whose name was Anton Wilhelm Amo, entered the ancient German University of Halle in 1727. After studying philosophy and law, Amo passed on to Wittenberg University and was there crowned with a doctorate of philosophy in 1733. On that occasion the Rector of Wittenberg University, after praising the scholars of the African past, welcomed Dr Amo as a man of high gifts, morality and civilisation. A third African to make his name in the world of letters was Olaudah Equiano, an Igbo who wrote in 1789 the first English book about Igboland, a work which helped to convince the British public of the evils of the slave trade.

All these men, soldiers and leaders, generals and statesmen, pioneers in farming, mining, and stock-raising, men of letters, were formed in their different ways by African ideas and values. They were as much the children of African civilisation as the European settlers in the Americas and Australia were the children of the civilisation of Europe.

The roots of our life now

Our study, in this book, ends in 1800. In that year, Europeans were ruling nowhere in West Africa, except on bits of ground where their castles stood and, indirectly, on a strip of Sierra Leone coast. But in 1900 Europeans were ruling or about to rule almost everywhere in West Africa.

Without knowledge of West African history, we may well ask how this could happen. For hundreds of years, as we have seen in this book, West Africans had dealt with Europeans and Americans as their equals. Attacked from the sea, West Africans had thrown off their attackers. Threatened from foreign-held castles, they had stormed and captured those castles. Tricked by foreign traders, they had brought such men to order and punished their tricks. Yet now, within less than one hundred years, this power of resistance would have collapsed.

The direct reasons for this collapse came after 1800. But we can see that the roots of the collapse were planted in West African life even before 1800.

These roots were partly planted by the slave trade, which pulled West Africa back and pushed Europe and America forward. They were also planted by other big processes of world history, such as the early development of science in Western Europe. All this meant that between 1700 and 1800 the leading European nations, especially the British and the French, developed big new sources of power, machine power, industrial power, while the Africans had no share in this development.

Look at the column marked 'Elsewhere' in the Table on page 306. There you see listed some of the machine inventions of the British before 1800. These and other such inventions gave the British much more power than the Africans. The British could develop a trading power, and then a military power, which other peoples would find they could not stop.

So the challenge that West Africa had to face, after 1800, took shape before 1800. It was not just one of military strength. It was above all the challenge by European nations which had modernised themselves by developing science and machinery.

This challenge was indirect before 1800: it took the form of the slave trade. After 1800, it became direct, and eventually took the form of colonial invasion.

That is one great example which shows why it is necessary to understand the past in order to explain the present. The strength and wealth and happiness of West Africa today were created by West Africa's history. But so were the problems of West Africa today: the problems, above all, of overcoming the handicaps of the past, the problems of giving West Africa a new and fully modern way of life.

Great men and women have their names in history. But it is ordinary people who make them great. And it is ordinary people who will solve the problems of today. These it is, the ordinary people whose names are not in the books, who were and are the true creators of history, the true founders of wealth and progress, the true builders of a better life. That is why our study ends as it began: with an Akan saying which points to the importance of ordinary people:

> I call Gold,
> Gold is mute.
> I call Cloth,
> Cloth is mute.
> It is Mankind that matters.

A note on sources

Students should have some understanding of the sources of historical knowledge and of the materials and methods used by historians to find out about the past. Some topics in this book, it will be noticed, are treated in precise detail while others are discussed in more general terms. This is because there are varying levels of historical knowledge available to historians. Some topics we know much about from many sources, while others we know little about from few sources.

The study of history is a continuous process of discovery. Many historians are at present researching into various aspects of West African history, bringing to light and studying new source material so that our knowledge of the distant past of the peoples of West Africa is being constantly amended and improved. Many sciences (for example anthropology, geography, linguistics, botany) can help the historian. But the most important sources of historical information are from three sources. These sources are: archaeology, oral tradition and written records.

Archaeology

Archaeology means the study of the material remains and ruins of the past. The job of the archaeologist is to find and carefully analyse ancient objects in a highly skilled and scientific way: for example, tombs, ruined cities, tools, pots and weapons. The materials of archaeology may be found on the surface or, more often, buried under the ground. After being found, they have to be examined in detail, often using advanced laboratory techniques (for example, carbon-dating), in order to find out as much as possible about the objects and the people who made them. Archaeology can provide information for all periods of history from the earliest origins of mankind to the very recent past. But it is most useful for the distant past, when other sources of information are often non-existent.

In West Africa, archaeology is a fairly new science. As it develops further, we can expect more exciting discoveries which should greatly improve our present knowledge of early West Africa. Already, however, much valuable work has been done. The excavation of Kumbi Saleh has greatly increased our knowledge of ancient Ghana. Archaeological work at Nok and other places in the middle belt of Nigeria has revealed a highly developed culture of the earliest iron age. The discovery of the buried Ife sculpture has revealed some of the richness of early Yoruba civilisation.

Archaeology can seldom tell us about exact dates and events, but it can tell us a lot about the way of life of ancient peoples and cultures which we would not otherwise know. In the wet coastal areas of West Africa, most materials (for example, wood) decay rapidly, leaving only objects that were made of stone or metal; but in the drier savannah areas a more varied range of objects may be preserved.

Oral traditions

West Africa is particularly rich in oral tradition or unwritten history. Stories, legends and myths passed down by word of mouth can all be forms of unwritten history and often provide the main source of historical knowledge in West Africa before the general introduction of writing. Many societies had (and still have) a special group of people whose job was to learn, remember and recite the traditions of their community. The oral history of many West African communities has still to be recorded and studied by historians. But already much has been learnt about the early history of some areas of West Africa by the careful study of tradition as in the case of the Bayajidda legend of Hausaland and the Oduduwa and Oranmiyan stories of Yorubaland and Benin.

Oral traditions are extremely difficult to interpret, so that historians have to use great skill in overcoming the many weaknesses of this form of source material. Oral history depends on human memory which is often unreliable. The sequence of events may be changed or events forgotten or left out on purpose, which means that the remembered story may be very different from what really happened. Moreover, such traditions usually deal only with the most important characters and events (for example kings, battles, conquests and migrations), and tell us little or nothing about the everyday life of ordinary people.

Written records

Written records (for example books, letters, inscriptions) provide the most precise source for the historian. But in West Africa, apart from the

Islamic areas of the Western Sudan, few written records exist for the period before the nineteenth century. The earliest written records dealing with West Africa deal with the medieval empires of the Western Sudan and were produced by Arab and North African travellers, traders and scholars from the tenth century onwards. For example the geographer al-Ma'sudi and the traveller Ibn Hawqal provide us with information about ancient Ghana, while Ibn Khaldun and Ibn Batuta give much detail about fourteenth-century Mali. Islam brought literacy to the Western Sudan, and by the sixteenth century many West African scholars and historians, such as Ahmad Baba of Timbuktu were working in the great cities of the Niger bend.

No written material on the coastal areas exists before the beginning of European contact in the fifteenth century. First the Portuguese, and later other Europeans, visited and wrote about the coastal peoples and afterwards about some peoples of the inland country. But these early European sources have to be treated with care, for they are often confused, misinformed and prejudiced. The Europeans very seldom travelled in the interior until the nineteenth century, so that until then almost no European written material exists for the large area between the coastal strip and the Western Sudan.

Book-list

Firstly some general books designed for students' use and covering large sections of the syllabus.

AJAYI, J. F. A. and ESPIE, I., *A Thousand Years of West African History*, IUP and Nelson, 1966.

AGBODEKA, F., *The Rise of the Nation States*, Nelson, 1969.

BOAHEN, A. A., *Topics in West African History*, Longman, 1966.

CROWDER, M., *West Africa: An Introduction to its History*, Longman, 1977.

DAVIDSON, B., *The African Past*, Penguin, 1966.

DAVIDSON, B., *Africa in History*, Paladin, 1975.

FAGE, J. D., *A History of West Africa*, CUP, rev. ed. 1969.

FAGE, J. D., *An Atlas of African History*, Arnold, 1958.

FYFE, C., *A Short History of Sierra Leone*, Longman, 1962.

OGINI, F. G., *An Outline History of West Africa 1000–1800*, Macmillan, 1973.

OLIVER, R. and FAGE, J. D., *A Short History of Africa*, Penguin, 5th ed. 1975.

OSAE, T. A. and NWAMBARA, S. N., *A Short History of West Africa 1000–1800*, Hodder and Stoughton, 1968.

STRIDE, G. T. and IFEKA, C., *Peoples and Empires of West Africa: West Africa in History 1000–1800*, Nelson, 1971.

THATCHER, P. F., *Longmans Certificate Notes: West African History*, Longman, 1974.

More specialised books giving detailed coverage of certain parts of the syllabus. Useful for reference purposes and for teachers' use.

AJAYI, J. F. A. and CROWDER, M. (eds), *A History of West Africa Vol I*, Longman, 1971.

AKINJOGBIN, I. A., *Dahomey and its Neighbours*, CUP, 1967.

ALAGOA, E. J., *A History of the Niger Delta*, Ibadan University Press, 1972.

ARMSTRONG, R. G., *The Study of West African Languages*, Ibadan University Press, 1964.

ibn BATUTA, *Travels in Asia and Africa 1325–54*, trans. H. A. R. Gibb, Routledge, 1957.

BAËTA, C. G. (ed.), *Christianity in Tropical Africa*, International African Institute and OUP, 1968.

BOVILL, E. W., *The Golden Trade of the Moors*, OUP, rev. 1970.

CROWDER, M., *The Story of Nigeria*, Faber and Faber, 1966.

DAVIDSON, B., *Black Mother*, Longman, paperback edition 1970.

DAVIDSON, B., *Old Africa Rediscovered*, Longman, paperback edition 1970.

DAAKU, K. Y., *Trade and Politics on the Gold Coast, 1600–1700*, OUP, 1970.

DIKE, K. O., *Trade and Politics in the Niger Delta*, OUP, 1956.

EGHAREVBA, J., *A Short History of Benin*, Ibadan University Press, 1960.

FAGE, J. D., *Ghana: A New Interpretation*, Wisconsin University Press, 1966.

FYFE, C., *Sierra Leone Inheritance*, OUP, 1964.

GRAY, J. M., *A History of The Gambia*, Cass, 1966.

HALLET, R., *Africa to 1875*, Heineman, 1974.

HODGKIN, T., *Nigerian Perspectives*, OUP, new edition 1975.

HOGBEN, S. J., *An Introduction to the History of the Islamic States of Northern Nigeria*, OUP, 1968.

HOPKINS, A. G., *An Economic History of West Africa*, Longman, 1973 (Chs 1–3).

IKIME, O., *Merchant Prince of the Niger Delta*, Heinemann, 1971.

LATHAM, N., *A Sketchmap History of West Africa*, Hulton, 1962.

LEVTZION, N., *Ancient Ghana and Mali*, Methuen, 1973.

LEWIS, I. M. (ed.), *Islam in Tropical Africa*, International African Institute and OUP, 1966.

NIANE, D. T., *Sundiata: An Epic of Old Mali*, Longman, 1965.

RYDER, A. F. C., *Benin and the Europeans, 1445–1897*, Longman, 1969.

SMITH, R. S., *Kingdoms of the Yoruba*, Methuen, new ed. 1976.

TRIMINGHAM, J. S., *A History of Islam in West Africa*, OUP, rev. ed. 1970.

WARD, W. E. F., *A History of Ghana*, Allen and Unwin, 1963.

WILKS, I., *The Northern Factor in Ashanti History*, Legon, 1961.

WOLFSON, F., *Pageant of Ghana*, OUP, 1959.

The following journals also include much useful material:
Journal of African History
Journal of the Historical Society of Nigeria
Tarikh
Transactions of the Historical Society of Ghana

Questions

These questions can be used for examination practice. They are similar to the type of questions set in the West African School Certificate Examination, but can also provide useful practice for examinations at a higher level. Since examination questions frequently require the use of material from several different sections of a syllabus, it would be unrealistic to list questions strictly under chapter headings. But these questions have been arranged in about the same order as the contents of the book, so that it should be easy to find questions dealing with any particular section of the book.

1 Outline the factors present in West Africa in about AD 1000 that helped the growth of large states in the Western Sudan.
2 Describe the part played by the Ghana Empire in the trans-Saharan trade, and show the benefits it obtained from this trade. (WASC June '73).
3 Explain the influence of the Almoravids on the history of the Ghana Empire.
4 Describe the Ghana Empire's geographical position and explain how geographical factors contributed to Ghana's strength.
5 Compare the contributions made by Sundiata and Mansa Musa to the growth of the Mali Empire.
6 In what ways did the trans-Saharan trade affect the lives of the people of the Mali Empire? (WASC June '75).
7 What factors helped to produce the decline of the Mali Empire during the century after the death of Mansa Musa?
8 Outline the important developments that occurred in the Sene-gambia area during the sixteenth century.
9 Briefly describe how *Askia* Muhammad came to power and the methods he used to rule Songhay. (WASC Nov. '73).
10 Why did the successors of *Askia* Muhammad fail to maintain the strength of the Songhay Empire?
11 Describe the internal events in Songhay in the sixteenth century which contributed to the easy conquest of the empire by Morocco,

and outline briefly the main effects of the conquest on the Western Sudan. (WASC June '74).

12 How was the trans-Saharan trade affected by the Moroccan invasion of Songhay?

13 Explain the importance to the history of the Western Sudan of two of the following; (a) Takrur, (b) the Dyula, (c) Ahmad Baba.

14 Outline the origin and development of any one of the following states: (a) Bono-Manso, (b) Gonja, (c) Denkyira.

15 Give a brief history of the rise and growth of the Mossi-Dagomba states, mentioning why they were able to resist the power of Mali and the force and influence of Islam. (WASC Nov. '73).

16 Explain the contribution of *Mai* Ali Ghaji to the growth of the Empire of Kanem-Bornu.

17 How was the government of Kanem-Bornu organised in the sixteenth century? What changes were introduced during the reign of *Mai* Idris Alooma?

18 How did the Hausa states originate? Choose any one of the major Hausa states and give a brief account of its development up to 1800.

19 Write briefly on any two of the following:
   (a) *Sunni* Ali's contribution to the founding of the Songhay Empire.
   (b) Ibn Battuta as a commentator on the kingdoms and empires of the Western Sudan.
   (c) The origins of the Mamprussi, Mossi and Dagomba Kingdoms.
   (d) The Poro Society in Sierra Leone in the pre-colonial days.
   (e) The 'Village Democracy' among the Igbo before 1800. (WASC June '75).

20 Explain the political and social organisation of either the Igbo or the Mossi before 1800.

21 Trace briefly the rise of any two of the following states: (a) Bullom, (b) Jolof, (c) Jukun, (d) Segu, (e) Akwamu. (WASC June '74).

22 In what ways did the presence of European traders, before 1800, affect the economic and social life of the peoples of the Guinea Coast? (WASC June '74).

23 Trace the origins of the transatlantic slave trade, and show why and how the trade increased in the eighteenth century. (WASC June '73).

24 How did Islam reach the Western Sudan? Trace the main stages of the spread and growth of Islam.

25 Describe some of the important political and social organisations of any one of the following peoples in pre-colonial times: (a) the

Mende, (b) the Akan, (c) the Igbo, (d) the Fon, (e) the Efik.   (WASC June '74).

26 Describe the Portuguese trade with the Empire of Benin in the fifteenth and sixteenth centuries. What effects did this trade have upon the Empire?   (WASC June '76).

27 Account for the decline in strength of the Benin Empire during the seventeenth and eighteenth centuries.

28 What were the strengths and weaknesses of the Oyo system of government in the period up to 1800?

29 Why were there frequent conflicts between Oyo and Dahomey during the eighteenth century?

30 Discuss the effects of the growth of the slave trade on the Niger Delta area in the period before 1800.

31 'A highly centralised state'. Is this an accurate description of the Kingdom of Dahomey in the eighteenth century?

32 What role did trade play in the rise and strength of the Asante Empire?

33 Describe the changes made to the system of government of the Asante Empire during the reign of Osei Kwadwo? How effective were these changes?

34 Explain the causes for the hostility between the Asante and the Fante during the eighteenth century and the attitude of the British to this conflict.

35 Give a short account of the rise and the political development before 1800 of either (a) the Wolof Empire or (b) the Bambara states of Segu and Kaarta.   (WASC June '75).

36 Why were there jihads (Muslim wars of religion) in the Futa states in the eighteenth century and with what results?

Table of comparative dates

| BC | West Africa | | | Elsewhere |
	WESTERN REGION	CENTRAL REGION	EASTERN REGION	
4000	The Old Stone Age family of languages used in West Africa begin to split up into the 400 or more different languages which are now spoken there			Early farming in Egypt. New Stone Age comes to an end with spreading use of copper for many purposes
3500	New Stone Age farming and cattle raising in the Sahara, at this time green and fertile. Old Stone Age (without farming) continues in the forest lands			Early states in Egypt
3200	The Sahara and Sudan are still green and fertile			Unification of two states of Upper and Lower Egypt. Beginning of the civilisation of Pharaonic Egypt
2500	Sahara begins gradually to dry up			Building of the Pyramids
2000	Gradual movement of farming peoples out of the Sahara, where water is now growing scarce			Great period of Egyptian history
1700-1800				Asians, called Hyksos, invade Egypt. They introduce use of horses and chariots.
1575				New Egyptian empire under Pharaohs of 18th dynasty.
1500				
1000	Carts and chariots drawn by donkeys or horses begin to be used for crossing the Sahara between North and West Africa			Rise of Berber civilisation in North Africa
800				Rise of civilisation of Kush on middle Nile. Soon Kush invades Egypt and holds most of it for a century.
814				Traditional date of foundation of Carthage by Phoenicians in Tunisia

300

West Africa

BC	WESTERN REGION	CENTRAL REGION	EASTERN REGION	Elsewhere
500	Farming begins to develop in the forest lands			
300	Iron-working begins to appear in West Africa south of the Sahara. The Nok Culture. Trade continues between North and West Africa across the Sahara			Greek kings (the Ptolemies) in Egypt
				Wars between Rome and Carthage. Rome wins and destroys Carthage
105	More Sudanese peoples learn how to make iron			Romans defeat King Jugurtha of the Berber Kingdom of Numidia. Much of Tunisia and Algeria are brought within the new Roman empire
100	Trans-Saharan trade now using increasing numbers of camels instead of horses and donkeys			Iron-working begins to appear in central South Africa
AD 300	Spread of iron-working through West Africa			Many fine and prosperous cities flourish in Roman North Africa
550				Emergence of Christian kingdoms in Nubia on middle Nile
622				The Prophet Muhammad enters Medina. The first year of Islam.
750	Ancient Ghana grows important	Origins of Gao	Sao culture (L. Chad)	Muslim conquests in North Africa and Spain far advanced
800	Ghana commands the international trade in gold and salt. Becomes a powerful empire	Islam begins to appear in West Africa through Muslim Berber traders from the Sahara	Traditional date for founding of early state of Kanem (about 850)	Egypt becomes a great centre of Muslim civilisation
1000	Ghana at height of its power	King of Gao accepts Islam (about 1010)	Kanem expands. Founding of early Hausa and Yoruba states	Fatimid Kalifate in Egypt (969-1171)

301

West Africa

AD	WESTERN REGION	CENTRAL REGION	EASTERN REGION	Elsewhere
1054	Almoravid Berbers capture Audoghast from Ghana	Early Songhay state of Gao. Its rulers are the Dia line of kings.		Almoravids set up new Muslim states in Morocco and Spain (1061-1147)
1076	Ghana begins to collapse under Almoravid attacks: its capital is taken by them			Arts and early sciences flourish in Muslim Spain and North Africa
1086			King of Kanem (Hume) accepts Islam	
1200	Time of confusion leads to end of Ancient Ghana		Early state of Benin under Ogiso rulers	Almohads set up new Muslim state in North Africa and Spain (1147-1289)
1230	Sundiata becomes King of small Mandinka state of Kangaba: defeats his enemy Sumanguru: founds early state of Mali, begins to conquer neighbouring lands			Ayyubids rule Egypt (1171-1250) Fall of Christian kingdoms in Nubia
1255	*Mansa* Uli (died 1270) continues to hold empire of Mali	Growing commercial power of Gao	Rise of first Kanem-Bornu empire to east and west of Lake Chad	Mamluk soldier-kings rule Egypt (1250-1517)
1300	Wolof states founded in Senegal	Early states in forest country	Yoruba states under spiritual leadership of Ife	Christians reconquer most of Spain. There remains only the small Muslim kingdom of Granada (1232-1492)
1312	*Mansa* Musa comes to throne of Mali. Dies in 1337 after expanding Mali far across both western and central regions of West Africa. Takes Gao into Mali empire in 1325			

West Africa

AD	WESTERN REGION	CENTRAL REGION	EASTERN REGION	Elsewhere
1335	Mali continues at height of its power	At Gao, *Dia* line of kings followed by first of a new line, called the Sunni kings		English and French fight feudal wars against each other
1375	Mali begins to decline	*Sunni* Suleiman-Mar of Gao wins back independence from Mali. Gao begins to grow in power	Bulala dominate Kanem east of Lake Chad. Kanem rulers temporarily much weakened	First detailed map of West Africa is drawn by Cresques of Majorca
1400		Songhay of Gao raid Niani, capital of Mali Bono-Manso and Mossi states in existence	Hausa and Yoruba states grow stronger and wealthier. Nupe and Jukun founded at this time	Kilwa on East African Coast (Tanzania) becomes rich and powerful; dominates gold trade with Arabia and Far East
1415		Timbuktu and Jenne are centres of Muslim scholarship		Portuguese, raiding overseas for first time, capture Ceuta, a port in north-western Morocco
1434	Portuguese begin sailing down Atlantic coast of West Africa. They are soon followed by other Europeans in small numbers who engage in more or less peaceful trade with many coastal states		Benin is now a big empire. Islam reaches Zaria (1456)	Egypt ruled by strong Mamluk Sultan Baybars (1422-37)
1464	Mali continues to decline	*Sunni* Ali comes to throne of Gao and begins to build the Songhay empire	Muhammad Rumfa of Kano (1465-99)	Empire of the Monomotapa (Zimbabwe)
1472		Songhay capture Jenne (1473)	Portuguese reach Bight of Benin. Christian missionaries soon follow them	Portuguese and Spanish attacks on Morocco, which is much weakened by them
1482	Much European trading on the coast of Senegambia	Portuguese build Elmina Castle on *Gold Coast*		Portuguese make contact with Bakongo Kingdom near mouth of Congo River (1483)

AD	WESTERN REGION	CENTRAL REGION	EASTERN REGION	Elsewhere
1492		*Sunni* Ali dies		Columbus reaches Caribbean
1493		*Askia* Muhammad becomes ruler of Songhay	Al-Maghili of Tuat at Kano and Katsina: writes *The Duties of Kings* for King Muhammad Rumfa of Kano	First Tudor king of England Henry VII (1485-1509)
1507		Big expansion of trade between Sudan and Guinea. Jenne becomes very prosperous	*Mai* Idris Katarkamabi becomes ruler of Bornu. Wins battle of Garni-Kiyala and regains control of Kanem	Spanish conquests in Caribbean and Central America
1517		Mahmud Kati of Timbuktu starts writing *Tarikh al-Fattash* at this time	Kebbi gains independence from Songhay empire. Attacks Gobir and Katsina	Ottoman Turks conquer Egypt and move west along the coast of North Africa
1528		*Askia* Muhammad followed by *Askia* Musa in Songhay		
1534	Mali asks help from Portugal			German states are the most advanced trading states in Europe
1550	Trading partnerships between European sea-merchants and African coastal states become established firmly in this period	The state of Gonja founded by Mandinka warriors at this time		Religious wars in Germany cause terrible destruction
1553	In Senegal, Cayor revolts against Jolof (1556), becomes independent	*Askia* Dawud rules Songhay empire (1549-82)	English visit Benin for first time	English fight Spanish at sea in these years
1559	Tenguella Koli establishes new line of kings in Takrur (Futa Toro). They were called the Denianke	Gold trade expands		Portuguese invasion of Kingdom of Ndongo (Angola) in wars which last many years

West Africa

AD	WESTERN REGION	CENTRAL REGION	EASTERN REGION	Elsewhere
1575			Hausa states revolt against Songhay	Portuguese invasion of Morocco smashed by Mulay the Victorious, who becomes king (1578)
1580		Songhay and Morocco clash at Taghaza	*Mai* Idris Alooma becomes ruler of Kanem-Bornu and establishes new empire by the time of his death in 1617	Spanish Armada fails to invade England (1588)
1591	Mali empire in last stages of decay	Songhay empire begins to collapse under Moroccan invasion (battle of Tondibi, 1591)		Judar leads a Moroccan army across the Sahara and defeats Songhay
		Ruin of Songhay empire as Moroccans occupy the cities and local peoples rebel against Songhay lords		Peoples of western Angola defend themselves against Portuguese invasion; are not defeated until middle of 17th century
1600	Wolof states in Senegal active in trade with sea-merchants	Gonja fights Dagomba. Timbuktu ruled by Moroccan pashas	Kanem-Bornu under Idris Alooma is most powerful state in this region	Dutch become strongest European sea-power. European powers now form their early chartered companies for trading with Africa and other distant countries
1650	Wolof states compete for trade with sea-merchants; many wars between them	Early Bambara state of Segu Rise of Denkyira Rise of Fon state in Dahomey under King Wegbaja, who reigns until 1685	Rise of Oyo Oyo empire extends over most Yoruba states and Dahomey Rise of new city-states in Niger Delta	Dutch make small settlement at Cape of Good Hope (1652): origins of South Africa British fight the Dutch for sea supremacy (1653-54) and (1665-67) British fight the Spanish and the French for supremacy at sea (1655 onwards). They come out on top

West Africa

AD	WESTERN REGION	CENTRAL REGION	EASTERN REGION	Elsewhere
1659	French found St Louis in Senegal			
1661	English rebuild Fort James on Gambia River	Asante states begin to combine		Reign of Louis XIV of France
1677-1681		Expansion of Akwamu under Ansa Sasraku	Kanem-Bornu enters period of confusion which leads to its gradual decline	
1705		Asante a strong power under Osei Tutu	Tuareg and Jukun raid North Nigeria (1670-1703)	War of Spanish Succession (1702-13)
1713	Europeans expand trade with Wolof and Takrur	Founding of Bambara state of Segu under Mamari Kulibali (1712-55)		With Treaty of Utrecht (1713) between Britain and France, British become the biggest buyers and carriers of slaves from Africa.
1725	Foundation of Imamate of Futa Jallon	Fon take control of city-states on Dahomey coast. End of Akwamu empire (1730)		Europeans in West Indies now making tremendous profits out of sugar grown by African slaves
1750	Spread of Muslim revival across Western Sudan	Asante predominates in central Guinea. Emergence of Baulé and Anyi states in Ivory Coast	Muhammad Teirab is Sultan of Darfur (1752-87)	Britain enters her *industrial revolution* with invention of important machines: 1733 Kay invents mechanical weaving shuttle 1738 Paul invents mechanical spinning roller
1753		Foundation of Bambara state of Kaarta	Niger Delta states at height of their trading expansion	1768 Hargreaves develops the 'spinning jenny' by which one worker can operate many spindles together 1776 Watt invents his mechanical pump
1765	Formation of British colony of Senegambia (ended in 1783)			(1803 Trevithick builds a steam locomotive to run on iron rails)

306

West Africa

AD	WESTERN REGION	CENTRAL REGION	EASTERN REGION	Elsewhere
1775	Foundation of Imamate of Futa Toro: end of Denianke line of rulers (1776)	Asante empire becomes very powerful	Decline of Benin. Oyo still powerful	Britain's North American colonies fight for their independence. They win
1789				French Revolution (1789)
1791	Foundation of Freetown			Toussaint declares independence of Haiti
1798		Mungo Park reaches Segu (1796)		French under Napoleon invade. Egypt (1798)
1804	Church Missionary Society in Sierra Leone. Methodists and others soon follow		Fulani conquest of Hausa kingdoms (1804-11)	British and French at war: European coalition against the French emperor, Napoleon, who is finally defeated in 1815
1806	Dakar independent under Diop family (1810). Later (1837) French take Dakar	Britain clashes with Asante, but peace is at once restored. Asante continues to dominate the greater part of central Guinea and neighbouring grassland countries	*Mai* Ahmad reigns in Kanem-Bornu (1793-1810) Collapse of Oyo empire	Rise of Zulu empire in Natal (South Africa): King Shaka begins reign in 1816

Subject index and guide to chapters

The chart below shows whereabouts in the book students will find the different parts of the WAEC 'O' level history syllabus I (History of West Africa, AD 1000 to Present Day), section A (West Africa, AD 1000–1800). Subjects are listed in the left hand column. The relevant chapters are listed in the middle column and the most useful page references, for facts and dates, are given on the right.

	General chapters	Pages
1 Peoples of West Africa about AD 1000	1, 2	12–20
2 The early states of the Western Sudan:	1, 2, 3, 4, 5, 6, 9, 11, 12, 13	20, 31, 34, 46
A Takrur		55, 59
B Ghana		34–45
C Kanem		98–105
D Mali		46–54
3 Islam in West Africa; introduction, dates, spread and influence	12, 20	50, 136–140 171–175 189–190, 267–273
4 The states of the Western Sudan between the fifteenth and eighteenth centuries	3, 7, 9, 11, 12, 13, 14, 20, 21	30–31, 65–67
A Songhay		68–78, 82–85, 262
B The Hausa States		105–111, 274
C Bornu		98–105, 276

Index of names

Abd al-Rahman as-Sadi, 161, 174–5
Abdelkadar, *Almamy*, 259
Abdullah ibn Yasin, 42
Abdullahi Burja, 108–9
Abiodun, *Alafin*, 218
Abomey, 228, 231–2; *see also* Dahomey
Abora, battle of (1806), 249
Abu Abdallah Muhammad, 68
Abu Bakr, 43, 44, 49
Abuakwa, 238
Aburi, 237
Accra, 93, 211, 237, 238, 248
Adamawa, 100
Adams, Captain John, 224n
Adansi, 89, 93, 239, 240
Adwuku, Iron Age pot found at, 88
Affonso, King Nzinga Mbemba, 286–7
Africanus, Leo *see* Leo Africanus
Agadès, 31, 191
Agaja, King of Dahomey, 232–3, 287
Age-sets, 115, 118, 123, 149, 177; *see also* Descent-lines
Agona, 237
Agonglo, King of Dahomey, 233
Agriculture: early (pre-1000), 7–8, 10, 13, 22; farming methods in central Guinea, 88; forest, 115, 120, 147, 186; Hausa, 274; Songhay, 186; subsistence, 148; tropical farming, 147
Ahmad, *Mai*, 278
Ahmad Baba, 173
Ahuan, *Oba*, 132
Aïr, 77, 98, 100, 278
Aissa Kili, Queen, 102
Ajase (Porto Novo), 218, 229
Ajayi, Professor J. F. Ade, 126
Akaba, King of Dahomey, 232
Akan, 4, 6, 12, 89–90, 151, 161, 240, 242, 251, 253, 263, 291; ancestors, 89; gold trade and expansion, 93–6, 139;

states, 89–93; traditional religion, 165–6; *see also* Asante
Akim, 236, 237–8, 245–6, 250
Akwa Boni, Queen of Baulé, 251
Akwamu, 89, 93, 211, 236–8, 244, 281
Akwapim, 238, 246, 250
Alafin of Oyo, 119, 126, 178, 185, 218–21, 233
Al-Bakri, 36–8, 39, 40–1
Albreda, 257
Alfa Askia Lanbar, 190
Alfa Muhammad Diobo, 273
Al-Fazari, 20, 139
Algeria, 33, 140, 191, 194
Ali, *Mai* (succeeds to throne c.1545), 100–1, 102
Ali, *Mai* (succeeds to throne 1657), 277, 278
Ali Ber *see* Sunni Ali
Ali Gaji, *Mai*, 100
Al-Ksar al-Kabir, battle of (1578), 83
Al-Kwarizma, 20
Allada *se* Ardrah
Almadiyya, 138
Al-Maghili, 138, 140, 190
Almeida, Francisco de, 193
Almoravids, 99, 204; invasion of Ancient Ghana by, 42–3, 139
Al-Omari, 51, 184
Alooma *see* Idris Alooma
Ama 'title societies', 117
Amayaa, Dyula Queen-mother, 89–90
Amina, Queen of Zaria, 110
Amo, Anton Wilhelm, 290
Amsa, Queen, 102
Ananse Kokrofu, 116
Ancient Ghana (Wagadu), 20, 27, 32, 34–45, 55, 60, 105, 139, 145, 155, 175; achievement of, 36–7; conquest of capital, 43, 44, 45, 62; early trade, 20,

312

Wagadugu (Ougadougou), 87
Walata, 31, 44, 50, 53, 62, 73, 74
Walo, 57, 59
Wangara *see* Dyula traders
Warebo, 251
Warri, 222
Wati, King of Mali, 49
Wegbaja, King of Dahomey, 231
West Africa, 3–22, 136–40, 143–62,
  282–91; cities, 159–62; civilisation,
  143–7; climate and geography, 4–6;
  coming of Europeans, 194–8, 208–12;
  colonialism, rise of, 285–6; creative
  arts, 166–8; culture, 156–76; daily life,
  147–50; early inhabitants, 7–20; and
  early states, 20–2; economy, 147–9;
  education, 168–71; geographical
  divisions, 4–6, 26–7; gold trade, 151–3;
  government, 177–8, 183–9; historical
  divisions, 27; Iron age, 13–20, 88, 136;
  Islam and, 136–40; law and order,
  188–9; monied economy, beginnings,
  147–59; Muslim centres of learning and
  scholars, 171–6; religions, 163–6,
  168–9, 189–90; slave trade *see* separate
  heading; social organisation, 177–90;
  Stone age, 7–12; subsistence economy,
  148–50; trade *see* separate heading

Western Imamates, 269–72
Whydah (Oudah or Fida), 228–9, 232,
  233, 237
Windward Coast, 252n
Wolof, 28, 53, 55–9, 61, 62, 63, 256,
  270; government and trade, 57–8;
  empire, 55–7; rivals to, 58–9
Wulliminden, 264

Yatenga, 74, 77, 87
Yawri, 106n
Yoruba, 3, 12, 59n, 66, 118–27, 217–21;
  Benin and, 127, 132–3; Dahomey and,
  230; government by, 56–7, 120–4, 164,
  185–6, 218, 254; growth of Oyo, 124–7;
  language, 119, 124, 126; military
  forces, 188; origins, 12, 118–20;
  religion, 123–4, 185, 218; sculpture,
  122, 124, 125; trade, 108, 126–7, 135,
  151; *see also* Oyo

Zaghawa, 98
Zamfara, 106n
Zaria (Zazzau), 106n, 107, 110–11, 135,
  274, 275–6
Zidan *see* Mulay Zidan, Sultan